WESTERN ESOTERICISM

A Brief History of Secret Knowledge

WESTERN ESOTERICISM

A BRIEF HISTORY OF SECRET KNOWLEDGE

KOCKU VON STUCKRAD

translated and with a Foreword by
Nicholas Goodrick-Clarke

Equinox Publishing Ltd

London   Oakville

Published by

UK: Equinox Publishing Ltd., Unit 6, The Village, 101 Amies St., London SW11 2JW
USA: DBBC, 28 Main Street, Oakville, CT 06779

www.equinoxpub.com

First published 2005

Library of Congress Cataloguing-in-Publication Data
A catalogue record for this book is available from the Library of Congress

ISBN   1845530330   (hardback)
        1845530349   (paperback)

Typeset by Forthcoming Publications Ltd
www.forthcomingpublications.com

Printed and bound in Great Britain by Antony Rowe Ltd, Chippenham

CONTENTS

FOREWORD

It gives me pleasure to introduce Kocku von Stuckrad's admirable survey of the Western esoteric traditions to the English-speaking world. As his own preface indicates, the time has come for a wider understanding of Western esotericism that transcends the medley of apparently unrelated and often suspect subjects on the shelves of esoteric bookstores. In the period from the 1950s to the early 1970s, such topics were typically grouped as 'occult', many of them graduating to 'New Age' interest by the early 1980s. But these tags conceal a more interesting and profound story of cultural transmission that involves Western self-understanding and philosophy.

Already between the two World Wars scholars were discovering a rich heritage of Neo-Platonic and Hermetic thought and practice in the West. A few examples will suffice to demonstrate the vigour and breadth of this enterprise, which sourced from the margins of academic and cultural discourse in order to illuminate pivotal linkages in European cultural history. Just as the Latin West had once assimilated Arab science, Jewish mysticism and Greek philosophy in response to geopolitical changes in the medieval and Renaissance periods, so the renewed persecution of the Jews in Central Europe in the 1930s led to the eventual translation of Aby Warburg's famous library from Hamburg to the University of London. A succession of brilliant scholars, German-Jewish and then British, including Edgar Wind, Ernst Cassirer, Frances Yates and D.P. Walker pioneered a history of ideas that bridged the Classical and European worlds, while embracing astrology, alchemy, magic, and their range of impact in the sixteenth and seventeenth centuries.

Other scholars also travelled to academic margins across cultural borders. Just as the nineteenth-century esotericists Helena Blavatsky and George Ivanovitch Gurdjieff sought an ancient wisdom in the East, so scholars of spiritual traditions returned with unexpected riches throwing light on forgotten East-West exchanges and shared traditions. Trained at the Sorbonne, Henry Corbin spent many years in Turkey and Iran assimilating the esoteric imaginaries of Sufi and Persian spirituality and his findings inspired another generation of Arabic scholars, whose work on Islamic mysticism has entered Western academic discourse. As the holder of the Sorbonne chair in mystical currents, François Secret unveiled the intricacies of Christian Kabbalah from the fifteenth century onwards, while his successor,

Antoine Faivre, developed the parameters of a formalised discipline following his pioneering works on theosophy, illuminism and the philosophy of nature.

As an emergent subject, not unlike 'science' in the seventeenth century, much of this work was also undertaken during the twentieth century in a non-university environment in professional societies and publishing programmes. Following a long tradition of British private scholarship, the Quest Society pioneered comparative religious studies in London during the 1920s, anticipating the notable Eranos Conferences in Switzerland attended by Carl Gustav Jung, Henry Corbin, Mircea Eliade, Gershom Scholem, Karl Kerenyi and D.T. Suzuki in the 1950s. In the 1970s and 1980s a circle of private scholars, including Ellic Howe, James Webb, Robert Gilbert, Leslie Price, Christopher McIntosh and myself, developed studies in the nineteenth-century occult revival, many of which found publishers and ultimately an academic readership. There were fruitful overlaps with other scholars in America, variously devoted to Platonism and Pythagoreanism, the history of the Theosophical Society, American Transcendentalism and German Romanticism. Joscelyn Godwin contributed studies of sixteenth-century panso-phists and musical philosophy, Arthur Versluis wrote on theosophy, and Allison Coudert (notably a Warburg émigré) examined the impact of Kabbalah on seven-teenth-century philosophy and mathematics. Joost Ritman's Bibliotheca Philoso-phica Hermetica was established in Amsterdam as a major collection and research centre. Publishers such as John Watkins, Donald Weiser, Jay Kinney, Christopher Bamford, Richard Grossinger, Ehud Sperling and Adam McLean provided an extended platform for scholarship that began to enter academic discourse in Britain, America and continental Europe during the 1990s.

Naming but a handful of individuals who toiled in the vineyard of Western esotericism is intended only to show the longer gestation and scope of these studies thus saved from the cul-de-sac of obscurantism and occultism. Western esoteri-cism is now a dynamic and growing subject at several universities across the world with professorial chairs at Paris, Amsterdam and Exeter, and faculty teaching students in the subject from Australia to Japan, from California to Scandinavia, from Italy to Russia.

Alfred North Whitehead, the philosopher of science, once noted, 'we are all footnotes to Plato', and Dr von Stuckrad's book shows indeed the breadth of this Platonic spirituality in the West, together with its Christian, Jewish and Muslim variants and imports. As a historian of astrology, he is well placed to observe the exchanges of the East and West in European history of religion and culture. As regards analysis, he advances a model based on ideas of fields, discourses, identity and communication, tradition and modernity, which participates in the latest dis-cussions of Hans G. Kippenberg and Burkhard Gladigow in Germany, the contri-butions of historians and sociologists of religion and the empirical studies of comparative religion.

His analysis of esotericism not only offers a fresh view of the European Ren-aissance as a dialogue with other faiths, but also shows how the blooming of esotericism coincided with the confessional differentiation of Christianity between 1450 and 1750. He thereby concludes, rather fashionably, that religious pluralism has been the norm in Europe since antiquity, not just in modernity. Even if Islam was not present in Western Europe, it featured in its literature and theological positions, both in common fields of discourse and as an *organisation of difference*, 'rehearsed again and again in councils, confessional writings, constitutions, social groups, political orders and legal systems'. Pluralism also is apparent in the interference between religion, politics, philosophy and science.

The study of Western esotericism draws on philosophy, religious studies and history. In this concise work we have a new analytical perspective that also discloses the cultural variety and historical interplay of ideas, seemingly marginal and forgotten, which have always lain at the heart of scientific and religious debates in the West.

Nicholas Goodrick-Clarke
Chair of Western Esotericism
University of Exeter

PREFACE

Almost everyone understands something by the concept 'esotericism', which, often linked with the 'New Age', has become an emotive word in the media and public over the past two decades. Likewise, both advocates and opponents of esotericism appear to have succumbed to the fascination of the 'occult' supposedly lying hidden in the background. An objective discussion of the subject is accordingly as necessary as it is difficult.

The last fifteen years have witnessed the emergence of a new field of academic research devoted to Western esotericism. Although the subjects usually seen as belonging to the field of esotericism had been studied intensively beforehand, the umbrella concept of esotericism has helped sufficiently to combine these various approaches and to demonstrate the important role of esoteric elements in the history of Western culture. Over against this very encouraging development it has to be noted, however, that academic research has not yet established a consensus on what is actually understood by 'esotericism' and what methodology is best suited for studying this phenomenon. This book is an attempt to take up the most recent academic research into Western esotericism and combine it with considerations relating to the characteristics of a European history of religion. Three suppositions are essential for this approach: First, from antiquity on, Western culture has been characterized by a religious pluralism that fostered identities by constructing an opposing 'other'; second, critical reflection on and negotiation of religious truth claims have been influenced by interaction between different cultural systems (such as religion, science, art, literature, politics, law, economics etc.); and finally, competing ways of attaining knowledge of the world provide a key to understanding the role of esotericism in Western discourse.

Given the highly controversial status of esotericism in popular and academic perception, some theoretical introduction to this study was indispensable. In the historical description of esotericism (Chapters 2–9) I have then focused on such examples, which clearly illustrate the role of 'perfect knowledge' in Western cultural history from ancient times to the present. This account is therefore neither complete nor to be read as a continuous history. Instead it offers an interpretation of esotericism within various aspects of European culture.

By speaking of *Western esotericism*, boundaries are already set upon the subject. I do not doubt that large parts of what I understand by esotericism can also be found in other cultures, and that a transcultural and comparative approach can be most valuable for our understanding of esotericism. Nevertheless, I derive my account from European and American culture and therefore wish to apply my findings to this field only.

While working on this book, many colleagues have assisted me greatly with their critical observations. I would like to express special thanks to Christoph Bochinger, Dylan Burns, Allison P. Coudert, Antoine Faivre, Steve A. Farmer, Olav Hammer, Wouter J. Hanegraaff, Andreas B. Kilcher, Hans G. Kippenberg, Monika Neugebauer-Wölk, Lawrence M. Principe, Matthew D. Rogers, Michael Stausberg and Steven M. Wasserstrom. Naturally I am alone responsible for any errors in the book. I am very grateful to the staff of the Bibliotheca Philosophica Hermetica, Amsterdam, for the procurement of literature and the preparation of illustrative material.

Kocku von Stuckrad
Amsterdam, March 2005

1

INTRODUCTION:
WHAT IS ESOTERICISM?

The concept 'esotericism' evokes widely differing responses among the public. Devotees of esotericism devour the stock of New Age bookshops with little discrimination and understanding of its historical provenance. Opponents of esotericism also have scant interest in its historical aspects. Given such controversy, an historical account of esotericism must clarify at the outset what is understood by the subject. For what, may one ask, does tea tree oil have to do with esotericism? Or Zen meditation for managers? Or pelvic gymnastics for women? Or *The Celestine Prophecies*? Or *A Course in Miracles*? Or Native American visionary quests in the Black Forest? All these subjects, with varying emphasis, are well stocked in specialist esoteric bookshops, but in actual fact they have little to do with esotericism as it is understood in this book.[1]

Extraordinarily enough, the public and media understanding of esotericism hardly corresponds at all to its scholarly discussion. Unnoticed by the broad public, the study of esotericism has crystallized into an academic discipline over the last ten to fifteen years. Many scholars have abandoned earlier concepts which characterised the esoteric wholly in the sense of the Greek meaning *esô, esôterikos* ('inner'), as that which is hidden, secret and only accessible to initiates.[2] Esotericism is understood rather as a particular world-view, which arose in natural philosophy,

---

1. Some scholars are content to define 'esotericism' simply as that which is sold as esotericism in the 'market of religions'. In this book I hope to show that such a definition is inadequate and also overlooks the esoteric current in European history of religion.

2. On the ancient usage of the word, see Gaiser 1988. An important overview and introduction to the academic study of esotericism is now provided by the *Dictionary of Gnosis and Western Esotericism* (Hanegraaff 2005). However, the dictionary strongly reflects the approach of Antoine Faivre (see below) and unfortunately neglects Jewish and Muslim esotericism. For instance, there is no entry in this 1228-page book on 'Kabbalah'; people interested in this field are referred to the entry 'Jewish Influences'. On the alternative approach presented in this book see also von Stuckrad 2005.

religious and literary traditions. Far from regarding it as something exotic, marginal or obscure, modern research seeks to present esotericism as a structural component of European history of religion and culture, while playing a significant part in the evolution of modernity.

SOME SCHOLARLY VIEWS

There have always been religious traditions, both within and outside Christianity, which differed from established views and were often in open conflict with them. A series of labels were given to these deviant currents: One spoke of 'Platonic-Hermetic Christianity', of 'Gnosis' or even of 'mysticism', in order to define these rival Christian and non-Christian world-views. All these attributions, except perhaps the first, derive from the perspective of Christian theology and served in former centuries to exclude suspected heresy and marginal beliefs from mainstream Christianity. In this process their actual links and connections were greatly distorted, thereby creating the impression that 'Gnosis' had little to do with Christianity, no more than the 'hermetic disciplines' of astrology, alchemy and magic.

By contrast the concept of 'esotericism' has a much shorter history. The noun 'esotericism'—in its French usage *l'ésotérisme*—was first used in 1828, at a time when alternative religious currents had already detached themselves from their Christian setting in the wake of the Enlightenment and the criticism of religion.[3] In the course of the nineteenth and twentieth centuries it became usual to locate esoteric traditions beyond Christianity as a kind of subculture, which had formed in the Renaissance and been excluded and persecuted by the dominant Church.[4] Up until the 1950s research into esotericism was undertaken by scholars who had specialised in mysticism and Gnosticism and presented these religious traditions as a counterpart to the scriptural religions of Judaism, Christianity and Islam (here one should mention Gershom Scholem, Henry Corbin and Mircea Eliade; also Martin Buber and Carl Gustav Jung). These scholars were themselves not infrequently part of a counter-movement against the rationalist 'disenchantment of the world'.[5]

Scholarship on esotericism received a major impetus in the 1960s through the works of Frances A. Yates (1899–1981). To be sure, scholars like Paul Kristeller, Ernst Cassirer and Eugenio Garin had already indicated that the so-called Hermetism of the Renaissance had played a much underestimated role in the development of modern science and culture. They disagreed with the view of most

3. For the history of the word *l'ésotérisme*, see Riffard 1990: 63-137.

4. The question of the relationship between Christianity and esotericism up to the present actually plays a decisive role in academic debate. On the one hand, it relates to the basic assumptions about the Christian West, and on the other to the connection between religious and rational scientific outlooks.

5. This is especially evident in the influential Eranos Conferences, which were held regularly in Switzerland since the 1930s; for which see Wasserstrom 1999 and Hakl 2001.

historians that an investigation of 'superstition' and irrationalism was not worthwhile. However, it was Frances A. Yates who succeeded at one fell swoop in bringing scholarship onto a new track. In her book *Giordano Bruno and the Hermetic Tradition* (1964) and successive essays she turned the tables by asserting that modern science had been fundamentally enabled by Renaissance Hermeticism. For many this seemed like a revelation: a forgotten tradition, suppressed by theologians, was suddenly visible; more, this 'Hermetic tradition' had in truth been the driving force of scientific revolutions. This hypothesis unleashed a vigorous debate and encountered bitter opposition, especially among historians of science. Although few now subscribe unreservedly to the 'Yates-paradigm', her works can be regarded as an important starting-point for modern scholarship on esotericism (see Hanegraaff 2001).

There followed a series of scholars who devoted themselves to research on esotericism and so saved it from the cul-de-sac of obscurantism and occultism.[6] In the meantime one can justifiably say that esotericism now represents a recognised branch of religious studies and cultural history.

ANTOINE FAIVRE AND ESOTERICISM AS 'A PATTERN OF THOUGHT'

Antoine Faivre has played a decisive part in the new scholarly definition of esotericism. Since the 1980s he worked intensively on the religious history of the Renaissance and early modern period, and developed an interpretative model of the esoteric, which systematically combines several traditions and disciplines. Among these belong the 'occult sciences' of astrology, alchemy and magic, whose roots stretch back to antiquity, but which were culturally re-positioned after the fifteenth century. These are joined by Platonic and hermetic thought, as well as (Christian) Kabbalah, which was regarded as ancient secret knowledge and linked with philosophical points of view. The links between these traditions were already recognised in the early modern period and given the Latin epithet *philosophia perennis* ('perennial/eternal philosophy'). This concept went along with the claim that one had found traces of a truth more ancient than all historical religions, and which found expression in different disciplines according to their nature. Out of these traditions Faivre developed a systematic model that characterised esotericism as a 'pattern of thought' (in French, *forme de pensée*). His heuristic and provisional definition, first presented in 1992, named four core characteristics of esotericism,

6.   An important step towards this new branch of research consisted in the establishment of a professorial chair for the 'History of Christian Esotericism' in the fifth section of the *École Pratique des Hautes Étude* of the Sorbonne, Paris in 1965, which was occupied by François Secret until 1979. Antoine Faivre held the chair until 2002 when he was succeeded by Jean-Pierre Brach, which was meanwhile renamed the 'History of Esoteric and Mystical Currents in Modern and Contemporary Europe'. Antoine Faivre's works have played a definitive role in shaping historical research into esotericism. In 1999 a further chair was established, dedicated to the 'History of Hermetic Philosophy and Related Currents', at the University of Amsterdam. In 2005 Nicholas Goodrick-Clarke was appointed to a new Chair in Western Esotericism at the University of Exeter.

which are complemented by two further characteristics that frequently occur but are not regarded as intrinsic or necessary (see Faivre and Needleman 1992: xi-xxx; Faivre 1994: 1-19). These characteristics are as follows:

(1) *Correspondences.* In Faivre's view, thinking in correspondences must be regarded as a basic component of all esotericism, namely the assumption that the various levels or 'classes' of reality (plants, humans, planets, minerals), similarly the visible and invisible parts of the universe, are linked through a series of correspondences. This connection is to be understood not causally but symbolically, wholly in the sense of the famous Hermetic motto 'As above, so below'. The universe is like a hall of mirrors, in which everything contains references to something else. Changes occur in parallel on all levels of reality. (2) *Living nature.* This idea comprehends the cosmos as a complex, ensouled entity, permeated by the flow of a living energy. This model in philosophy of nature influenced the so-called *magia naturalis* of the Renaissance as well as those pantheistic, monist and holistic conceptions of the cosmos that have remained an integral element in the history of European religion from the Middle Ages until the present. (3) *Imagination and mediations.* These terms indicate that esoteric knowledge of correspondences demands great power of symbolic imagination, which is also significant in practical magic. Moreover, this knowledge is revealed ('mediated') by spiritual authorities (gods, angels, masters or spirits). Hence, it is possible to decipher the 'hieroglyphs of nature'. (4) *The experience of transmutation* posits a parallel between outer action and inner experience. Analogous to spiritual alchemy, esotericism seeks to refine the human being upon a spiritual path and so enable an inner metamorphosis. This metamorphosis can also be grasped in metaphors of realization and reason, namely in the understanding of higher or absolute knowledge, which totally transforms the human being.

Following Faivre's model, these four core components are joined by two further elements: (5) *the practice of concordance* strives to find a common denominator or 'fundament' among the various teachings, which simply appears in a different light in various historical epochs; (6) *transmission or initiation through masters* is a sociological element of esotericism, because the teaching is frequently transmitted by spiritual authorities and the transformation of the believer becomes externally visible through rituals of initiation.

As already indicated, the advantage of such a taxonomy consists in its capacity to compare varying traditions, including philosophy of nature, Hermeticism, Gnosticism, magic, astrology and alchemy, with one another in a systematic fashion. Even the occasional precarious conceptual definition of those traditions is, so to speak, defused by this concept of esotericism. A pattern of thought becomes visible, which has helped fashion European religion and philosophy since the Renaissance and must therefore be considered an essential part of modern intellectual history. Instead of contrasting the esoteric in an antithetical position with the Enlightenment and with science, as was the former practice, recent historical scholarship increasingly recognises the *inner connections* between esotericism, science and the Enlightenment.[7]

The last decade has shown that one can arrive at very fruitful analyses with the aid of the 'Faivre paradigm'. However, critics have also pointed to the weakness of the theory, chiefly that Faivre extrapolated his typology from a very specific phase in modern religious history and thereby excluded other aspects from the outset.[8] The result is a tautology, which only includes in its definition of esotericism whatever served as the basis of its definition. To be specific: because Faivre mainly drew on Renaissance Hermeticism, philosophy of nature, Christian Kabbalah and Protestant theosophy to generate his taxonomy, some areas are excluded from research, which might actually be decisive for a comprehensive survey. Historically, this concerns the ancient world, the medieval and modern periods; from the point of view of content, Jewish and Islamic esotericism, and for modernity also Buddhism, which strongly influenced twentieth-century European esotericism. If one should like a general description of (Western) esotericism, which included those historical and cultural aspects, one would have to test the taxonomy once more for its utility. For this reason, I describe esotericism from another point of view. As I will shortly explain, I use a model of European history of religion that proceeds from the idea of religious pluralism, an idea which therefore regards Christianity, Judaism and Islam, but also the many European polytheisms as established elements of European culture. In this historical account, I am seeking to describe the continuities and breaks, the overlaps and changes of 'esoteric discourse' in a specific historical context.[9]

7. It must be emphasised that Faivre's definition of esotericism has an *ideal-type* character (contrary to Faivre's own depiction). It should not therefore be understood essentially, by drawing conclusions from it as to what esotericism *really* is and is not. It is rather an instrument for clarifying what *should, according to this definition*, be understood by esotericism. This is a major methodological distinction. Moreover, an ideal-type definition certainly does not mean that the described characteristics have to be present in the same way or in their 'pure form'; in actual fact this is rarely the case (at any rate Faivre insists that esotericism is only that which exhibits *all* components, a claim which is hotly debated by scholars). Faivre's definition is no more and no less than a scholarly construct to elucidate connections and traditions, which have shaped the cultural history of Europe over a long period of time.

8. See, for instance, McCalla 2001, who focuses his critique on the religionist elements in Faivre's work, arguably of less importance in his later writings.

9. Even if our investigation starts in the history of ideas, it cannot remain there, but must closely examine the historical context of esotericism. The same point is also emphasised by historians. Reinhart Koselleck already indicated in his 1954 dissertation (see Koselleck 1973), that it was the *arcanum*, the mystery of the Masonic lodges, which undermined the absolutist state, by protecting the enlightened citizen from its power. Social history can throw light on those groups responsible for transmitting esoteric ideas. Esoteric milieus and discourses, as we will repeatedly discover, run contrary to membership of religious denominations. Unlike other scholars (for example Neugebauer-Wölk 2003) I do not consider it important to relate the esoteric by definition to Christianity—whether inclusively as a deviant part of Christianity or exclusively as a tradition irreconcilable with Christianity.

Religious Pluralism and the 'Esoteric Field of Discourse'

Nowadays historians like to talk about a 'history of cultural memory', which no longer follows a simple sequence of historical events, but describes the 'simultaneity of the diverse'. According to Dan Diner, 'memory represents a plurality of pasts which transcends time in a simultaneous fashion' (Diner 2003: 7). The history of cultural memory regards historical events as akin to a palimpsest on which two or more successive texts have been written, but where the original is still legible. While the model of a strictly successive historical development reached its zenith in the nineteenth century, the model of the history of cultural memory is indebted to twentieth-century concepts of culture.[10] Historical writing is not the representation of what 'was', but that which is remembered and appears important to contemporary observers. History is always a construction of the past in the light of present interests.

This leads to the analysis of specific historical contexts. If one asks *why* particular events were remembered or particular historical narratives constructed at particular times, one must consider the social, political, economic, legal and cultural circumstances which lent esoteric traditions their particular significance. In order to distinguish the various approaches to history, I will talk about traditions and discourses.

Traditions and Discourses

Within Christianity, Judaism or Islam there certainly exists a self-contained core of traditions, which can be described in the form of literatures and their reception. However, once one looks at the specific formulations of these traditions in their historical contexts, one finds that this core is actually quite slight. Much more frequently such a core is *used* in the light of contemporary questioning and thereby significantly transformed. At this point religious discourses come into play, which describe, as it were, challenges which are divided into respective historical contexts by adherents of divergent religious traditions. Discourses are not identical with traditions, but instead represent *the social organisation of tradition, opinion and knowledge.*[11]

In this sense, the question of the significance of historical events and their incorporation in a doctrine of salvation is an example of a discourse. While Shiites in the Middle Ages related the astrological doctrine of so-called Great Conjunctions to the date of the return of the Hidden Imam, Jews could relate the same doctrine theologically to their expulsion from Spain in 1492 and to the exile, which would soon give way to a messianic era. Christians again used this doctrine in terms of apocalypticism and eschatology to escalate the confessional tensions of the sixteenth and seventeenth centuries. I call both these discussions and, most importantly,

---

10. Jan Assmann and Erik Hornung have used the example of Egypt to show that the 'decoding of memories' has great significance in the history of esotericism; see Assmann 1997 and Hornung 2001.

11. For my description of 'discourse' in religious studies, see von Stuckrad 2003a.

their social and political implications, *fields of discourse*.[12] In the case above, one could speak of an apocalyptic, redemptive or even an astrological field of discourse.

Fields of discourse are not restricted to specific traditions. They develop rather from common challenges and contemporary interests. Indeed, fields of discourse *change* religious identities and lead now and then to astonishing alliances and parallels between supposedly separate religious traditions. The boundaries often run not between Christianity, Judaism and Islam, but much more clearly between Platonists and Aristotelians, between scholasticism and nominalism, or between literal interpretations of the Bible and mystical or esoteric vision. There are intensive exchanges between Christian, Jewish and Muslim traditions, which often bear little relation to their original religious purpose.

THE PLURALITY OF IDENTITIES

This process has consequences for religious identities. Research into religious socialisation has shown that in the twentieth century it is not possible to speak of a closed religious identity according to the motto 'one person, one faith'. This is not just a phenomenon of modernity, even if modernity is characterised by a differentiation of religious options and choices. A glance at earlier centuries shows that religious identities were not formed along clearly defined religious traditions, but according to fields of discourse, biographical narratives and a tension between the perception of self and other, albeit to a far lesser degree than today. Christians who practice Zen meditation today rarely lose their Christian identity, and the latter was not compromised by pantheistic thought or esoteric disciplines like astrology and alchemy in the early modern period. A certain pastor Johann Rist (1607–1667) erected in his vicarage at Wedel a complex laboratory, in order to research the basis of life. In 1664 he declared: 'I can scarcely describe the pleasure I derive from these pursuits'. When an acquaintance reproached him for his alchemical operations, saying, 'the alchemist and his like are seeking to become demi-gods!', the pastor gave the lapidary response 'and why should that not be possible?' (see Trepp 2001: 103f.).

In this book I will repeatedly introduce personalities that demonstrate the multilayered nature of religious identities. Guillaume Postel (1510–1581), for example, cannot be simply described as a Jesuit, but also as a kabbalist, a scholar of Islam, and as a prophet of the return of the Holy Virgin Mary. Thinkers like Guillaume Postel are the nodal points, where religious exchanges can be observed. Even if their interest was occasionally polemic in nature, they ensured that philosophical, theological and esoteric concepts found a reciprocal echo.[13]

---

12. In so doing I draw on the discourse theory of Michel Foucault as well as the field theory as formulated by Burkhard Gladigow in response to the ideas of Ingo Mörth: 'Cooperation and complementarity, polemics and dialogue, exclusion and inclusion in systems and the carriers of such systems can best be described as a "field"' (Gladigow 1995: 28, with reference to Mörth 1975).

13. Two further examples can make this even clearer: the Muslim conception of *wahī*, namely the revelation of the Qur'an through a divine source, can easily be equated with an esoteric

Religious identities arise through processes of communication. They are not pre-existing but negotiated (see Kippenberg and von Stuckrad 2003a: 136-46). Here religious alternatives play a critical role. The process of identification is firstly stimulated by the debate with other options, which can be adopted affirmatively or within limits. This applies to individuals such as Guillaume Postel, Pastor Rist or Christian Zen practitioners as well as to religious communities, who require a contrasting 'other' in order to define themselves. In this process, petty differences are often exaggerated into radical contrasts, a good example being the blooming of esotericism and the confessional differentiation of Christianity between 1450 and 1750.

PLURALISM AND THE EUROPEAN HISTORY OF RELIGION

Religious pluralism has been the norm in Europe since antiquity, not just in modernity. Even if there were times, when Islam was not institutionally present in parts of Europe, it was always present in the sense of its literature and theological positions, as well as being a counterfoil for multifarious Christian and Jewish identities. It was shared in common fields of discourse.[14] Here one recognises the difference between plurality and pluralism: while plurality only describes the objective content of a multiplicity of religions, the concept of pluralism stands for the *organisation of difference*. The other contemporary religious options are known— they are the object of debate and serve the generation of identities. What is different is not only perceived in its presence, but constructed as the Other. Both sides therefore form a discursive unity. The organisation of difference is rehearsed again and again in councils, confessional writings, constitutions, social groups, political orders and legal systems.

As the organisation of difference, religious pluralism is a structural element of European cultural history. If one wishes to analyse this history, one must take the 'Other' into account, which is constantly produced by the 'Self'. Seventeenth-century scholars in Basle, Venice and Paris were not concerned with Muslim

concept of mediation, as the Arabic word approximately signifies 'mysterious non-verbal communication'; *wahī* is, as it were, the canal through which the truth flows from an absolute source into the human realm. The kabbalistic model of emanations of divine energy seeks to describe something similar. My second example is drawn from the kabbalistic interpretation of history. Isaac Luria produced a highly elaborate explanation of the Creation, which culminated in the redemptive restoration of the original state. The theosophical metaphor of the contraction of divine energy and the creation of the universe through emanation in primordial space was so powerful that Schelling and other German philosophers were still making use of this kabbalistic idea in the nineteenth century. That process of restoration, which Luria called *Tiqqun*, reflects the same interpretative model as Postel's *Restitutio*, which offers hope for the imminent achievement of a universal realm of peace in times of extreme religious tension.

14. In a pioneering study Michael Stausberg has made a similar claim for Zoroastrianism, which was present in Europe 'only' in imagination: In his 'history of reception', Stausberg combines his analysis of the external European perspective on Zoroaster (the 'history of the Other') with an analysis of the inner-European contexts of reception (see Stausberg 1998: 22).

theology and scripture due to a neutral interest in the Qur'an, nor simply because they wanted to 'refute' Islam. Their opponents were always those of a different persuasion *within* the Church. In 1716 the Dutch theologian and orientalist Adrian Reland wrote: 'Whoever wants to disgrace a doctrine, needs only to say forthwith that it is a Muslim doctrine'.[15] In the case of esotericism a further factor is discernible: Jewish and Muslim philosophy and esotericism were not studied merely because one 'wanted to beat the enemy with his own weapons', but due to an interest in an alternative reading of the cosmos, which had much to teach Christians. Not until one accepts pluralistic reflection as a factor in the history of religion, can one recognise these connections.

The Other not only comprises alternative religious options, but also the discursive interweavings between religious systems and political or economic systems. Precisely this reciprocal relationship of the religions as well as their involvement with cultures of knowledge is a feature of the European history of religion. Scholarly interpretations can themselves become generators of 'meaning', whereby philosophy and philologies play a critical role.[16] If one adopts such a cultural model of interpretation, one cannot represent esotericism as an independent tradition divorced from Christianity, empirical science or the Enlightenment, but only in its encounter with these, which more often than not led to a fruitful exchange.

THE ESOTERIC AS AN ELEMENT OF DISCOURSE

From the foregoing, one must draw the conclusion that one needs a concept of esotericism, which illustrates not only continuities, but also the dynamics and processes of forming identities. Such a concept must involve the *discursive transfer* between the individual areas of European culture, especially religion, natural science, philosophy, literature and art. Since we are trying to construct an analytical instrument, we must emphasise something from the outset: 'Esotericism' does not exist as an object. 'Esotericism' exists only in the heads of scholars, who classify objects in meaningful way to themselves, in order to analyse processes of European

15. Hartmut Bobzin rightly draws the conclusion: 'The motives for studying Islam and particularly the Qur'an as 'a box of heresies' can only be understood against the background of theological debates in the whole context of the Reformation' (Bobzin 1995: viii).

16. 'For many centuries philosophy and philologies have presented or revived traditions, which no longer had active "carriers", or which had never had carriers (in the Weberian sense), by passing them on through the medium of science. The Renaissance, Humanism and Romanticism have taken their alternatives to Western Christian culture largely from the sciences. A revived Platonism could have the closest engagement with Christianity, or alternatively continue as a theory of magic and irrationalism up to the eighteenth century. Gnostic ideas and notions of salvation could make connections with Asian religions imported through philology; monism could be absorbed into a Christian pantheism or constitute a new religion' (Gladigow 1995: 29). In order to avoid misunderstandings, Gladigow declares that 'this process—it is important to remember—is not a matter of mixing systems of meaning or syncretism, but of a "semiotic" which combines the individual religions, their constructions of meaning of social groups, like signs in a system of signs' (Gladigow 1995: 37).

cultural history.[17] Put differently: definitions are tools of *interpretation*; they should not be used essentially.

For this reason it is often better to talk about *the esoteric* rather than *esotericism*, because the esoteric is an element of cultural processes, while the mention of esotericism suggests that there is a coherent doctrine or a clearly identified body of tradition. One only finds the latter in particular sequences of influence. An account of discourses does not, therefore, offer an unbroken history of the development of esotericism in Europe.[18] Whenever I talk about 'esotericism' in this book, I conceive of the esoteric much more as an *element of discourse* in the European history of religion. This element of discourse can be identified as follows: the pivotal point of all esoteric traditions are *claims* to 'real' or absolute knowledge and the *means* of making this knowledge available. This might be through an individual ascent as in Gnostic or Neo-Platonic texts, or through an initiatory event as in secret societies of the modern period, or through communication with spiritual beings, as in the 'channelling' of the twentieth century. In the following chapters it will be evident that such means of acquiring knowledge can also be found in scientific contexts.

The means, through which a discourse of absolute knowledge unfolds, relates to the *dialectic of the hidden and revealed*, thus with 'secrecy', but not in the sense that esoteric truth is accessible only to initiates. What makes a discourse esoteric is the rhetoric of a hidden truth, which can be unveiled in a specific way and established contrary to other interpretations of the universe and history—often that of the institutionalised majority. Mediation may be conceived as such a means: the link between hidden and revealed knowledge, between transcendence and immanence, is frequently attributed to specific authorities—for example Hermes or Zoroaster—who act as mediators and place a 'perfect' knowledge at the disposal of human beings. That eternal knowledge, the *philosophia perennis*, can be achieved by some distinguished persons even without mediation,[19] but the notion of a chain of 'initiates' and sages, who determine the course of revelation, is a recurrent motif in the history of esotericism from ancient times up until the present. This claim to knowledge is often combined with an emphasis on individual *experience*, wherein a seeker attains higher knowledge through extraordinary states of consciousness.

The concept of 'otherness' also acquires a significant role in the analysis of discourse. 'Otherness' or 'deviance' are interpretative tools in cultural studies, which illustrate the construction of difference. Once there is a majority, deviant

17. This not only applies to the concept of esotericism, but also to other analytical categories like 'Gnosticism' and 'Mysticism'. Even such common concepts as 'Religion', 'Christianity' or 'Science' raise problems within this perspective.

18. 'Nobody will wish to construct a new "grand narrative" out of the discovery of new discursive segments, as for example, "it was occultism that made modernity possible" or similar statements. Instead one should insist on the complexity of each individual historical fact as a nodal point of innumerable discourses in each specific constellation' (Introduction to Baßler and Châtellier 1998: 25; see also Bettina Gruber's Introduction to Gruber 1997).

19. Consider Abulafia's quest for direct, ecstatic access to the absolute truth or Hegel's 'conclusion of philosophy'.

minorities develop, and moreover both through the exclusion of the 'Other' on the part of the majority, as well as through the conscious tendency of the minority towards its own constructions of meaning. Those claims of making 'actual knowledge' individually accessible has sharpened this encounter. Many manifestations of esotericism form a spectrum of deviant religious options, be these Christian 'heresies', or polytheistic and pantheistic models that dissent from a monotheistic world-view.[20]

This crystallisation of esoteric discourses in ever new constellations, that is in a *field*, I describe as *motifs* or *themes*. These motifs have usually merged from a conception of the cosmos, which one can call *holistic* or *monistic*. These signify projects that consider material and non-material levels of reality as a unity and focus their interest on the links between these levels: thinking in terms of correspondences constructs these connections and reflections, for example between transcendence and immanence, between planets and terrestrial events, between body and soul, or spirit and matter. The examples can be multiplied, but what is important is the means of describing reality. The conception of a living nature is also usually developed in a holistic context, whereby world and cosmos are conceived as a dynamic plait of connections. These kinds of animistic traditions can be found in nature–philosophical, pantheistic and animistic world-views that have recurred throughout European cultural history. The notion of a *prisca theologia* or *philosophia perennis* also counts among the motifs which stimulate an esoteric discourse. The reception of Gnostic doctrines or texts like the *Corpus Hermeticum* or the *Chaldæan Oracles* produces a recurrent topos, to be analysed in the sense of constructing alternative identities.[21]

One might ask: What is actually gained by such a concept of esotericism? I hope to make clear in the following chapters that this analytical model enables us to demonstrate the complexity of European cultural history, without playing off religion against science, Christianity against paganism, or reason against superstition. In reality these large factors are inseparably related to each other and their relationship is the most interesting aspect of the history of esotericism in Europe.

20. This is not a matter of static conditions. For example, early forms of Christianity may be regarded from such a perspective as deviant phenomena, because their concept of individual salvation consciously distinguished them from the Roman majority religion. Initially excluded by Rome as an illegitimate religion, because non-public, the Christian state religion later presented itself as the public and legitimate religion of Roman law and excluded alternative concepts on its part as illegitimate. What Michel Foucault calls the 'control of discourse' runs like a red thread through the history of European Christianities.

21. It must be emphasised that I do not conceive such motifs and themes—in contrast to typological approaches to esotericism as propagated by Antoine Faivre—as *determining elements* of the esoteric, but rather as 'material' of the discourse.

2

ESOTERICISM IN THE ANCIENT WORLD

Modern esotericism emulates its ancient origins in two respects. On the one hand, its principal motifs were adopted and developed in ancient philosophy and the major religions of antiquity. Moreover, these esoteric motifs played a vital part in contemporary debates in the ancient world. On the other hand, the textual foundations of modern esotericism also date from the first centuries BCE. The reception of Hermetism is only valid when the hermetic texts are trusted as a foundation and viewed in their own context. The same is true for the so-called *Chaldæan Oracles* as well as for astrological, alchemical or Neo-Platonic world interpretations—all crucial elements in the history of esotericism. What is more, the latter texts were by no means lost for over a thousand years as was the case with the *Corpus Hermeticum*.

PHILOSOPHICAL RELIGION, RELIGIOUS PHILOSOPHY

Esotericism has always occupied that charged field between philosophy and religion. Esotericism shares with certain philosophical traditions views on man (anthropology), on existence and reality (ontology), and on the condition of the cosmos and nature. The transition to religion arises in questions relating to the sacralisation of nature and the self, to the perceptive capacity of man—which links him to the divine—and to revelation—when human beings receive knowledge from transcendent sources—and similar themes.

The idea that the microcosm and macrocosm reflect each other assumes many forms in the history of esotericism. This holistic notion of a cosmos ordered through correspondences is found in many cultures, not only in the Mediterranean area and the civilisations it gave rise to.[1] However, the similarities do not lie in their specific formulation, but rather in the way the cosmos is described. Already in the earliest times, namely in the Babylonian cults of the third and second

---

1. This systematic description of correspondences between levels of reality is sometimes termed a 'correlative cosmology', e.g. Farmer *et al.* 2000. This enables a cross-cultural comparison between European, Chinese, Indian and Latin American cosmologies.

millennia BCE, we find the idea of correspondence between the heavenly and terrestrial world, which may be regarded as the fundamental characteristic of the temple traditions of Western Asia. The Jewish community of Qumran (second century BCE–70 CE) held similar ideas and Philo of Alexandria (first century CE) also considered the mystical dimensions of the Temple. Although these Jewish sources are quite distinct from Babylonian cult theology in terms of their content, they do indicate a comparable scheme of interpretation.

No one culture can claim to have invented the idea of correspondences. It is a different matter, however, once one considers the *elaboration* of such ideas into a comprehensive way of thinking. It is then apparent that Hellenistic Egypt has made a major contribution to the elaboration of the micro–macrocosmic idea. At the same time, it is difficult to make a clear distinction between individual traditions, because Pythagorean philosophy and Stoicism also made their own contributions to the development of this idea, as did Egypt. All these factors led to a particular syncretism in Hellenistic Egypt.

FOOTNOTES TO PLATO

Let us turn to the philosophical foundations of ancient esotericism. It is almost commonplace to say that we now are all footnotes to Plato. That is of course an enormous exaggeration and yet there is more than a grain of truth in this saying, because esoteric ontology and anthropology would hardly exist without Platonic philosophy.[2]

Plato (427–347 BCE) is the first known Greek philosopher to make a mytho-logical connection between the arrangement of the heavens and terrestrial destiny. In his later work *Timæus* he speaks of the fixed stars as 'living beings of a divine and immortal nature' (*Timæus* 40b). Plato also relates the planets directly to time, which God, the *demiurge* ('craftsman') simultaneously created with them. He con-tinues:

> When the heavenly bodies jointly needed for the production of time had been given their appropriate motion and had become living creatures bound by the ties of the soul, they started to move with the motion of the Different, which traverses that of the Same obliquely and is subject to it, some in larger circles, some in smaller, those with the smaller circles moving faster, those with the larger moving more slowly. (*Timæus* 38e)

Symbolic correspondence—the ties of the soul in Plato—remains a prominent part of astrology right up to the present day. Even the conception of the cosmos as a living being in which all parts are interconnected is an unshakeable foundation of esotericism and philosophy of nature ever since Plato. Plato's *doctrine of souls* has had an equally far-reaching significance. Indeed, the notion that man possesses only one soul, which can be divided but survives the death of the body in its entirety is 'the critical psychological turning-point in the European history of religion'

---

2. For a more detailed discussion see Runggaldier 1996.

(Gladigow 1993: 122). This change was completed very early, namely in the fifth century BCE, when Plato discussed the immortality of the soul with Socrates' suicide as an example in *Phaedo*. Before he drinks the cup of hemlock, Socrates is asked by Crito: 'But how shall we bury you?' Socrates' reply sounds initially cryptic: 'As you wish, he said, if you really will have me and I have not eluded you' (115c), but then Socrates adds with a smile, when one carries the apparent Socrates to his grave, he will be somewhere quite different. '[I will] then remain no longer with you, but depart…to some wonders of the blessed' (115d).

This was a novel view. The earlier relationship between the soul and the body can be seen by comparing Homer's *Iliad* from the end of the eighth century BCE. Here one encounters the word *psychê* for the first time, but in quite a different usage from Plato. At the very beginning of the epic 'many powerful souls' of heroes are thrown before Hades, but the goddess created them 'as the quarry of hounds and to feed the birds'. Here the person is by no means identical with their soul, but with their body, which is thrown for the animals to devour.[3] By contrast, Plato was firmly convinced that the soul should be regarded as the 'real' or 'true' centre of man. Only the soul partook in the Highest Good and the Divine, while incarnation in a body was tantamount to the exile of the soul from its homeland. The body became the 'tomb of the soul' (*Gorgias* 493a; *Phaedo* 250c; *Nomoi* 958c).

The archimedean point in the European interpretation of the soul came with Neo-Platonic and Christian influence, mostly between the first and fourth centuries, especially through the influential philosophy of Plotinus (205–270). The motif of the soul as an exile in the body was now linked to the option of redemption, whereby the soul could follow a path back into the realm of light thanks to its inclination towards the divine. In Gnostic contexts this path could be trodden even in life, which often involved a devaluation of the physical being (see below). The assumption that only the soul had a share in absolute truth and that the path of knowledge led through the inner side of man was also elaborated. There arose the notion of the 'inner person' contrasted with the 'merely outer, superficial person', which would then prevail throughout the course of European religious and intellectual history.[4]

---

3. Burkhard Gladigow states: 'Here, in short, are two fundamentally opposed views of the person: one that links the self with the body…and another, which assumes a "soul", distinct, separable and autonomous from the body, which contains it like a shrine. The former requires any maintenance of postmortem existence to concentrate on the external form and any "change of being" must be conceived as a *metamorphosis* through a change of masks and clothes. In the latter case, the body is regarded as rather incidental to the soul, leading to all the unfortunate consequences in the treatment of the actual body' (Gladigow 1993: 116).

4. See Assmann and Sundermeier 1993. A casual glance at the publications of the 'New Age' movement suffices to show that the Neo-Platonic concept of the soul is the centre point of present-day esoteric viewpoints. Quite rightly Edmund Runggaldier calls the fundamental anthropological principles of contemporary esotericism '*dualistic*. Man is not identical with his body.' The complementary assumption 'True knowledge is nothing else but *remembrance*' is similarly Platonic. He concludes: 'Esoteric notions of the *ascent* of souls and their *union* with the ultimate principle of

The notion of the unity of the world also carries Neo-Platonic associations. Plotinus had already reflected at great length on the relationship of the individual soul to the Absolute or the world-soul. According to his explanation, the human soul had separated itself from the purely spiritual, intelligible world, by directing its effective energy towards something specific and incarnating in a body, and yet it always remained linked to the world-soul and represented a part of the whole. The soul, arising from *Nous* (Being), adopts a mediating position between the spiritual and material world. The influence of this argument in European religious and intellectual history can hardly be overestimated. Not only is the separation of body and soul anticipated here, but also the divisibility of the soul, without which there could be no notion of multiple personalities, and finally the assumption that the 'real' soul, identical with the cosmos, is perfect and consequently divine.[5]

PYTHAGOREANS AND ORPHICS

Plato was not the first to think about the soul in this way. He could refer to speculations current at the end of the sixth century BCE predominantly linked with the name of *Pythagoras*. We know regrettably all too little about the life of this influential philosopher. It is known that Pythagoras (c. 580–500 BCE) left his home Samos around 530 BCE and gathered disciples around him in the southern Italian town of Crotona. His followers came from the aristocratic class and clearly differed from the majority in their religious and philosophical outlook. During his lifetime many legends gathered around Pythagoras, who helped to develop many esoteric fields of discourse. His concept of the soul inspired Plato and others (see Bremmer 2002: 11-26). More explicitly than Plato, Pythagoras taught the doctrine of reincarnation, that is the rebirth of the soul, which moved him to advise caution in the consumption of certain meats—one could inadvertently eat a person reincarnated as an animal. Unlike his successors, above all Parmenides, Empedocles and the Orphics, who regarded the consumption of meat as cannibalism on the basis of reincarnation, Pythagoras was not a rigid vegetarian. However, his doctrines ensured that the Pythagoreans formed their own social group on the grounds of their strict regime. Some scholars described this lifestyle as 'puritanical', because Pythagoras taught a clear division of body and soul (whereby the physical was devalued in relation to the spiritual), a certain asceticism, and a link between individual guilt and punishment.

reality…are typically Gnostic' (Runggaldier 1996: 12f.). This evaluation is justified even if one considers that many advocates of modern esotericism propagate a unity of soul, body and world, since the restoration of (paradisial) unity presupposes that a separation has occurred, a separation which is usually interpreted as the 'Fall'.

5.   C.G. Jung's discourse on the individuation of the person belongs to this tradition of sacralising the psyche, as Wouter J. Hanegraaff has described in 'New Age' conceptions and the motto of the 'I am God' motif (Hanegraaff 1996: 203-24). We will meet this idea of the world-soul again in the Renaissance.

Pythagoras made a further contribution to esoteric discourse in his interpreta-tion of the cosmos. Aristotle and others tell us that Pythagoras was the first to make a serious study of mathematics (though Pythagoras' theorem may not actually be his). The Pythagoreans developed the idea that mathematical principles, and therefore numbers, were also the principles of all being. The ratio of numbers and proportions are accordingly images of the harmony of the universe, which is then described (for the first time) as a 'cosmos', as an ordered unity, and the oppo-site of chaos. The mathematical or 'grammatical constitution' of the cosmos would via Jewish mysticism develop into a central motif of medieval and modern esotericism.

Pythagoras was interested in music as a further expression of this comprehensive harmony of all beings. The intervals of music correspond to the cosmic propor-tions, and the heavenly bodies in motion produce notes in specific intervals. This leads to the Pythagorean doctrine of the 'harmony of the spheres', which through Neo-Platonism influenced the speculations of renowned Renaissance scholars and other schools as far as twentieth-century esotericism.[6]

The so-called *Orphics* also count among the groups that were influenced by Pythagoreanism in the fifth century BCE. This group was earlier regarded as a small Greek sect, but new discoveries show that the Orphics, who included many women, practised a mystery religion with individual initiation following Dionysus Bacchus, thus in contrast to the Great Mysteries of Eleusis or Samothrace. The 'ecstatic' elements of this cult are still visible in the Roman bacchanalia. Unlike Pythagoreanism, the Orphic doctrine was not attributed to a specific founding figure but to a legend. Its content related to the creation of the world and man (a theme that had previously aroused no interest in Greece), and to eschatology, that is the doctrine of the end and a new beginning of history, and with reincarnation (see Bremmer 2002: 15-24).

Platonism, Pythagoreanism and Orphism clearly show the rich variety of Greek philosophical and religious discourse and how certain concepts of man and the world developed into important building-stones of ancient esotericism. Finally, we must consider Stoicism for a proper understanding of esotericism, for here the above-named traditions were absorbed and transformed into a new form.

FATE, COSMOS AND SYMPATHY: THE STOICS

Around 300 BCE Zeno from Citium gathered his pupils in the *stoa poikile*, a colon-naded hall in Athens. This place gave its name to the Stoic movement, soon counted among the most influential philosophies of the ancient world. More remarkably, fragments have been preserved of the Early Stoics (Zeno, Cleanthes, Chrysippus) and the Middle Stoics (Panaetius, Poseidonius) which must therefore be squared with the reports of the Later Stoics. The Early Stoics succeeded in transcending the limits of their school and developing a kind of popular ethics,

---

6.   Joscelyn Godwin has written several studies on this subject. See, e.g., Godwin 1987.

which found general approval in Rome. The most important authors of this trend were Seneca, Epictetus and Marcus Aurelius.

The distinction between what is in our power and what is not lies at the heart of Stoic doctrine. Only that which pertains to the sphere of our conceptions, namely opinions, desires, appetites and aversions, is subject to our control. Physical existence, property and prestige are not our work. The Stoic life consists in distinguishing one from the other and adapting oneself to the laws of those things outside our control. These laws are divine in nature and reveal a perfect order, which human reason can understand. The law of causality is thereby regarded as fundamental to any explanation of the world. Because nothing exists without a cause, there is no room in the cosmos for chance and arbitrary events, especially in view of the fact that all chains of causation are linked with each other and the universe forms a total unity. The Stoics described this compelling mechanism with the concept of *heimarmene*, which initially meant only 'fate', but has little to do with our notion of fate. *Heimarmene* is rather a cipher for the regularity of the cosmos, not as static, but as a dynamic system of forces, which develops and undergoes processes of change like a living being. Sometimes *heimarmene* is described in two respects as *energeia*, thus as an 'energy' which drives cosmic administration, and as *ousia*, as a 'being' or the 'world-soul', which represents as it were a personified energy. In this sense the *heimarmene* can even be described as a goddess responsible for the administration of causality. The concept of *sympatheia* (sympathy) is related to this. If all parts of the cosmos are regarded as being linked to each other— philosophy of nature speaks of *monism* or even *holism*—then the principles of causality have a simultaneous effect upon all parts. The connection between various levels of the cosmos, even if these are naturally subject to causality, can be interpreted as a connection of correspondences. For esotericism in general and astrology in particular the consequence is that the stars, which are just as much part of the world-soul as men, stand in a dynamic relationship of correspondence to the terrestrial Earth. The observation of their movements provides information about developments on Earth.

The Stoics were ultimately superseded by other philosophical movements. The reasons lay not so much in philosophical debate as in the social and political changes of the first centuries CE, which created a new spiritual and intellectual climate. Middle- and Neo-Platonism especially took the place of Stoicism. Neo-Platonism naturally assumed aspects of Stoic doctrine, for instance the idea of the cosmos as a living being or the role of the planets as effective agents. However, thinkers like Philo of Alexandria and later the most important Neo-Platonic philosopher Plotinus linked such thoughts with Hermetic and astral-mystical ideas in the sense of Plato, and thereby established a model which recognised *heimarmene* as a principle of fate but simultaneously offered man the prospect of redemption, which would have far-reaching significance for Gnostic ideas.

HERMETISM: THE FOUNDING OF A TRADITION

Holism and monism were established aspects of ancient natural philosophy. Both the idea of correspondences and the idea of nature and cosmos as a living being were already prominent in religious and philosophical discourse. However, the idea of mediation whereby transcendental knowledge is imparted to man by gods or intermediaries in a revelation was less familiar in Greek and Roman thought. (The practices of oracles and divination were different.) The origins of this discursive element in esotericism can be found in Jewish and Christian traditions. Since the third century BCE, Jewish circles had developed the idea that divine knowledge was granted to chosen groups through mediation, by the revelation of angels, which could flit between transcendence and immanence. The most important angel of revelation (*angelus interpres*) in the Jewish tradition was Enoch, who was specially predestined for this role. According to Gen. 5.23-24: 'And all the days of Enoch were three hundred sixty and five years; and Enoch walked with God, and then he was no longer there, for God had taken him'. Thus, according to Jewish interpretation, instead of dying like the other heroes of the Genesis story, Enoch lived on and could inform men of heavenly things. A literary genre developed around the figure of Enoch and his revelations, whereby the number 365, corresponding to the days of the year, was accorded a special astronomical and astrological significance, as we know from the texts of the Qumran community (see von Stuckrad 2000: 316-65).

The idea that chosen persons could enter the heavenly realms also arose early among the Jews, moreover in connection with Ezekiel's vision of the throne on the chariot (Ezek. 1 and 10). Combined with Gnostic traditions, the journey to heaven and the vision of the divine chariot would become an important element of Jewish mysticism in late antiquity. But then another personage came into play, who would become a key figure in esoteric thought up to modern times: Hermes Trismegistus.

IN SEARCH OF THE GREAT HERMES

During the Hellenistic period ancient Egyptian traditions merged with Greek religion and mythology. The union of the Egyptian Thoth and Greek Hermes has had an enduring impact on the history of esotericism. This connection was made at the time because both gods were concerned with the priestly art of writing and the revelation of hidden truths. From the third century BCE onwards, Thoth-Hermes came to be known as Hermes Trismegistus, the 'thrice-greatest Hermes' (see Koch 1993: 610-22). Hermes Trismegistus was regarded as the god who revealed all magical and occult traditions to his initiated priests. These included teachings of science, writing and especially astronomy and astrology. Here one should distinguish on the one hand the genre of the *Hermetica*, where Hermes plays a prominent role, and on the other a specific collection of texts from the early Christian period called the *Corpus Hermeticum* (see the survey in Copenhaver 1992: xiii-lxi).

As far as the *Hermetica* are concerned, the material is far from uniform and even displays variations in the nature of divine revelations. The 'Pseudo-Manethon' (V, VI, 1ff.), a text probably dating back to the Ptolemaic period, describes how the god has carved his teachings about the effects of the stars onto the columns and walls in the sanctuaries of Egyptian temples. Clement of Alexandria (c. 150–211 CE) refers to an extensive literature bearing the name of the god Hermes, stating that Hermes authored forty-two 'quite indispensable books'. The priests had to know these books 'by heart and always be able to quote them' (*Stromateis* VI, 4, 35, 2-37,1). In terms of their content, the works attributed to Hermes Trismegistus practically covered the entire magical, alchemical, astrological and natural philosophical knowledge of Hellenistic Egypt, in which older traditions were blended with Greek philosophy. In this respect, the following areas are particular interesting.

The so-called *General Discourses* (*Genika*) treat the whole area of mundane and universal astrology, namely the investigation of terrestrial change in connection with cosmic events. This includes the doctrine of rulers over particular world epochs and speculations about the expected end of the world, as already found in Greece. This simultaneously involved a discussion of the *thema mundi*, or the natal horoscope of the world. Statements about eclipses, meteorological phenomena (lightning, thunder, winds—the so-called 'brontologies'), about comets and earthquakes, probably formed a part of the 'original' Hermetic literature.

The text usually known as the *Salmeschiniaka*, the subject of scholarly controversy, contains besides detailed astronomical data a collection of remedies, amulets, and various means for avoiding cosmic influences. Medical astrology played an important role in the Hermetic writings. This is seen, for example, in the work *Iatromathematika*, which treats the subject of medicinal correspondences, and in the fact that the Greek god of medicine, Asclepius, was regarded as an astrologer and linked with Thoth-Hermes in the Hellenistic period. This aspect of Asclepius can be easily related to very ancient Egyptian views, for example 'the warnings of Ipuwer' of the Middle Empire or the *Oracle of the Potter* in the Ptolemaic period. The survival of the divinized Egyptian sage Imhotep (c. 2650 BCE) in the guise of Asclepius clearly illustrates the close proximity of Hermetic–Greek philosophy to Egyptian wisdom teachings (see Hornung 1999: 54-58).

These writings all share the assumption of a *sympathy* (as it is called in Greek and Roman philosophy), which integrates the correspondence between macrocosm and microcosm within a theosophical system of thought. This doctrine would soon become a fundamental motif of esoteric discourses. In the second century CE—and then prominently in the *Corpus Hermeticum*—a Neo-Platonic element is added, which describes the ascent of the adept through the planetary spheres, according to the secrets which Hermes Trismegistus vouchsafed to his son Tat (= Thoth) in an initiation. The Platonic 'home of light' of the soul is also the place of Christian redemption from the sufferings of the world. The tradition can be adapted to the most varied religious and social contexts. To the Christians in Nag Hammadi, Hermes Trismegistus was an Egyptian sage, who had already foretold in his teachings the salvation through Jesus.

From the point of view of their form and content, the *Hermetica* are related to texts attributed to the names Nechepso and Petosiris in the Hellenistic and Roman period. The authority of 'King Nechepso' could be traced to Necho II, who reigned in the 26th Dynasty (677–672 BCE), but nothing more definite is known about him. The same is true of the 'high priest Petosiris', for whose actual existence in the Ptolemaic period there is no evidence. One therefore usually assumes that the Hellenistic authors of these books chose these names in order to lend their writings a venerable age and thus greater authority. The similarities of their contents with the books of the *Hermetica* are extensive.

THE CORPUS *HERMETICUM* BETWEEN CHRISTIANITY, NEO-PLATONISM AND EGYPTIAN TRADITION

The *Corpus Hermeticum* represents a collection of seventeen Greek treatises (*logoi*) gathered by Byzantine scholars in the tenth century. The original writings are usually dated to the third century CE, especially as three of the texts were also found in the Nag Hammadi Codex (NHC) (see below). The *Corpus Hermeticum* plays a prominent role in the history of esotericism, especially once it was redis-covered in the fifteenth century and then regarded as evidence of an ancient wisdom tradition.

It is extremely difficult to establish the authorship of these texts. They might derive from the same cultural milieu as the other *Hermetica*, namely that complex weave of Greek and Egyptian culture during the Ptolemaic period, subject to Roman and then Christian overlays.[7] It is noticeable that in the *Corpus* the disci-plines of astrology, magic and alchemy play only a subordinate role in contrast to the practical orientation of the *Hermetica*. Instead, the treatises concentrate on theological and philosophical questions about the perceptive capacity of man, the origin of the world, and on moral topics of divine and human existence. Such questions also recur in the Latin *Asclepius*, in the forty Hermetic fragments, which *Stobæus* collected in his anthology, and in the Nag Hammadi texts. There are also other differences. In the *Corpus Hermeticum* there is far less emphasis on an alien god who wishes to hinder man's understanding as in Gnostic texts. The saviour figure who defeats the enemies of God is also usually absent. Despite these differ-ences it is possible to talk about a shared field of discourse, because certain themes and arguments link the individual groups. The Hermetic discourse of late antiq-uity embraced quite varied groups, above all the educated elite found in Christian, Gnostic and Roman circles. They also shared the same interest in the revelations of Hermes.

Knowledge as understanding is a key word of Hermetism. Already in the first treatise of the *Corpus Hermeticum* (CH), also known as *Poimandres*, we find the

---

7.   'What can be asserted is that Hermetism represents the sort of pagan intellectual milieu with which Christian Gnostics could feel that they had something in common' (Fowden 1993: 114). John Dillon (1977: 384-96) defines this field of discourse as 'the underworld of Middle Platonism'.

apodictic words: 'Holy is god who wishes to be known and is known by his own people' (CH I,31). The perceptive capacity of the believer is again inseparably bound up with the specifically Hermetic conception of the soul, whose Platonic origins are plainly evident. It is a basic Hermetic assumption that the soul, which still always carries within itself a divine spark, incarnates on Earth by descending through the heavenly spheres and is there subject to the laws of the archons, and thus to *heimarmene* (see *Poimandres*, CH I,9), from which it can liberate itself through the knowledge (*gnôsis*) of its condition (Fowden 1993: 104-105). The redemption of man from the shackles of matter and his reascent into the home of light proceeds in tandem with ethical demands which the adept must accept.[8]

The description of the soul's ascent through the spheres in *Poimandres* clearly shows a similarity with Gnostic ascent scenarios, but also with those in Jewish, Persian and Hellenistic sources:

> Thence the human being rushes up through the cosmic framework, at the first zone surrendering the energy of increase and decrease; at the second evil machination, a device now inactive; at the third the illusion of longing, now inactive; at the fourth the ruler's arrogance, now freed of excess; at the fifth unholy presumption and daring recklessness; at the sixth the evil impulses that come from wealth, now inactive; and at the seventh zone the deceit that lies in ambush. [26] And then, stripped of the effects of the cosmic framework, the human enters the region of the ogdoad [the eighth sphere]; he has his own proper power, and along with the blessed he hymns the father. Those present there rejoice together in his presence, and, having become like his companions, he also hears certain powers that exist beyond the ogdoadic region and hymn god with sweet voice. They rise up to the father in order and sur-render themselves to the powers, and, having become powers, they enter into god. This is the final good for those who have received knowledge: to be made god (CH I,25f.; trans. Copenhaver 1992: 6).

This passage is a key example of the Hermetic view of the redemption of man from the power of *heimarmene*, the result of the ascent through the cosmic spheres and successful passing of trials. Even the merging with God is quite unambiguous.

In the *Corpus Hermeticum* it is the *inner disposition* of the believer which enables him to ascend, not an external act of grace nor a cultic activity. The goal of the believer is therefore not redemption, but deification, as can be gleaned from the quotation in *Poimandres*. A series of other passages from the *Corpus Hermeticum* bear witness to this intention,[9] as do some from the Nag Hammadi Codex (NHC): 'He rises in stages and enters on the path of immortality. And in this fashion he attains knowledge of the Eight, which reveals the Nine' (NHC VI.6.63, 9-14). The passage from the NHC VI.6 refers to a Hermetic text, clearly indicated by the use of the name Hermes Trismegistus as well as the words, the adept will 'keep things secret that Hermes has said' (VI.6.63, 24). The fact that Hermetic treatises were among the texts discovered at Nag Hammadi is evidence of intellectual relations between the two social groups.

---

8. Cf. CH I,22; VI,5; IX,4; X,9; XVI,11; *Asclepius* XI,29 with NHC VI.6,56f. 62,28-33.
9. CH I,26; X,7; XI,20; XII,1; XIII,3.10.14; *Asclepius* VI,22.

Considering these relations more closely, it is evident that the concept of 'redemption' also had the connotation of 'deification' in diverse Gnostic circles, as is well known from their *theurgic* connections. While the Gnostic usually seeks ascent following death, there are also indications of a deification in this world and thus of immortality.[10] Starting with the so-called *Chaldæan Oracles*, the mystical and magical movement of theurgy flourished throughout the whole ancient world, thereby touching Hermetism, Gnosticism and sections of Jewry in the second century CE (see Lewy 1978; Johnston 1997; Berchman 1998). Theurgy was a religion for proven experts. These typically came from the intellectual elite and practised magical techniques, which were highly ritualised and contained liturgical elements. Although they were not widely known, their influence on mystical circles of the period should not be underestimated. When Georgios Gemistos Plethon asserted in the fifteenth century that the author of the *Chaldæan Oracles* was no lesser person than Zoroaster, an entire 'mnemonic history' of esoteric identities was elaborated around this motif.

But let us return to the *Corpus Hermeticum*. Mystical Neo-Platonism overlaid with Christianity made a deep impression on the concept of the soul, and questions regarding the perceptive capacity of man, which can also be seen in the idea of reincarnation. For example, the thirteenth treatise of the *Corpus Hermeticum* contains a dialogue between Hermes Trismegistus and his son Tat on the question of reincarnation. Tat wishes to have more precise information about the Hermetic doctrine that nobody can be saved before they have been reincarnated (CH XIII, 1). Hermes thereupon explains that man is tormented by twelve sins and thus trapped in the 'prison of the body'. These tormentors withdraw one by one from the man who receives God's mercy and this is the manner and teaching of reincarnation (CH XIII, 7). The rule of the 'Twelve' [sins] is broken by the arrival of the 'Ten' [virtues], which lead to a spiritual birth as well as to the deification of man (CH XIII, 10). This is not easy to understand and even Tat asks why the Ten should triumph over the Twelve. His father therefore gives a fuller explanation:

> This tent—from which we also have passed, my child—was constituted from the zodiacal circle, which was in turn constituted of…entities that are twelve in number, one in nature, omniform in appearance. To mankind's confusion, there are disjunctions among the twelve, my child, though they are unified when they act… Strictly speaking, then, it is likely that the twelve retreat when the ten powers (the decad, that is) drive them away. The decade engenders soul, my child. Life and light are unified when the number of the henad, of spirit, is begotten. Logically, then, the henad contains the decad, and the decad the henad… This, my child, is rebirth: no longer picturing things in three bodily dimensions… [T]hrough this discourse on being born again that I have noted down for you alone to avoid casting it all before the mob but [to give it] to those whom god himself wishes (CH XIII,12-13; trans. Copenhaver 1993: 52).

---

10. Cf. NHC VI.6.60,4-5; CH XIII, 1.22 and also *Asclepius* 41.

The body is the prison, which is composed of twelve zodiacal signs. The signs of the zodiac represent the coarse material of the body, which is clearly devalued in Gnostic and Hermetic thought in favour of the subtle body, which is granted to man through spiritual rebirth.

WHAT IS 'GNOSIS'?

'Gnosis' is a difficult concept, not least because it is not the self-description of individual ancient communities, but a polemic employed by the established Christian Church.[11] This leads to difficulties in the nomenclature of religious communities. By adopting the rhetoric of the Church apologists, scholarly discourse runs the risk of identifying with their strategy of exclusion. The early Church already exhibited a wide diversity of viewpoints arising from regional, social and political differences. Within that wider perspective one finds many Christian groups expelled on suspicion of heresy from 'true Christianity' in the course of Church history.

GNOSIS AND THE CHURCH

This applies particularly to the 'Gnosis' which is readily juxtaposed to the 'Church' or to 'orthodoxy'. A glance at the self-descriptions of the Gnostic groups illustrates the dilemma of this position. Ecclesiastical apologists tended to use the term *Gnostics*, unless they named these groups 'Valentinians', 'Marcionites' and so on after their founders. For example, Hippolytus gives a definition: 'All these people prefer to call themselves "Knowers" [Gnostics], because they alone have drunk the wonderful "knowledge" [*gnôsis*] of perfection and goodness' (*Refutatio* V, 23, 3). These kinds of appellation are nowhere to be found in the newly discovered primary sources. Instead, the original writings tend to reveal the inner conflicts of different forms of Christianity with regard to the accepted theological interpretation. This conflict had concrete political and social implications. The *Testimony of Truth* is strongly polemical:

> The foolish—thinking [in] their heart [that] if they confess, 'We are Christians,' in word only (but) not in power, while giving themselves over to ignorance, to a human death, not knowing where they are going nor who Christ is, thinking that they will live, when they are (really) in error—Hasten towards the principalities and the authorities. They fall into their clutches because of the ignorance that is in them. For (if) only words which bear testimony were effecting salvation, the whole world would endure this thing [and] be saved.[12]

11. There is a great deal of debate over 'Gnosis' and 'Gnosticism' in scholarly circles. On the one hand, there are some who regard the concept of Gnosticism as relevant for the description of concrete historical religions as well as their intellectual influence in history; on the other hand, there are those who criticise the discourse of 'Gnosis' and 'Gnosticism' as fundamentally artificial and seek alternatives, as Michael Allen Williams has in an important study (1996).

12. NHC IX.3,31,22-32,12; trans. Robinson 1990: 450.

The believers behind this text doubtless regarded themselves as *Christians*, and moreover as 'orthodox' Christians. Accordingly, they could brand rival Christian communities as heretics in the same way as the 'Church' apologists did. The NHC text mentions the Valentinians as well as the followers of Basilides and Simon. The problem becomes even more acute when one considers that prominent Gnostics, above all Valentinus, regarded their communities as a church (Gk. *ekklesia*).

Instead of adopting later simplified attributions, one must endeavour to regard the various Christian groups on their own terms and to take them seriously. One can then detect certain alliances reflecting the contemporary religious and social language. In the second century Celsus may not have been so mistaken when he admitted no conceptual division between 'Church' and 'Gnosis'; finally, even Irenaeus himself complained that the majority of Christians no longer saw the Valentinians as heretics and could not name their differences with orthodox doctrine.[13] Not only were the labels 'Gnosis' and 'Christianity' exceedingly flexible, but even their social and political consequences illustrate the lack of clarity in ancient opinions. The highly regarded (Gnostic) theologian Valentinus might almost have been elected Bishop of Rome, and by contrast, leading ecclesiastical apologists are later found among the ranks of heretics. Thus Epiphanius of Salamis calls Origen 'the chief of the heretics', Hippolytus was condemned by Pope Kallistos, and the writings of Tertullian were declared heretical by the Gelasian Edict of 495 CE. One should recall that Epiphanius (*Prooemium* I, 4, 3-8) listed sixty Gnostic groups in his incomplete register of heretics.

NEW SOURCES FOR THE HISTORY OF EARLY CHRISTIANITY

The discovery of the Nag Hammadi texts in 1945 have greatly increased our understanding of these groups' own outlook. Their writings comprise a corpus of thirteen volumes composed in the middle of the fourth century. Some scholars suspect that these texts came from the library of a monastery, others see in them the writings of a Gnostic community. More recent scholarship is less certain in this regard. Alongside the *Pistis Sophia* first published in 1778, the *Books of Jeû* published in 1891, and the *Papyrus Berolinensis*, these texts written in Coptic represent the most important source for research into Gnosticism. On the basis of the Nag Hammadi texts, we are now in a position to scrutinise the theology of the Gnostic groups in their own documents, as opposed to relying only on secondary sources.

One must consider both sides of this debate if one wishes to understand the social implications of certain formulations of esotericism.[14] The Christian

---

13. Irenaeus, *Adversus haereses* III,16,6-8; on the whole subject see Pagels 1979, Chapter 2.

14. The most important Church writings which had an almost canonical influence on the Gnostic debate up to our own century were as follows: *Adversus haereses* by Irenaeus of Lyons (c. 140–200) written between 185 and 189, the *Refutatio omnium haeresium* of Hippolytus of Rome (d. c. 235), which he composed three years before his death, the work *De praescriptione haereticorum* by Tertullian (c. 160–222) and finally *Panarion haeresium* by Epiphanius of Salamis (c. 315–403). Justinus (d. between 163 and 167), Clement of Alexandria (c. 200) and Eusebius (first half of the fourth century) are also informative with regard to esotericism.

controversy over what we call esotericism, then chiefly focused on questions of astrology and magic, is moreover part of a wider social debate. It is simply impossible to understand Gnosticism without reference to other religious phenomena of the ancient world. To form a balanced view one cannot just consider Christian hostility towards Gnosticism. One should also examine documents of a non-Christian origin relating directly or indirectly to Gnostic discourses.

GNOSIS AND GNOSTICISM

Ancient religious communities created an esoteric network, which in turn throws interesting light on their own historical interaction. On the one hand, we see the historical growth and interweaving of religious phenomena, and on the other we have the concepts 'Gnosis/Gnosticism' drawn from the history of ideas. It is often difficult to distinguish between them, because there never was a Gnostic institution or a binding Gnostic canon, except at most in the case of the Marcionites and Manichaeans.[15]

Christoph Markschies has conceived of Gnosis as a *typological model*, describing movements that establish their special interest in the rational conception of insight ('knowledge') in theological systems. The latter are as a rule characterised by a certain combination of ideas or motifs in their texts (see Markschies 2003, Chapter 1). Markschies identifies eight core ideas in this combination: (1) the idea of a completely transcendent, remote, and supreme God; (2) the introduction of further divine figures or the splitting of existing figures into those that are nearer to man than the distant supreme God; (3) the evaluation of the world and matter as an evil creation and the consequent Gnostic experience of being in an alien world; (4) the introduction of a creative deity or assistant, usually called the demiurge according to Platonic tradition, seen as both ignorant and as a counterfoil to the Deity; (5) the explanation of this state through a mythological drama, in which the divine element falls from his own sphere into the evil world, slumbers as a divine spark in a certain class of men, and can then be liberated; (6) knowledge ('Gnosis') about this situation, which is often achieved through a transcendent redeemer figure descending from a higher sphere and then returning; (7) redemption through an understanding that God is living as a spark in man; (8) a variable tendency towards dualism, which can be expressed in the concept of deity, in the juxtaposition of spirit and matter, and in anthropology.

15. The attempt of the Messina Conference in 1966 to distinguish 'Gnosis' as a categorical or systematic concept from the phenomenological, historical aspect of 'Gnosticism' did not satisfy scholars for long. Both concepts have such a close relationship that their separation can only lead to artificial and ultimately false conclusions. This does not mean that 'Gnosis' cannot be understood in the sense of a certain spiritual attitude. Once removed from its original historical context, Gnosis was able to influence European intellectual history in ever new variations through the centuries. Thus Eric Voegelin (1953/54: 43) can regard the modern period as the 'gnostic age', while Hans Blumenberg (1983: 144) constrastingly sees the modern period as prevailing over the 'gnostic relapse'. Due to these confusions, the concept 'Gnosis' appears philosophically and historically useful only when in agreement with an historically founded typology, even if this must remain open on all sides.

There is obviously an overlap between Gnostic and esoteric motifs. Both groups of ideas intersect at many points without, however, being identical.

SELF-EMPOWERMENT OF KNOWLEDGE

Even if knowledge is frequently revealed to fallen men in matter by intermediary figures, Gnostic thought does not exclude the possibility of self-knowledge and its consequent self-salvation. As in the case of theurgy, dividing lines can be seen between individual Christian and Jewish groups of late antiquity, whose importance for the ensuing period can scarcely be overestimated.

The philosophical schools already discussed were primarily responsible for this. Gnostic ideas about the creation of the cosmos and man, involving the redemption of man and his soul through an ascent through the astral planes, are very close to the philosophical discussions surrounding *heimarmene* and astrology. Hippolytus already clearly made this point: when he stated the views of the heretics 'have their origin in the wisdom of the Greeks, in philosophical outlooks, in borrowed mysteries and in wandering astrologers' (*Refutatio* I,8; see also Porphyry, *Vita Plotini* 16).

The tension between human freedom and the cosmic powers which determine terrestrial fate assume a central importance in Gnosticism. The astrological idea of *heimarmene* is thereby adopted, with the archons as representatives of divine power simultaneously relegated to demons, who cannot ultimately resist liberated man's longing for knowledge. The detailed investigation of those astral powers is thus a natural concern of the Gnostic quest. The human soul is threatened by the powers of the heavens and the demonised planetary spheres. Against these, the believer posits the *gnôsis*, which can free him from the shackles of the *heimarmene*. In this sense, Gnosis has been appropriately called a religion of self-liberation or the *self-empowerment of the knowing subject*.[16] The *Corpus Hermeticum* (CH XIII,15) explicitly refers to the adept's ability to know *all things by oneself*. The same is seen in CH I,20, when Poimandres scolds the adept: 'You behave like a person who has not given thought to what he has heard. Did I not tell you to think?'

The motif of self-empowerment and knowledge of absolute truth, irrespective of whether it is called 'Gnosis' or not, recurs throughout esoteric discourses.

TRANSMISSION INTO THE MIDDLE AGES

The Christianisation of the Roman Empire and the establishment of Christianity as the state religion created a new context for some traditions of the ancient world. Others were excluded from the mainstream of Christianity in its orthodox sense. This particularly applied to those forms of Christianity which followed an

---

16. 'The critical factor…is the conviction [of the Gnostics], that the truth is accessible to man through his *own* insight and authority. The Church fathers insisted that God's decrees were not comprehensible to his flock of sheep. Thereby they sought to silence doubts regarding the authority of the Church and to extricate themselves from the vicissitudes of biblical exegesis' (Pauen 1994: 36).

individual path of salvation or regarded as authoritative other scripture besides the New Testament, soon to become canonical. However, one should not conceive of the success of Christianity as a majority religion in too linear a fashion. Not only were there still countless wings of Christianity, which jockeyed for recognition, but Christianity's understanding of itself was also significantly influenced through its debate with non-Christian religions. The pagan religions which still had their adherents played this role in the Mediterranean region, while Manichaeism and Zoroastrianism represented a particular challenge in the Middle East. The rise of Islam then led to a confrontation, which has marked European history of religion right up to the present.

Esoteric motifs were transmitted primarily by groups apart from the state Christianity of Rome. Judaism, Manichaeism and a multiplicity of 'Gnostic' communities ensured that such religious and philosophical thought was fostered. Swiftly blooming in a diverse variety of schools, Islam also adopted many Hermetic and esoteric motifs and integrated them into a new context.

THE MANICHAEAN SWITCHBOARD

The *Religion of Light* was one of the great contemporary religions, deriving from its founder Mani (14 April 216–276). Manichaeism, as outsiders called the new religion, arose from Judaeo-Christian baptist movements in Syria and the strong influence of Gnostic theology. From the outset Mani took special care that his words became Scripture and could only be interpreted by appointed individuals in a tightly organised network. The adherents of his religion regarded themselves as the 'true church of Christ', again demonstrating that there were many Christian-inspired communities competing as the legitimate followers of Jesus in the third century.

From the fourth century onwards Manichaeism was heavily persecuted by the Roman Church and it was only able to survive in the East in the peaceful coexistence of Manichaeism, Christianity and Buddhism along the Silk Road. In the eighth century Manichaeism even became the state religion of the Uighur Empire, until the Mongol attack led to its eclipse in the thirteenth century. A few traces survived until the seventeenth century in Buddhist sanctuaries of China. Manichaeism thereby assumes a major importance in the history of religion in late antiquity, especially in regard to the interaction between East and West, and the continuities between the Roman world, the Syrian cultural zone, and the areas under Muslim jurisdiction. Scholarly research into this extremely complex period of religious history has made great progress in recent decades, largely due to the discovery of new primary sources, including the Cologne Mani Codex, the Tebessa Codex from Algeria and the most recent finds at Kellis in the Dakhleh oasis of Egypt. All these sources can now be compared with the already known *Kephalaia* of Mani, the central document of his religion.[17]

17. An impressive description of Manichaeism, making use of these newly accessible primary sources, is BeDuhn 2000.

The importance of Manichaeism for esotericism is illustrated by the role of astrology. In the Manichaean system the planets possess a comparable status to that in Gnostic and Hermetic writings. They represent the evil powers of *heimarmene* and are responsible as archons, that is, ruling powers, for hostile cosmic regions. The planets rule in the fourth region of the universe together with the twelve houses of the zodiac. They give power over war and peace, order and chaos, the captivity of the soul, desire and property. At the end of time, heralded by revelation and the mission of Mani, their reign will reach its conclusion and the soul of the elect will be freed from their power. Up until this point Mani still conforms to Gnostic and Hermetic references. The seven planetary powers have, however, been modified, because Mani excludes the Sun and the Moon from being negatively regarded as archons. But in order to preserve the traditional numerical system of seven, he replaces these two lights with the two lunar nodes.

The exclusion of the Sun and the Moon is Mani's own achievement. It is a consequence of the important role of Sun and Moon in the journey of the human soul back to its home of light. Both lights are described as 'ships', which transport the souls illuminated by Mani. They are simultaneously 'guardians of the gate', which sort the wheat from the chaff at the entrance to the heavenly realms of light. Thus Mani confidently asserts in the Cologne Mani Codex:

> I have demonstrated the truth to my travelling companions, I have proclaimed peace to the children of peace; I have preached hope to the immortal race; I have selected the chosen and I have shown the path which leads up above, and I have shown it to them, who ascend in accordance with this truth. (67)

This positive regard for the Sun and the Moon did not escape others. Epiphanius, for example, characterised the Manichaeans as follows: 'They pray to the Sun and the Moon…they proclaim the Seven and the Twelve, according to them there are lucky stars and destiny, and they are zealous in the art of the Chaldæans' (*Panarion* LXVI,13). This description certainly accords with the facts, for Mani himself relates that he advised a man 'to rest, to pray and kneel down before the heavenly lights' (Cologne Mani Codex 127f.; cf. 141f.).

Mani thus develops a complex astrological doctrine in his instructions which forms a dialogue within his *Kephalaia*. It is interesting to note that he does not regard the connections between the sphere of the planets and the terrestrial world as causal but symbolic in nature. In the view of the 'illuminator', the planets and houses of the zodiac are linked to corresponding planes via their 'roots' and 'conduits'. Connections are visible in both directions. In reply to the disciples' question how the relationship between the 'conduits' and the zodiac should be conceived—for the former could be entangled in the latter—Mani explained: 'The reason that the conduits shall not be cut is that they are *spiritual*' (*Kephalaia* 49, trans. Iain Gardner). It is similar to when a ship sails through the water: at first the prow divides the water and causes waves, but the surface swiftly closes behind the ship and its course can no longer be seen. The 'conduits' are thus subtle and ultimately spiritual links between the levels of reality—clear evidence of the esoteric idea of correspondences.

THE MYSTERIOUS SABAEANS

The Manichaeans were certainly not the only religious community to pass on and rearrange esoteric motifs. Muslim circles also took them directly from Syria and Mesopotamia into their doctrines. But there is another group besides the Gnostic, Manichaean and Persian religious communities which is of particular interest in the elaboration of esoteric traditions, namely the Sabaeans. The name 'Sabaean' gives recurrent rise to mythical speculations, first, in connection with the mysterious 'Queen of Sheba', then on account of a puzzling link with the Nabataeans, whose empire likewise lay near the Silk Road, and finally due to claims about the city of Harran in northern Mesopotamia, famed since yore for its important cult of the Moon.

The Moon Temple of Harran was destroyed by Christians in 386, but this did not prevent the local population from adhering to the local astral cult. In 639 the town was occupied by Muslim conquerors, and if one can believe the later Arabic documents, the people of Harran very soon requested permission to rebuild the Moon Temple. The important chronicler an-Nadīm writes in the tenth century that the Harranians employed a ruse to gain the protection of the Muslims: they simply called themselves 'Sabaeans', because this religious community is mentioned by name in the Qur'an; according to the prevailing law they could not then be persecuted (see an-Nadīm's *Fihrist* in Dodge 1970: 752). They evidently even tried to make use of biblical tradition to make good their claim: Abraham was said to have come from Harran and was described as the adherent of an astral cult, whereby the Sabaean religion could be regarded as the precursor of Islam. The Muslim authorities were convinced and endorsed the Sabaeans.

The matter is further complicated by the fact that around 875 a group of scholars in Baghdad called themselves 'Harranians' and stood in high regard as Sabaeans until the eleventh century. Even if the actual links between the two groups of Sabaeans are obscure, the documents are unequivocal that there was, until 1081, when the second Moon Temple was destroyed, a community in Harran and Baghdad, which practised a pagan religion, studied Greek philosophy and accorded Hermes an important position in their doctrine (see Walbridge 2001: 37-42). We know from the Muslim astrologer and natural philosopher al-Būrûnî (973–c. 1050), that the Harranians traced their religion back to Solon, the forefather of Plato. They counted Hermes, Agathadaemon, Asclepius, Pythagoras and others among the prophets of their religion. Given their proximity to the Hermetic tradition it is quite possible that the 'book' one had to possess to come under Islamic protection was a collection of texts resembling what is known today as the *Corpus Hermeticum*.[18] After all, the *Fihrist* hands down a saying of the scholar

18. John Walbridge goes so far as to suggest that 'some form of the *Corpus Hermeticum* was probably in use as scripture, at least among the philosophical elite. Certainly, this high Sabianism

al-Kindī, that he had 'examined a book, in which the people [of Harran] believe. It consisted of excellent treatises of Hermes regarding the divine unity, which he wrote for his son.'

The Sabaeans are a single chapter in the long history of the reception of Hermetic and Neo-Platonic motifs, which produced an abundance of literary works and esoteric speculations in Islam.

contained exactly the mix of philosophical, occult, and scientific ideas that we would expect in a late Neoplatonic cult' (Walbridge 2001: 40).

3

THE KABBALAH:
UNDERSTANDING THE HIDDEN
IN THE REVEALED

Jewish mysticism has decisively influenced the development of European esotericism again and again since late antiquity. Given the magical and theurgical aspects of Jewish mysticism, Jews in late antiquity and medieval times were initially fascinated by Neo-Platonic interpretations of the hidden meaning of texts. With the rise of the Kabbalah in the twelfth century, esotericism acquired an extremely complex form of theological and philosophical mysticism whose influence was soon felt beyond Jewry. From the fifteenth to the seventeenth century Kabbalah developed into such a major movement within European Jewry that a schism almost resulted between kabbalistic and rabbinical Judaism. For their part, Christians absorbed kabbalistic ideas and transformed them into a specifically Christian Kabbalah, the ideas of which were still influential on nineteenth-century philosophy. The Kabbalah is thus not only an important tradition of Jewish, Muslim and Christian esotericism but also a nodal point in European history of religion, where alternative religious options are polemically contrasted with each other.

PREHISTORY: HEKHALOT MYSTICISM AND ESOTERIC BIBLICAL EXEGESIS

The Hebrew–Aramaic Bible represents the pillar of religious thought and practice in the Jewish tradition. It was believed that God had revealed everything concerning world events and their interpretation, but as the literal sense of the text offered no simple answer to all questions, the Jews constantly sought deeper levels of meaning in the Bible beyond the obvious. For example, in the first century CE, Philo of Alexandria developed an allegorical interpretation of the Bible, in which biblical statements could be regarded as a code for an *idea* lying behind the text in a Platonic sense. He was less concerned with the actual Temple in Jerusalem, destroyed by the Romans in 70 CE, than with the idea of the Temple, which existed beyond time and space and symbolised a fundamental truth always accessible to the Jews. The allegorical interpretation of the Bible was an important tool for rabbinical exegesis developed between the second and eighth centuries, finding expression in the principal works of Jewish religious literature such as the Mishnah, the Talmud and the Midrash.

The ingenious inventory of rabbinical hermeneutics contained yet another tool: the unveiling of the *sôd*, the secret of a scriptural passage. In order to detect this secret, one could, for example, convert the letters of the text into numbers and examine these for hidden correspondences and connections. Alternatively, one might vocalize the Hebrew consonantal text in such a way that it suddenly disclosed quite different dimensions of meaning. Both techniques relied upon specific properties of the Hebrew language. Like Aramaic and Arabic, the Hebrew script is a consonantal script, that is, one without characters for vowels. When reading a text, one must retrospectively supply the vowels. This is at times a highly creative process, since different vocalisations produce quite different meanings. Although a normative vocalisation of the biblical text became standard at an early stage, rabbinical scholars were always aware that this could form only one of many variations of the content and that the sacredness and inviolability of the texts solely resided in its consonants.

One can illustrate this problem well with a much discussed example. The Bible begins with the consonantal series *BR'Sh(Y)T*, which is usually read as $B^eR^eSh^iT$ and translated as 'in the beginning'. But if one vocalised the word as $B^aR^aSh^aT$, it would mean 'with the head', that is 'with reason'. In fact this version had many supporters. Aramaic translations of the Bible in the first few centuries give the first sentence of the book of Genesis as 'With reason did Elohim create heaven and earth'. But this is not all. The Aramaic word for 'reason' is *hokhmah*, which once again in a kabbalistic reading means that God created the world with the power of the second *Sefirah*, namely Hokhmah (I will deal with the *Sefirot* below). The unveiling of the secret meaning of the text leads to the attainment of levels of meaning which were not initially apparent. So thought Menahem ben Solomon Recanati (*fl.* 1300), when he said: 'Know then that we must understand the hidden from the revealed'. Gershom Scholem, the founder of the scholarly study of Kabbalah, wrote:

> Those secret signatures (*Rishumim*), which God concealed in things are as much veils of his revelation as a revelation of his veiling… Therefore the revelation is one bearing on the name or names of God, which reflect the various modes of his Being. The language of God has no grammar. It only consists of names. (Scholem 1962: 34)

Another property of the Hebrew language is similarly important for kabbalistic interpretation: namely that each of the 22 consonants is assigned a numerical value. Applying this to a scriptural passage, new connections become apparent which would remain hidden to the untrained eye. The numerical sum of individual words can correspond to that of another word—or even to the numerical value of individual names of God. Whole sentences can have a mysterious connection with other sentences in this manner. Such an interpretation was a matter of debate in rabbinical hermeneutics and usually subordinate to literal and allegorical means, but this playing with numerical relationships formed an established part of kabbalistic exegesis.

THE CHARIOT THRONE AND HEAVENLY HALLS

Esoteric speculations can already be found in the Bible, for instance with regard to Enoch (see above, p. 18), in Ezekiel's visions of the heavenly throne (Ezek. 1 and 10) and especially in the cult theology practised by the Qumran community. However, the basic features of what one can call 'Jewish mysticism' were first developed in rabbinical times. Through the discovery of an enormous cache of treasure, which medieval Jews had deposited in the Cairo *Genizah*—a repository for writings which could not be destroyed as they contained the names of God— our knowledge of this magical and mystical tradition is far greater than a century ago.

In antiquity there was an entire literary genre concerned with the ascent of specially elect persons into heavenly realms. It was mostly the heroes of Holy Scripture—Enoch, Moses, Solomon and others—who found admittance to the divine spheres and on their return gave their contemporaries 'below' an account in the form of a revelation. The texts attributed to them were then known as an 'apocalypse' ('revelation') or a 'testament'. In the rabbinical period the biblical heroes were increasingly joined by rabbis like Rabbi Aqiba or individual mystics, whose transports to heaven engaged believers. The fascination of such excursions was by no means restricted to Jewry.

There developed a broad literary genre known as Hekhalot mysticism.[1] *Hekhalot* is the Hebrew word for the heavenly 'halls' or palaces visited by the mystic. In the seventh hall stands the chariot throne of God, which the prophet Ezekiel once saw in his vision. The Hekhalot mystic is a representative of the people of Israel, who, once enraptured into heavenly spheres, communicates with the world of angels and intercedes with God on behalf of Israel. The heavenly spheres, regarded as the concentric circles of the planets in accordance with contemporary cosmology, through which the mystic ascended, also related to astrological ideas, as can be deduced from the major significance of the numbers seven and twelve.

The mysteries of the Merkabah and the Creation, the two foremost themes of early Jewish mysticism, were among the most subtle topics of theological contemplation. The *ma'asê merkavah* ('Work of the Chariot Throne') and the *ma'asê b^ereshît* ('Work of Creation'), as these secret doctrines were known in rabbinical terminology, were subject to severe restrictions. The Mishnah (second century CE) states: 'One shall not explicate about cases of fornication before three persons, about the Work of Creation before two, and about the Merkabah before one person, but only if he is wise and can understand' (Hagiga Tract 2:1).

---

1. For a comprehensive account see Schäfer 1991.

These ideas find expression in magical and theurgical terms. The ascent is described as a dangerous undertaking and the adept will do well to know the passwords and oaths required for the voyage into the heavenly spheres:

> If you want to be lifted in the world,
> To be shown the secrets of the world and the mysteries of wisdom,
> Then learn this Mishnah and walk carefully in its ways until the day of your departure.
> Do not ascertain what lies behind you, and do not query the words from your lips.
> You should fathom what is in your heart and keep silent,
> To be worthy of the beauty of the Merkabah.
> Have careful dealings with the magnificence of your Creator... (see Schäfer 1991: 68f.)

The sense of a theurgical invocation is plainly evident in the passage:

> Praised be his name,
> The great, fearsome, strong,
> Bold, powerful and noble one
> Whom our eyes have seen
> And with whose name we conjure:
> I conjure you, MQLYThW, with the name...[2]

As in the case of Gnosticism and Hermeticism, Neo-Platonic concepts have contributed to the elaboration of such ideas (see Scholem 1991 [1957]: 43-86, and Davila 2001). However, in this case it is the collective knowledge and salvation of the people of Israel that is now centre stage.

SEFER YETZIRAH

The platonizing cosmologies and anthropologies so widespread in late antiquity also entered Jewish mysticism. Towards the end of the Talmudic era, in the late seventh century, these traditions began to be systematized, thus creating the first really mystical work of Jewish literature: the *Sefer Yetzirah*, the 'Book of Formation (Creation)'. A longer and a shorter version of this work have survived, but older variant texts can also be reconstructed (see Gruenwald 1971). The final version was probably compiled in the ninth century. Here, the esoteric doctrine of correspondences between the microcosm and the macrocosm are introduced, often in a cryptic fashion, ranging from astrological and astronomical correspondences through considerations of anatomy to an interpretation of time and historical periods. These doctrines are linked with the traditional theology of the Torah and simultaneously packed with exhaustive discussions of the symbolism inherent in Hebrew language and characters.

The Sefer Yetzirah divides the 22 consonants of the Hebrew alphabet into three groups, known as three 'mothers', seven 'doubles' and twelve 'singles'. The latter are then associated with the twelve zodiacal signs, the group comprising seven with

---

2. See Schäfer 1991: 68. The name *MQLYThW* is an anagram of consonants whose meaning is ambiguous.

the seven planets, the seven days of the week and corresponding parts of the body. The letter Taf claims a key position as the last letter, since it closes the circle to the first letter—Aleph—which is one of the 'mothers'.[3]

This is the first attempt to systematise esoteric motifs in a comprehensive manner while employing traditions of theological and hermeneutic interpretation. The book is also highly significant inasmuch as it mentions the *Sefirot*, which later achieve such importance. The Hebrew word *s'firah* (Pl. *s'firot*) actually means only 'number' or 'counting', and this is how it was used in the Sefer Yetzirah. The Sefirot are simple numerical sequences for the ordering of individual letters and their cosmological and anthropological correspondences. There are already indications of a Platonic interpretation of these correspondences as 'fundamental principles', but several centuries would elapse before a refined Sefirot doctrine developed as the core of kabbalistic thought.

The Classical Kabbalah: From Southern France to Israel

'Kabbalah' as a collective term can signify quite different currents even just within a Jewish context. Due to social and religious change over the centuries, there arose distinct forms of mystical speculation and practice, which each in their time claimed to represent the 'authentic' Kabbalah.[4] The roots of the kabbalistic movement can be traced back to southern France in the twelfth century.[5] From the perspective of the history of religion, it was no coincidence that kabbalistic and mystical ideas developed in Provence. Between the twelfth and fourteenth centuries this same region experienced the marked rise of oppositional Christian sects, chiefly the Cathars and Albigensians, whose claims to represent 'true' Christianity against the established Church could only be met with violent suppression. Even if it is still disputed whether there were exchanges between these often esoteric forms of Christianity and the representatives of the early Kabbalah, one can assume that they were aware of each other.[6]

Beginning with a few individuals, who gathered a rapidly growing number of students in the twelfth century, there developed a mystical movement speculating on the operation of divine powers in the world. These were closely related to terrestrial events—especially the pious observance of the Torah by the people of Israel—and so formed the total framework of the world process. Owing to their secret character, these doctrines were not initially written down; nevertheless, they gained wider and wider circulation until they found their first literary expression

---

3.   On this subject see Maier 1995: 38-43.

4.   Whoever seeks a detailed account is referred to the pertinent literature. The writings of Scholem are still landmarks of scholarship, which have been supplemented today by Idel 1988 and 2002.

5.   The standard work on the following subject is Scholem 1962.

6.   For the exchange beween Judaism, Christianity and Islam, see also Nederman 2000 and Meyerson and English 2000.

around 1180 in the *Sefer ha-Bahîr*, the 'Bright Shining Book', which speculates on the ten divine powers described as 'rays', 'lights', 'crowns', 'kings', 'roots' and such terms. The 'flowing' and 'pouring' of transcendental powers, clearly inspired by the symbolism of Neo-Platonic emanationism, was linked with the traditional ideas of biblical and rabbinical literature. It must be emphasised that Kabbalah never considered itself as a protest movement. On the contrary, by calling themselves *mᵉqûbbalîm* ('accepted adepts') of an ancient tradition, the early kabbalists stressed the traditionalism of their doctrine; even the word *qabbalah* means 'tradition'. In point of fact, the Kabbalah 'despite its speculative innovations proved to be the most effective agent for the preservation and deepening of Torah piety in the Jewish religion' (Maier 1995: 47).

FROM SEFIROT MYSTICISM TO THE SEFER HA-ZOHAR

A further systematisation and literary formulation of the kabbalistic secret doctrine occurred in the thirteenth century. In this process the elaboration of Sefirot symbolism became a focal point of interest. To gain a clearer understanding of what the Sefirot signified at this time, it is helpful to look at the writings of Joseph ben Abraham Gikatilla (1248–c. 1325) from Segovia, whose structured works still offer one of the best introductions to kabbalistic thought. In 1274 his *Ginnat 'egôs* ('Nut Garden') appeared, followed after 1293 by *Sha'arê tzedeq* ('Portal of Justice') and *Sha'arê 'ôrah* ('Portal of Light'), all works on the interpretation of the variety of divine names and revolving around what was universally understood as the 'Sefirot'.

I have already indicated in the context of the Sefer Yetzirah that the Hebrew word *sefirah* simply means 'number' or 'counting'. However, this proved insufficient and there developed explanations to help evaluate the idea in a Platonic sense, for example by its derivation from the Greek *sphaira* ('sphere'). These derivations cannot be proven linguistically and from the point of view of content the Sefirot do not relate to the spheres of ancient cosmology but to the *effective means of the deity* in a complex system of relationships which is called *middôt* ('qualities', 'properties') in kabbalistic jargon. A whole series of metaphorical expressions was used to describe the emanation of divine power between the transcendent world of the divinity and the revealed world of men. These metaphors ranged from 'rays' and 'speaking tubes' through 'lights' to 'emanations' (Heb. *'atziliyôt*). The notion of 'crowns' (*kᵉtarîm*) is a further development of the traditional conception of the god-king and courtly state from the mystical tradition.

According to Joseph Gikatilla and others the system of the Sefirot lies between the absolute divine Being, which cannot be described other than *Ein Sôf* ('The Endless'), and the world of the angels and spiritual intermediaries which in turn provide contact with the material world. The ten effective powers of God are usually ranked in the form of a 'Tree', whose 'branches' are connected with each other in various ways. (Illustration1 shows a common version from the seventeenth century.) Vertically considered, there are two opposed 'columns' whose duality is balanced by a central column. Horizontally, the highest Sefirot (I–III) are located so near to the transcendent divinity that scarcely any mortal can reach them, while the lower Sefirot, especially IX and X, represent the most important references for the people of Israel.

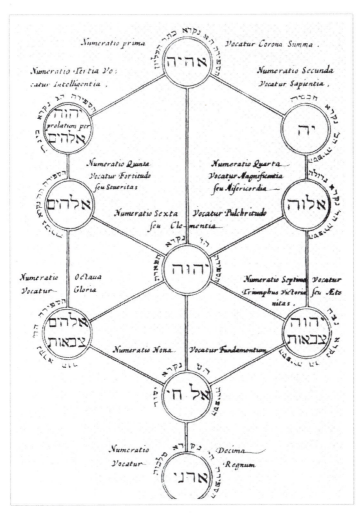

Illustration 1. This representation of the *sefirot* on the Tree of Life, taken from a 1642 edition of the *Sefer Yetzirah*, gives the names of God in Hebrew letters corresponding to the individual *sefirot*. The Hebrew explanations printed around the *sefirot* indicate their Hebrew names together with their Latin translations. (Rittangelius, *Id est liber Jetzirah* [1642]. Bibliotheca Philosophica Hermetica, Amsterdam [BPH], arch. No. R 46 622/10)

The kabbalist regards the system of the Sefirot both as a complete image of the effective means of God as can be deduced from the Bible and also a model for describing the historical course of Jewish salvation. Only when all Sefirot are in harmony and balance will the people of Israel do justice to their cosmic responsibility. Such disturbances as arise from evil powers or through Israel's neglect of Torah piety hinder a harmonious enactment of divine salvation. This explains why kabbalists were so 'conservative' and put such a high value on the exact fulfilment of biblical commandments. It also shows how magical and theurgical elements found a place in the kabbalistic system. By applying prayers, meditations and rituals to specific Sefirot, kabbalists believed they could influence the course of the world and finally unite with the effective power of God (see Swartz 1996). This branch of Kabbalah has been described as 'ecstatic' or 'prophetic' Kabbalah and linked with the name Abraham ben Samuel Abulafia (1240–after 1291) (see Scholem 1991 [1957]: 128-70). Abulafia is the best known representative of a kabbalistic current, which strove to achieve 'absolute knowledge' by direct experience and not through expert biblical interpretation nor mediations by intermediaries. Joseph Gikatilla was among Abulafia's pupils but later devoted himself entirely to a more 'theosophical' Kabbalah. The platonising magic of the 'ecstatic' Kabbalah was seized upon with great interest in the fifteenth century by thinkers like Marsilio Ficino and especially Pico della Mirandola, as it could very easily be combined with their own holistic view of the cosmos.[7]

By the second half of the thirteenth century kabbalistic ideas, now known as such, had spread in many districts of southern France and the Iberian peninsula. Besides Joseph Gikatilla and Abraham Abulafia there were other important representatives of this early Kabbalah, now increasingly committed to writing. An important contribution was made by Moses ben Shemtov de Léon (d. 1305), who worked in Spain and made the acquaintance of Joseph Gikatilla in the 1270s. Both authors henceforth strongly influenced each other. Moses de Léon composed parts of a work, which thanks to the influence of Isaac Luria two hundred and fifty years later would become an almost canonical text of kabbalistic Jewry: the *Sefer ha-Zohar*, the 'Book of Splendour'. The history of this work's origin is to some extent still obscure. One reason for this is that the authors of the Zohar did all in their power to cover their traces. A kabbalistic reading, right up to the present, insists that the Zohar is an ancient text composed by Shimon bar Yohai in the second century CE. Moses de Léon and his fellow authors sought to create an impression of the text's great antiquity by using Aramaic, which often seems artificial, and thus made it difficult for medieval readers to penetrate the mysteries of the work. These methods were not representative of 'forgery', but were a firmly established stylistic element of religious literature, intended to enhance the legitimacy, gravity and authority of the text.

---

7.   This subject was addressed by Yates 2002 [1964]: 66-145.

The Zohar, its first versions circulating towards the end of the thirteenth century, is formally regarded as a commentary on the Torah by Shimon bar Yohai. Each book of the Torah (the five Books of Moses) was examined for its secret meaning and interpreted with the aid of kabbalistic hermeneutics. The symbolism of the Sefirot and the interpretation of the divine names played a prominent role in this process. Besides the first main part on the Pentateuch, almost wholly written by Moses de Léon, the Zohar consists of a second part (*tiqqûnê ha-zôhar*) and a third part (*zôhar ha-chadash*), which after the first printings were composed of quotations. However, its contents essentially reflect the ideas of Moses de Léon, which on the one hand indicate many similarities with the Kabbalah of Joseph Gikatilla, and on the other independent developments arising within the circle of Moses de Léon.[8] These included a strong interest in the pantheistically tinged aspects of the doctrine rooted in magic, theosophy and natural philosophy. Questions about the Creation and its relationship to God, the representation of God as the unity of all Being, simultaneously regarded as transcendently unknowable and yet revealed in nature, the emphasis on sexuality as an important element of purity, and the role of ethics in the maintenance and restoration of cosmic order are all aspects of kabbalistic thought which increasingly gained importance (Scholem 1991 [1957]: 224-66; Giller 2001).

The feminine aspect of divinity was also strongly emphasised. Jewry had never known those forms of physical aversion and devaluation of the feminine, as had developed from the notion of 'original sin' in Christian circles, and the *shekhînah* as the feminine principle of the deity was highly valued in kabbalistic thought (see Schäfer 2002). In ancient Judaism the Shekhinah was known as the cultic presence of God in the Holy of Holies in the Temple. This was now linked to the tenth Sefirah, Malkhut. As this tends downwards towards immanence, it is also a symbol for the (oral) Torah and the people of Israel. It is the 'principal addressee' for prayers and acts of piety. Since Israel is identified with the Schekhinah, a sexual metaphor comes into play, because God longs for his people just as Israel longs for its God. Israel, the Shekhinah, is the 'bride of God'. The Lurianic Kabbalah would invest this idea with soteriological speculations concerning salvation.

ISAAC LURIA

The year 1492 was an important turning-point in the European history of religion and not only because Columbus discovered America, but also because the *Reconquista* of the Iberian peninsula by the Christian Church signalled the end of an important episode of Jewish and Islamic culture in Europe. Jews and Muslims were expelled from Spain and Portugal or compelled to convert, albeit precariously, to Christianity. One can only understand the major scale of this cultural

---

8.   Scholem 1991 [1957]: 171-223. A good introduction to the Zohar is Green 2004. Arthur Green also provided a very helpful introduction to the ambitious project of the first (!) scholarly translation of the Zohar, the so-called 'Pritzker Edition'; see Matt 2004.

disruption against the background of the high development of Jewish cultural and religious life in Spain. The Spanish or Sephardic Jews generally considered themselves superior to the Ashkenazi Jews of Germany and Eastern Europe. Even if continuities survived and the Iberian peninsula was regarded as a mixture of Muslim, Jewish and Christian cultures by many non-Spaniards (see Meyerson and English 2000: 309-22), the expulsion was a catastrophe for those involved. In Jewish memory it is often mentioned in the same breath as the destruction of the Temple at Jerusalem in 70 CE.

Such an event necessarily had an impact on patterns of religious interpretation. In point of fact, the situation of exile acquired increasing meaning in the sixteenth century, together with voluminous speculations concerning its soteriological, apocalyptic and messianic consequences. The Jews were not alone in this respect. The various Reformations of the early sixteenth century leading to a schism in the Church and division of Christianity into denominations had also generated apocalyptic and eschatological speculations as a commonplace of European culture, even to the point of hysterical expectations of an imminent flood (see von Stuckrad 2003b: 234-41).

The strongest impulse on the Jewish side of this debate came from a mystic, who left no writings but whose thought, quite contrary to his intention, spread through his circle of pupils right across Europe.[9] This was Isaac Luria (1534–1572), who with some like-minded followers created a kabbalistic centre at Safed in Upper Galilee, which became the essence of a 'new Kabbalah'. Luria was regarded by his pupils as an inspired mystic, indeed as a saint, who lived in constant contact with the spiritual world. Numerous legends surrounding his life survive right up to the present day. As often occurs with saints, the systematic presentation of his thought was not Luria's own work. This was undertaken by others, especially Moses ben Jacob Cordovero (1522–1570), one of the most philosophical and systematic representatives of the later Kabbalah, who wrote a large commentary on the Zohar. The work was also done by Luria's most important pupil, Hayyim Vital (1543–1620), likewise a busy author, who presented the Lurianic Kabbalah in his life's work *Etz Hayyîm* ('Tree of Life'); and finally by Joseph ibn Tabul, also a pupil of Luria, who wrote down the important elements of the new doctrine. As the most intimate circle of pupils forbade publication of the writings, these texts reached the public around 1587 through secret copies procured by bribing Vital's brother. They only achieved an open circulation once another kabbalist, Israel Sarug, propagated the new doctrine in Italy between 1592 and 1598, falsely claiming he was a pupil of Luria.

But what exactly was new in these kabbalistic systems and how did it match the spirit of the age? The reputation of the Lurianic Kabbalah essentially resided in Luria's successful formulation of a coherent model explaining the process of Creation. He not only discussed the existence of demonic powers, without invoking

---

9.   For a comprehensive account see Scholem 1991 [1957]: 267-314, and Fine 2003.

the familiar dilemma of pantheism,[10] but simultaneously applied this model to historical processes. Luria thereby also located the catastrophes of Jewish history in a meaningful pattern of divine developments and messianic expectations that were general in the sixteenth century.[11]

Luria regarded the Creation as a process of God's 'self-exile' in his own primeval space. By an act of withdrawal (Heb. *tzimtzum*) he made space for the created world, which came into being though his light emanating into the free space and causing a kind of primal man (*Adam Qadmon*) to arise. Once again the Sefirot act as emanations of the divine. However, as only the higher three Sefirot can contain the perfect light, while the lower seven burst (the so-called 'breaking of the vessels'), the pure divine light separated into many potsherds or sparks and became mixed with impure matter. This posits the exile of God, which is now assumed by the people of Israel, insofar as it is the task of every Jew to piece together the fragments though prayer and Torah piety, a process described as *Tiqqun*.

Here too the Shekhinah assumes a central position. According to Scholem,

> The exile of the Shekhinah is not a metaphor, it is a genuine symbol of the 'broken' state of things in the realm of divine potentialities. The Shekhinah fell, as the last Sefirah, when the vessels were broken... To lead the Shekhinah back to her Master, to unite her with Him, is in one way or other the true purpose of the Torah. (Scholem 1991 [1957]: 302)

While Jews work towards the goal of restoring their original spiritual image (Adam Qadmon), they are ultimately helping God to overcome his exile. The destruction of the Temple and the expulsion from Spain were therefore actual representations of the salvific process of exile and the restoration of cosmic order, a process in which God needs Israel as much as Israel needs its God. The 'coming world' of the messianic age was therefore one which Israel itself had to create. The advent of the messiah was simply the confirmation of this achievement, which was the exclusive responsibility of Israel.

MESSIANIC IDEAS IN SABBATEANISM AND HASIDISM

One sees how closely woven esoteric motifs are with social and cultural developments. The apocalyptic ideas current in sixteenth- and seventeenth-century Europe ensured that the Lurianic doctrines were not only absorbed within Jewry but also far more widely disseminated. But let us return to the Jewish literary developments. The 'new Kabbalah' in general and its salvific concentration fascinated many educated European Jews, as it offered clear guidance in times of religious and political confusion. The interpretations attributed to Luria were expanded and altered in various ways.

---

10. One such dilemma is as follows: Either God is perfect, and can only be thought of as transcendent in view of the evil in the world, or evil is itself part of God, in which case he cannot be perfect.

11. For the importance of this interpretation in the history of religion, see Kippenberg and von Stuckrad 2003: 114-26.

The explosive power of kabbalistic interpretations of the world and history is evident once the Kabbalah became a serious rival to rabbinical Judaism in the seventeenth and eighteenth centuries. A large section of European Jewry favoured the kabbalistic world-view—though to what extent this was truly Lurianic is questionable—and was drawn towards messianism, when millions of followers thronged around Shabbatai Zvi (1626–1680), probably the most important pseudo-Messiah in Jewish eyes since Jesus of Nazareth.[12] In 1665 this mystic from Smyrna in Turkey was proclaimed the Messiah, who would fulfil the biblical prophecies by his 'prophet', Nathan of Gaza (1644–1680). Whether Shabbatai Zvi showed every sign of a manic-depressive psychosis, as Scholem and others suspect, need not detain us here (Scholem 1991 [1957]: 317-19; cf. Sharot 1982). What is more important is that the messianic movement, based on the promise of the all-embracing *Tiqqun*, succeeded in attracting large sections of European Jewry within just two years, and moreover on such a scale that it almost suffered a schism. In order to check the movement and its attendant religious and social unrest, Shabbatai Zvi was swiftly arrested by the Ottomans. In 1666 he converted to Islam under threat of a death sentence. Whoever thought that this was the end of Sabbateanism was deceived. Not only did Shabbatai Zvi observe the Jewish doctrines in secret, but many of his followers still regarded him as the Messiah. The Sabbateans exercised an influence on Jewish mysticism in the following period, especially on Jacob Frank (1726–1791). A loyal following of Sabbateanists, which had made an apparent conversion to Islam, preserved itself under the name 'Doenmeh' in Thessalonica right into the twentieth century.

The religious commotion unleashed by Sabbateanism had effects elsewhere. Among the Ashkenazim of Germany and Eastern Europe it was so-called *Hasidism*, which transformed and popularised kabbalistic doctrines. The Middle Ages had already witnessed an important mystical tradition among German Jewry, which crystallised around the 'pious of Ashkenaz', the *Hasidei Ashkenaz* (see Scholem 1991 [1957]: 87-127). However, the concept of the Hasidim underwent a change in the eighteenth century, when it combined with a new movement that had emerged from Sabbateanism. Its most important founder was the saint and mystic Israel Baal Shem-tov ('Master of the Holy Name', abbrev. 'Besht', d. 1760). He succeeded in establishing a mystical and ecstatic form of Judaism as opposed to its rabbinical variety, which still prevailed among wide sections of Russian and Polish Jewry until 1850. As Hasidism found the greatest support in those regions where radical Sabbateanism was particularly successful, it is no surprise that Hasidism was also inspired by a messianic idea. The Baal Shem clearly distinguished himself from the nihilistic forms of Sabbateanism that had taken root in Podolia and Wolhynia during the first half of the eighteenth century. One characteristic of East European Hasidism is its emphasis on mysticism and ecstasy and its focus on a

---

12. An excellent analysis of the prophetic and messianic discourse, which Sabbateanism was part of, is Goldish 2004.

spiritual leader upon whom messianic hopes often lit. Right up until the present Hasidism and its successor movements have particular importance in the context of apocalypticism and the belief in prophecies, which are repeatedly expressed in explosive political terms.[13]

13. On the whole subject see Scholem 1991 [1957]: 356-85; Idel 1998. For its political consequences see Kippenberg and von Stuckrad 2003: 164-72.

4

THE RENAISSANCE:
RE-INVENTING THE ANCIENT WORLD

What is the 'Renaissance' and when did it begin? A question easily asked but hard to answer. As with all labels for historical eras, the Renaissance (or 'rebirth') is a matter of construction, which characterises, usually in hindsight, specific periods as something unique, as an event *sui generis*, highlighted in a longer time-span due to its particular qualities.[1] The Renaissance as the 'rebirth of the ancient world' is an invention of special significance for the history of esotericism, as many scholars tend to speak of a kind of watershed between the 'early periods' of esotericism and its 'actual' formulation in the Renaissance. This notion of the Renaissance as a distinct period, like that applied to the Enlightenment, has come under fire in recent years, as it stems from a nineteenth-century construction.[2]

The fifteenth and sixteenth centuries by no means signified a watershed of esoteric and religious traditions, but the boundaries of discourse did change in ways which one could not have expected in the tenth or eleventh centuries. These changes were driven by the rediscovery of key Hermetic texts, by the invention of printing, and by the enormous cultural, religious and political upheavals which followed in the wake of the sixteenth-century Reformations. During this period philosophical, religious and scientific positions were polemically contrasted and thereby underwent major change.

1. For a full account see Herzog and Koselleck 1987.
2. Although Francesco Petrarca (1304–1374) already speaks of the 'dark ages' (*tenebrae*), caused by the invasion of Rome, 'the civilised world', by the 'nordic barbarians', his contrast does not signify a contrast between the pre-Christian and Christian worlds. The medieval consciousness of *rinascita* (the Italian precursor of the Renaissance concept) was first expressed by Giorgio Vasari (1511–1574) but still restricted to the context of art history. *Rinascita* did not become an historical concept in Italy but in France, there known as *Renaissance*, through Voltaire (1694–1778) and other Enlightenment writers. The cultural circumstances of the nineteenth century first produced the concept of the Renaissance as a prominent and unique cultural age of preparation for 'modernity'. This occurred between 1820 and 1830, before Jules Michelet's great study *La Renaissance* (c. 1855) and Jacob Burkhardt's classic *Die Kultur der Renaissance in Italien* (1860) finally established its usage. The notions of the nineteenth century are more reflected in this concept than the actual universality of events in the fifteenth century.

Esotericism in the Middle Ages

Two Prejudices

At least two prejudices are still widespread concerning the Middle Ages. The first is apparent in the characterisation of the era as a 'middle age', for this suggests that this was a time of transition or incubation before a more positively valued 'modern age', leading through constant progress to the achievements of the present. Only with the Renaissance did Europe supposedly awaken from the deep slumber of the Middle Ages, recalled the sciences and culture of the ancient world, shook off its magical and mystical habits of thought, and finally blossomed in the Enlightenment. This suggestive historical construction distorts the real meaning of those periods following antiquity. It is true that many Christian theologians in Rome and Byzantium conducted a fierce battle against the ancient cultures of knowledge, but generalisations can be misleading. On closer examination, one finds great differences from region to region and from ruler to ruler. Quite a few Christian potentates demonstrated an unbroken interest in fostering these sciences, and it was the monastic schools of the Middle Ages that busied themselves with the classical texts of philosophy and science. There is therefore some justification in speaking of the 'medieval enlightenment' (see Flasch and Jeck 1997).

The second prejudice is the assumption that the West is Christian. This idea has hindered the perception of Europe as a region of religious and cultural pluralism right up to the present, and still remains the core of a rhetorical 'European identity', to be defended against the Islamic East, with all its implications for European Muslims today. Against this, one should see that the Christian domains were not established in a vacuum, but were linked with the empires under Muslim authority through various economic, political, cultural and of course military contacts. This led to processes of exchange and mutual fertilisation, which even found an institutional basis in some countries, as for example in the Kingdom of Castile. There were naturally vast areas in the Christian domains where scarcely anyone could read and write, let alone understand Greek, Hebrew or Arabic. But there were also numerous Christian courts, where the classical sciences were maintained and taught. As time went on, a need to catch up with Islamic culture made itself felt, leading to a growing interest in natural science and philosophy from the tenth century onwards. For this reason the Middle Ages may be regarded as a shared cultural space, in which several interacting religions gave rise to a distinct pluralism often heightened by polemics and rhetoric (see Meyerson and English 2000, and also Brann 2002).

Such prejudices often prove an obstacle to the description of esotericism in the cultural and religious context of the Middle Ages and the supposed Renaissance of the fifteenth century. In this respect, esotericism offers a particularly good example of the diverse transfer of knowledge between religious and cultural systems.

MUSLIM ESOTERICISM

Our earlier treatment of the Manichaeans and Sabaeans already suggests that the reception of esoteric motifs in the Islamic context played a much greater role than was the case in the medieval Christian world. Many Muslim rulers were extremely receptive to philosophy and science and interested in the preservation and study of ancient texts. In the early phase of its expansion, Islam produced competing religious currents, which fostered the process of pluralism, and this enabled mystical or esoterically minded groups to establish their own traditions. This religious variety found a parallel in the numerous philosophical schools of Islam. Alongside the dominant interpretation of Aristotle by Avicenna (Ibn Sina, c. 980–1037), there were always Neo-Platonic schools more receptive to esoteric ideas. The latter had a great influence on Shiite communities, Sufism, and Islamic mysticism.

The example of the Iranian philosopher Shihāb al-Dīn Suhrawardī demonstrates the efflorescence of esoteric discourse in medieval Islam. This mystic was executed at the age of 37 at Aleppo in 1191 and his theosophical school achieved an influence in the East comparable to that of Avicenna in the West. Earlier scholarship assumed that Suhrawardī's doctrine had assimilated Zoroastrian ideas from Iran, but recent studies have made it clear that his thought actually reflects the reception of Platonic philosophy in a Persian context (see Walbridge 2000: 3–11).

Suhrawardī's philosophy is characterised by a combination of Zoroastrian, Hermetic, Pythagorean, Platonic and other ancient teachings. He himself describes his doctrine as an 'intuitive philosophy' of mystical experience compared with the speculative philosophy of the Aristotelians. The *Ishrāqī* school, which traces its descent from Suhrawardī, is therefore called the school of 'Illumination' or the 'Illuminati' (which naturally have no connection with the Illuminati of the eighteenth and twentieth centuries). In his major work, *The Philosophy of Illumination*, Suhrawardī gives a full account of his spiritual practice directed towards the attainment of absolute knowledge. In his view, the illuminated masters of his philosophical tradition are exemplars of the mystical vision of the final verities.

> In everything I have said regarding the science of light and what is and what is not based on it, I have the support of those who have walked on the path to God. This science is precisely the intuition of the inspired and illuminated Plato, the leader and master of philosophy, and of those preceding him since the time of Hermes, the 'father of philosophy', including such mighty pillars of philosophy as Empedocles, Pythagoras and others. The words of the ancients are symbols and irrefutable. (*Hikmat al-Ishrāq*, §4)

Suhrawardī regards the history of philosophy as beginning with Hermes, the 'father of philosophy'. The genealogy of knowledge, with which he identifies, passes through Pythagoras, Socrates, Plato and Aristotle (no Greek philosophers are named after Aristotle). It is noteworthy that Zoroaster, Mohammed and Jesus have no prominent position in his thought, a clear deviance from the lineages constructed among Sunni and broad sections of Shiite Islam. He also exemplifies how esotericism validates claims to knowledge deriving from direct individual experience of the absolute, while regarding 'merely rational' knowledge as an alternative and a complement.

Suhrawardī founded an influential current of theosophical Shia in the East, scarcely less important than that of Ibn Arabi (d. 1240) in Spain. Qutb al-Dīn al Shīrazī (1237–1311) continued to assert this harmonization of Greek and Iranian philosophy in the thirteenth century. Important parts of this teaching were also absorbed by Jews, especially in those circles described as 'interconfessional groups' by Steven Wasserstrom (2000). Later on, the famous 'School of Isfahan' among the Safawids of the fifteenth and sixteenth centuries descended in a direct line from the teachings of Suhrawardī. Although cross-connections between the School of Isfahan and the 'Platonic Academy' in Florence are possible from a point of view of content and chronology, the influence of Muslim esotericism on the West has scarcely been investigated yet.

A great number of *Hermetica*, mostly devoted to alchemy, astrology and magic, under the alleged authorship of Hermes as the forefather of the sciences circulated among the Muslims during the Middle Ages. Among the most influential treatises in the later period was the famous *Tabula Smaragdina* ('Emerald Tablet'), which had been known to Europe since the twelfth century and is cited again and again up to the present day as the quintessence of esoteric doctrine (see Ruska 1926). According to tradition, Hermes himself inscribed the tablet with sentences such as 'As above, so below' and, with reference to the 'Philosophers' Stone', 'His father is the Sun, his mother the moon'. Frequently combined with emblematic engravings, the *Tabula Smaragdina* was a major influence on alchemy in the early modern period.

CONTINUITIES AND BREAKS

The continuities of esoteric themes between the tenth and sixteenth centuries were greater than the 'watershed' notion of the Renaissance suggests. Alchemical knowledge preserved in the Muslim world found its way early into Christian circles of Western Europe. There was little in fifteenth-century astrology which was not already known or had to be 'rediscovered'. The same could also be said of magic (see Schütt 2000: 157-415; von Stuckrad 2003b: 159-206; Klaassen 2003). Not only did Christian demonology foster the survival of ancient beliefs in the existence of demonic powers and methods of controlling them, but the ritual magic of Marsilio Ficino, Trithemius and Agrippa had highly developed precursors in the Middle Ages. Consider the Benedictine monk Jean de Morigny, whose *Liber visionum* ('Book of Visions'), written in the first two decades of the fourteenth century, represents an inventory of numerous ancient and medieval magical traditions, with whose help absolute knowledge might be attained. The *Liber visionum* was classified as heretical and burnt at Paris in 1323, although Jean de Morigny was convinced that magic could be reconciled with orthodox Catholic doctrine. For this purpose he used another known text of medieval ritual magic, the *Ars notoria*, in which the adept achieves his knowledge through the mediation of the Holy Spirit and the angels in conjunction with ritual practices like fasting, praying and meditation (see Fanger 1998). The *Ars notoria* also had a great influence on the famous 'Mirror of Astronomy' (*Speculum astronomiae*) of Albertus Magnus (1193–1280), as well as on the *Liber visionum*. An extremely important link between the late Neo-Platonism of Iamblichus and Proclus and the 'occult philosophy' and magic of the fifteenth century was the so-called *Picatrix*, a magical text known as the 'Goal of the Wise' (*Ghayat al-Hakīm*) in the medieval Muslim world (Kiesel 2002). Composed in the eleventh century, the four books of the *Picatrix* treat a variety of philosophical, astrological and magical topics, and with reference to 224 books of 'an old sage', indicating a similar chain of transmission to the *prisca theologia* in the Hermetic and esoteric tradition.

Despite the numerous continuities in respect of specific ideas, there were also profound changes at this time. One of the most important was the transition from Aristotelian philosophy as practised in medieval scholasticism and in the Islamic world towards a greater emphasis on Neo-Platonic philosophy, with consequences in religion, esotericism and science. The Aristotelian world-view saw the cosmos beyond the sphere of the Moon as unchanging, but the Platonic view of reality allowed that processes in the sublunary world could be transposed to the transcendent world. This created a holistic model of a unitary cosmos, which subjected the higher spheres to change and thereby made them accessible to human purposes. This change in cosmological thinking lends an extraordinary importance to Hermeticism and esotericism for the development of science. The rhetorical struggle between Aristotelianism and (Neo-)Platonism was a crucial element in European cultural history at the beginning of the 'modern period'. These battle-fronts did not run between the religions but rather between cosmological conceptions, challenging all religions in equal measure.

The growing knowledge of sources in the history of religion also signified a major change. The knowledge of Greek philosophy and science was increasing thanks to the intensive translation work undertaken in medieval centres. The rediscovery of the *Corpus Hermeticum* in the fifteenth century and its translation into Latin alongside the writings of Plato and the Neo-Platonists by Marsilio Ficino was moreover a decisive turning-point for esotericism. The idea of the *prisca theologia*, namely the 'original' unity of all religious and philosophical schemes, could now make reference to a supposedly very ancient layer of documentation. The new interpretation of the *Chaldæan Oracles* by Pletho and other contemporary philosophers played a similar role to the *Corpus Hermeticum*.

Finally, the invention of printing signified a further change. This revolution in the history of communication had an enormous effect on esotericism. As esoteric writings were now accessible to a much greater readership, esoteric and Hermetic ideas were henceforth carried by new social groups. Whereas these ideas were previously discussed in monastic and courtly circles, or in the madresses of the Muslim world, now merchants, university teachers or private individuals could learn about these subjects. A new market was developing that would change the face of esotericism.

THE BIRTH OF MODERN ESOTERICISM

The rise of Italy to a leading cultural region in the fifteenth and sixteenth century owed a great deal to the flight of Byzantine scholars once the Byzantine Empire had been conquered by the Ottoman Turks. The Ottoman Empire had grown from a small Turkish emirate, which had constantly led attacks on Constantinople, the capital of Eastern Christianity. Under the leadership of sultans such as Osman I, Orhan and Murat I, the Ottomans began a series of swift campaigns of conquest at the beginning of the fourteenth century. Seeking to block this advance the Christian Balkan states under the leadership of the Serbian nobility raised an army, which was crushingly defeated in the year 1389 in the Battle of Kosovo. Sultan Bayezid I could then conquer Bulgaria and attack Hungary. Their expansion towards the East was arrested for some time after 1402 by the Mongols led by Tamerlane. However, in 1453 Constantinople could no longer withstand the pressure of the Turkish armies, and Sultan Mohammed II the Conqueror took power over the Bosporus. The Ottoman Empire became an important player on the cultural stage of Europe and remained such right up to the nineteenth century.

These upheavals must be taken into account if one is to understand the religious, political and philosophical shifts of the fifteenth century. In Eastern Christendom traditions which had been lost in the West were preserved, primarily through the orientation towards the Greek language. Among the emigrants setting off for the rich cities of Italy were many scholars who subscribed to a Neo-Platonic world-view and broadcast this in the West (see Monfasani 1995). They gave important momentum to what is usually called the 'Plato–Aristotle debate'.

THE 'PLATO–ARISTOTLE DEBATE'

Scarcely anyone in the ancient world and the Middle Ages thought of making a radical distinction between Plato and his pupil Aristotle. It is true that in *The Metaphysics* Aristotle attacked Plato's theory of the forms, in *The Politics* Plato's theory of the state, in *De Anima* Plato's idea of the soul, and in his other writings the Platonic conception of time and eternity. However, Aristotle directed an equally combative critique against the Pre-Socratic philosophers and it is true that he always refrained from writing a treatise against his teacher, whose statements he rather took and developed further. This was the view in late antiquity, which seldom distinguished between Plato and Aristotle as two mutually exclusive schemes of thought. The ancient debate was usually conducted between Sceptics (who had taken over the Platonic Academy in 270 BCE), Stoics and Epicureans. Furthermore, Middle Platonism and Neo-Platonism combined Aristotelian and Platonic ideas. Even Plotinus, although he rejected particular Aristotelian doctrines, was strongly influenced by the commentary on Aristotle by Alexander of Aphrodisias, and Plotinus' famous pupil Porphyry actually wrote an introduction to Aristotle's *Categories*. The Neo-Platonists thereby exemplified the philosophy of late antiquity, which was oriented towards integration and averse to polarities.

Throughout the Middle Ages it was still customary to imagine a 'division of labour' between the two philosophers, whereby Aristotle was seen as the master of logic and physics, and Plato the teacher of metaphysics and theology. Once Latin translations made Aristotelian works known in the West, there arose in the twelfth century a specifically Christian interpretation of Aristotle opposed to the Platonic tendencies in Christianity. Scholasticism, namely the philosophy taught in Christian universities and places of education, followed this interpretation, while Muslim scholars such as Averroes (Ibn Rushd, 1126–1198) worked in parallel on their own authoritative commentaries on Aristotle. This situation changed in the fifteenth century due to Latin translations of the works of Plato and, just as importantly, the writings of Plotinus. First, Neo-Platonic thought became known in this way; second, the humanistic clamour grew louder for an abandonment of the Christian reformulation of ancient philosophy and a return to the original sources.[3]

There now arose a polarised debate under the implicit assumption that Plato and Aristotle represented the totality of philosophical knowledge. The Plato–Aristotle controversy of the Renaissance is thus a unique moment in the history of philosophy. Between 1439 (George Gemistus Pletho, *On the Differences between the Platonic and Aristotelian Philosophies*) and 1597 (Jacopo Mazzoni, *A Comparison between Plato and Aristotle*) there developed a whole genre of literature devoted to a comparison between the two philosophers, often marked by those polemics so typical of humanistic discourse.

A religious rather than philosophical controversy lay behind this comparison. Critics of Scholasticism, the dominant Christian philosophy, opposed Platonism to Christianity. The most important of these was Pletho, whom I will discuss in more detail in the following section. Others, such as Marsilio Ficino, tried to combine Plato with Christianity, and reproached the Scholastics for having forced Aristotle into a straitjacket of ossified concepts. Basically, everyone was at liberty to make use of the ancient masters for their own argument. Thus one should look beyond the subjects of this controversy to its motivating *issues*, which were entirely theological in nature.

One issue was the question of whether the *soul* was immortal or not. Aristotle denied this, on account of which Christian Platonists attacked him. But Plato's doctrine of the transmigration of souls and his idea that knowledge was nothing but remembrance seemed strange to many theologians and they set about 'diluting' Aristotle in order to deploy him more effectively. The various notions of the soul also raised the question of how the human soul stood in relation to the world soul. Renaissance Neo-Platonists developed the idea that the individual soul could in principle merge with the world soul, whereby it became possible for human beings to participate in the universal wisdom of the cosmos. Christian theologians felt this was human presumption in God's realm, and therefore rejected this doctrine and

3.   See Hankins 1990 and Allen 1998.

held fast to the scholastic Aristotle, who described God as 'the first unmoved mover', surpassing all human curiosity.

Another conflict arose over the question of *destiny and free will*. Neo-Platonists of late antiquity had combined Plato with the Stoic doctrine of *heimarmene* and sympathy (see above, p. 17) and thereby developed a determinism which created problems for Christian ethics (and also for Jewish and Muslim thinkers), as it was no longer possible to punish sinful conduct if man was not responsible for his actions. The doctrine of sympathy had yet another consequence, because if everything was connected with everything else and the cosmos was held together by a unified power, then not only could everything be ascertained in principle, but both the transcendent realm and the gods were subject to this causal principle. Precisely this was asserted by Renaissance Platonists like Pietro Pomponazzi (1462–1524), thereby assuming a radically anti-Christian position. Not only was the freedom of man at stake, but the freedom of God. There was yet a further concern: if transcendence was included in the sympathy doctrine, then the heavenly world would also be subject to change. It is then difficult to uphold the Aristotelian view that changes only occurred in the sublunary region, while the gods and heaven were eternal. The discussion of this topic reached a crisis when the geocentric model of the cosmos was replaced by the heliocentric model through the work of Copernicus, Kepler and Galileo (see von Stuckrad 2003b: 219-22, 252-64).

A third area of conflict concerned the *scientific intelligibility* of the universe. Early medieval thought was characterised by the primacy of theology over philosophy. This meant that the study of nature was by no means an end in itself for human knowledge, but solely served to read 'God's truth' in the world of material revelation. The 'Book of Nature' was interpreted as an analogue to the Bible, while one applied theological exposition to the contemplation of nature. An empirical science proceeding inductively from experiment and fact to the processes of nature was thus suppressed in favour of deductive reasoning which proceeded from the reality of God's revelation to its discovery in nature. Although there were already the beginnings of an empirically oriented science in the Middle Ages, several centuries would elapse before such a method could enjoy broad acceptance. This method was basically founded on the nominalistic alternative, which makes the *nomina* (the 'names', thus the externals) the actual object of enquiry, while the *essentia* (the 'inner Being') eluded scientific grasp. If this distinction were maintained, then empirical research was acceptable to theology. One made a simultaneous distinction between theology, which concerned the transcendent (*natura naturans*, i.e. the formative power of nature), and science, which concerned itself with revealed nature (*natura naturata*). The Renaissance Platonists contested the primacy of theology in understanding the *natura naturans*. The investigation of nature was now concerned with 'God's sway' behind revealed reality and this was a God who cast his personal attributes aside in order to merge with a Platonic 'idea' of the Highest Good.

This leads to a fourth area of conflict: the *pantheistic controversy*. The Neo-Platonists of late antiquity, especially in their 'Gnostic' garb, proposed a dualistic world-view, by elevating sparks of divine light from the dark matter into which they had fallen. By contrast, the Renaissance Neo-Platonists, like the theurgists of late antiquity, tended towards a monistic or holistic world-view. Both the Platonic doctrine of emanationism and the reverence for a universal life-force, permeating the whole cosmos as *natura naturans*, often leads to pantheism, which is contrary to a monotheistic theology. Pantheism ('everything is divine' or 'God dwells in everything') is closely linked to the esoteric notion of living nature. A distinctly pantheistic philosophy was developed by Baruch Spinoza (1632–1677), and this discourse can be traced via John Toland (1670–1722), Lessing, Mendelssohn, Schopenhauer, Schleiermacher, Friedrich Max Müller and Wilhelm Dilthey, to name but a few, right up to the twentieth century. Pantheism was problematical for traditional Christian theology, because a danger arose if nature was no longer seen as something separate from God and assigned to human purposes and control ('subdue the earth'), but was itself the object of deification and worship. The reproach of paganism and the suspicion of heresy was an inevitable consequence for pantheistic Neo-Platonism.

Despite all attempts of the Christian Neo-Platonists to prove the compatibility of their views with the Christian faith, there can be no doubt that Renaissance Neo-Platonism actually represented a powerful rival to the established forms of Christianity. The esoteric discourse ultimately subjected God to the autonomous human will to know and command.

PLETHO: PLATONIC POLYTHEISM

George Gemistus (1355/1360–1454) was both one of the most important scholars of the declining Byzantine Empire and a pioneer of the Italian Renaissance. Following his participation in the Council of Ferrara (later moved to Florence) to discuss the unification of the Western and Eastern Churches, he used the pseudonym 'Pletho' to identify himself as a successor, or even immodestly as a restorer, of Plato.[4] In the first decade of the fifteenth century Pletho had settled at Mistra in the vicinity of ancient Sparta, where he worked as a teacher of philosophy and gained a reputation for his political and legal advice, leading to his invitation to attend the Council of Ferrara.

Little is known regarding Pletho's own education. His opponent, George Scholarius (Gennadius II, 1405–1473), the first patriarch of Constantinople under Turkish rule, states that Pletho was already in his youth under the sway of 'heretical' Neo-Platonists like Proclus, Plotinus, Porphyry and Iamblichus. He also mentioned the influence of the Jew Elisha, regarded as a 'Hellenistic pagan', who had introduced him to the doctrines of Zoroaster and other non-Christian authors. It is still uncertain whether this Elisha was actually a historical person, but it is

---

4.   On the life and work of Pletho see Woodhouse 1986; Blum 1988.

interesting that Scholarius cited a 'polytheistic' Jew as the source of Pletho's heresy, because Jewish scholars could achieve high office in the administration of the Ottoman Empire under Murad I. Many of these Jews were followers of Suhrawardī (see above, p. 46). There is no doubt that Jews were important intermediaries, but it is uncertain whether Pletho knew the relevant literature.

Pletho was an extremely productive author. Unfortunately many of his works have survived only as fragments, because they were considered heretical and destroyed. This is also true of his most influential work, *Book of Laws* (based on Plato's *Laws* and the Torah). On receiving the book for examination after Pletho's death, Scholarius consigned it to the flames, preserving only the table of contents and Pletho's hymns to the gods to justify his decision. Thanks to partial copies made by Pletho's pupils, about a third of his total works have been preserved. From these fragments we know that Pletho advocated a complete restoration of the Greek pantheon and religion. Pletho also proclaimed the dominance of *heimarmene*, namely destiny, the all-embracing law of the supreme god, whom he called Zeus. These notions led to a bitter debate at the Council of Ferrara. One of his most severe critics, George of Trebizond, wrote later:

> I myself heard him in Florence when he said that within a few years the whole world would have one and the same religion, one mind, one soul, one sermon. And when I asked him if it would be the faith of Christ or that of Mohammed, he replied: neither of these, but another faith which is not so different from that of the gentiles. I was offended by these words, and have always hated him; I have a horror of him as of a poisonous snake, and I could not look at or listen to him any more. I heard, however, from some Greeks who had fled here from the Peloponnese, that before dying, almost thirty years ago now, he had publicly stated that, quite soon after his death, Mohammed and Christ would be forgotten, and that absolute truth would flower again throughout the whole universe. (Quoted in Garin 1983: 83)

The surviving sections of the *Laws* indicate that Pletho's utopia was less a restoration of ancient religion than an inventive new creation in Platonic garb. While Pletho uses the names of the Graeco-Roman gods, he supplies his own conceptions concerning their function and mythology. For him the gods are Platonic 'ideas', representing specific forces and mechanisms of the cosmos, which are revered by the true sages, who should also be the political leaders. Moreover, Pletho's ideal state well demonstrates that polytheism is not necessarily more tolerant than monotheism. His exclusive polytheism suppresses alternative notions and would have led to a totalitarian rule of initiates, had it ever been realised.[5]

THE REDISCOVERY OF THE CORPUS HERMETICUM
Italian scholars and merchants also participated in these heated debates over Platonism and Aristotelianism, Christianity and the 'rebirth of paganism' at the waning of the Byzantine Empire. Cosimo de' Medici (1389–1464) was hardly

---

5. For this reason Pletho's utopia is not a continuation of the previously inclusive ancient polytheism, but a response to the exclusive monotheism of the Christian church.

involved in the discussions but he used his enormous wealth to patronise aspiring scholars. In 1462 Cosimo gave the young and still unknown Marsilio Ficino (1433–1499) several Greek manuscripts from his own extensive library. Among these was a codex containing Plato's entire works, a great rarity in the fifteenth century since even the Vatican library did not possess a whole collection of Plato. It is likely that Cosimo had this codex copied during the Council of Florence or possibly received it directly from Pletho, as earlier Byzantine versions were evidently in his possession. This codex alone was the basic inspiration of the famous 'Platonic Academy', which Cosimo was said to have established due to Pletho's impressive appearance in Florence: now the patron only needed a suitable translator (see Hankins 1991). Political considerations may even have played a role in the matter.

In any case, Marsilio Ficino was entrusted with the task and after he had completed the first part of his translation of Plato in April 1463 he received in payment a house and estate at Careggi near Florence. A few years later Ficino appears to have organised a kind of private grammar school, an 'Academy', in which he taught young students rhetoric, vernacular literature, Bible knowledge, astrology and 'spiritual medicine'. The young scholar also drew attention to himself through public debates and symposia as well as his sermons, regularly given in the Church of Santa Maria of the Angels much to the annoyance of the ecclesiastical authorities.[6] A revised translation of Plato circulated in manuscript from 1482 and was printed in an edition of 1025 copies in 1484. A second edition was soon published in 1491. In Ficino's view, the year 1484 was an *annus mirabilis*. Ficino and many of his contemporaries regarded the major conjunction of Jupiter and Saturn as the herald of the Golden Age and the renewal of Christianity (see Hankins 1990: 302-304). Ficino also calculated that twelve hundred years had passed between Porphyry's last celebration of Plato's birthday and his own time, namely a world year which made a historical upheaval all the more likely. Ficino finally cited the prominent constellation of Jupiter and Saturn in his own horoscope to present himself as the 'restorer of ancient things'.

Besides his translations, Ficino also produced exhaustive commentaries and introductions to Plato, including the famous commentary on *The Symposium*, which he completed under the title *De amore* ('On Love') in the summer of 1469. Thanks to Ficino even the Neo-Platonic texts became known. So great was the influence of his translation of Plotinus (1492), which he regarded as his crowning achievement, that it can scarcely be overestimated. In 1496 appeared the translation of Dionysius the Areopagite, whom Ficino regarded as the culmination of Platonic philosophy and the pillar of Christian theology. Finally, in 1497 there followed his translations of Iamblichus, Proclus, Porphyry, Psellos, Synesius, Xenocrates and other Neo-Platonists under the title *De mysteriis et alia* ('On the mysteries and other subjects'). From this bibliography it is plain that Ficino and his contemporaries viewed Plato through the spectacles of the Neo-Platonists in late antiquity.

---

6.   On the significance of this phase of his work see Allan and Rees 2002: 15-44.

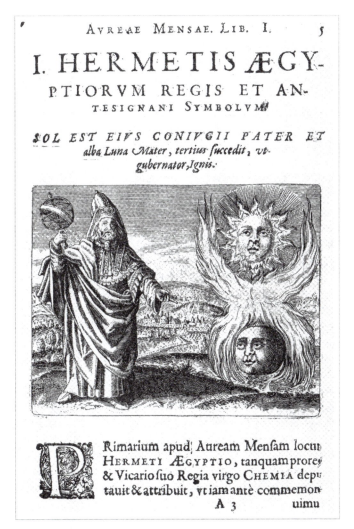

AVREAE MENSAE. LIB. I.   5

I. HERMETIS ÆGY-
PTIORVM REGIS ET AN-
TESIGNANI SYMBOLVM

*SOL EST EIVS CONIVGII PATER ET
alba Luna Mater, tertius succedit, vt-
gubernator, Ignis.*

Rimarium apud Auream Mensam locu
HERMETI ÆGYPTIO, tanquam prore
& Vicario suo Regia virgo CHEMIA dep
tauit & attribuit, vt iam antè commemon
A 3   uimu

Illustration 2. In Michael Maier's work *Symbola aureae mensae* (1617) Hermes Trismegistus is portrayed as the 'Egyptian' forefather of alchemy and the occult arts, carrying in his right hand a globe with a zodiacal band indicating his astrological knowledge. With his left he points to the conjunction of the Sun and Moon, a key to understanding the alchemical process. (Michael Maier, *Symbola aureae mensae* [1617], BPH/Photo: Wim Dingemans)

Important as Ficino's dissemination of Platonic and Neo-Platonic literature was for esotericism, the rediscovery of the *Corpus Hermeticum* had even greater consequences. The Graeco-Egyptian god and revealer Hermes Trismegistus had been known as the forefather of the occult sciences throughout medieval alchemy and astrology, especially in the Islamic world (see Illustration 2). However, the original texts, compiled as we now know in the first centuries CE, were not available to medieval scholars. It is true that Psellos (1018–1078) mentions the entire collection of the *Corpus Hermeticum*, but leaving aside the slender chance that the Sabaeans preserved the book in the Muslim world (see above, pp. 29-30), only the *Asclepius* was known in a Latin version.

Given this background, it is easy to imagine how electrified scholars were, when in 1463 a Greek collection of the *Corpus Hermeticum* was discovered in Macedonia. The text was brought to Cosimo de' Medici at Florence, and Marsilio Ficino was instructed to translate the collection into Latin even before working on the Plato translations. This was logical, insofar as it was accepted that Hermes Trismegistus was far older than Plato, even than Moses, and therefore revealed to mankind something akin to 'primal knowledge'. The translation was printed in 1471 under the title *Liber de potestate et sapientia Dei* ('Book of the Power and Wisdom of God'), also known as *Pimander*, a name actually denoting only the first treatise of the *Corpus Hermeticum*, but which Ficino applied to the whole collection. The printing press enabled Ficino's translation to appear in no less than twenty-five new editions together with translations into other languages up to 1641. The original text of the *Corpus Hermeticum* in Greek was published for the first time at Paris in 1554.

This widespread publication demonstrates the great interest of contemporary scholars in this ostensibly ancient document. In this fashion the Renaissance discovered the *philosophia perennis* ('eternal philosophy'), regarded as the common denominator of Egyptian, Greek, Jewish and Christian religion. The legendary reputation of the Hermetic documents remained intact (even up to the present day among esotericists), despite the fact that a more differentiated humanistic critique of the early dating of the *Corpus Hermeticum* was already in circulation by the second half of the sixteenth century. This reached its climax in Isaac Casaubon's proof (1614), that the texts were no older than the first Christian sources (see Grafton 1991: 145-77; Mulsow 2002). If this sounded the knell of Hermetism from the perspective of literary criticism, many authors still continued to refer to the *Corpus Hermeticum*. These included Ludovico Lazzarelli, Symphorien Champier, Nicolas Copernicus, Francesco Giorgi of Venice, Henry Cornelius Agrippa of Nettesheim, John Dee, Francesco Patrizi, Giordano Bruno, Robert Fludd, Ralph Cudworth and Athanasius Kircher as well as the representatives of Christian Kabbalah Giovanni Pico della Mirandola, Johannes Reuchlin, Pietro Galatino, Guillaume Postel and Christian Knorr von Rosenroth. These early modern Hermetists reflected a veritable *Who's Who* of contemporary natural philosophy and esotericism.

PRISCA THEOLOGIA: GENEALOGIES OF KNOWLEDGE
Now they had access to texts supposedly more ancient than Judaeo-Christian sources, fifteenth-century scholars and philosophers directed their gaze towards the alternative traditions of antiquity. Questions arose relating to the genealogies of esoteric knowledge and their possible connections with monotheistic revelation.

The answers to these questions directly impinged on the inter-religious tensions of the age. The various religions were understandably much affected by the new discoveries with their implications for the antiquity of each religious tradition and its proximity to the 'original truth'.

There was a special significance in the debate between Christian thinkers like Marsilio Ficino and Pico della Mirandola on the one side and Jewish philosophers and kabbalists on the other.[7] Two distinct models for the genealogy of esoteric knowledge emerged: the unilinear model assumes a continuous chain of sages who bequeath the original knowledge to succeeding generations, while the multilinear theory accepts that absolute knowledge can derive from different traditions. This may seem an academic question at first glance, but the very claims of Jewish, Christian and Muslim theology to knowledge are actually at stake. With the multilinear model it is legitimate to seek knowledge beyond the revelations of the scriptural religions, an ambiguity fully recognised and hotly debated in the fifteenth and sixteenth centuries.

The identity of Jewish kabbalists had always rested upon a unilinear theory, which believed the revelation of the Torah the fount of all knowledge and that non-Jewish authorities had received the teachings from Jewish sages like Moses or Abraham. This view was already current in antiquity, witness the writings of Artapanus, Alexander Polyhistor, Flavius Josephus and others. Many Renaissance authors, for example Yohanan Alemanno and Isaac Abarbanel, reacted to the question of the supposed age of the Hermetic texts by regarding Hermes as identical with the biblical Enoch. Yohanan Alemanno, a contemporary of Ficino and acquainted with Pico, went so far as to claim Platonic philosophy for Judaism. In his commentary on the *Song of Solomon* he described two types of philosophical schools:

> One ancient school stretches from venerable antiquity up to the generation in which prophecy ended. These philosophers and their sons and pupils drank thirstily from their [i.e. the prophets'] words up to Plato, who lived at the time [of the prophets]. The second group began when prophecy ended and evil arose, from the time of Aristotle and later up to our own times.[8]

But now several Christian authors of the Renaissance broke with this model.[9] Interestingly, the 'pagan' Pletho introduced the name of Zoroaster into the discussion as a source of valid knowledge beyond the Judaeo-Christian revelation. Pletho did this indirectly by using the (late ancient) *Chaldæan Oracles*, which he attributed to Zoroaster and his 'magicians'. He was the first to make this link explicitly and thereby helped launch the European fascination with Zoroaster. In his new edition

---

7. This has recently been demonstrated by Moshe Idel, see Idel in Allen and Rees 2002: 137-58.

8. Bodleian Library, Oxford, MS Or. 1535, fol. 162v.

9. Suhrawardī might once again be cited as a precursor of this alternative interpretation.

of the *Oracles*, essentially influenced by Michael Psellos,[10] to which he added a commentary, Pletho makes no comparisons with Christian theology. In the concluding section of his commentary he writes that many people, especially the 'Pythagorean and Platonic sages' had clearly harmonized their doctrine in some way with the *Oracles* of Zoroaster's pupils. Plato's philosophy moreover accords with the doctrine of Zoroaster as presented by Plutarch. At the end of his commentary Pletho states that Plutarch regards Zoroaster as very ancient, living five thousand years before the Trojan War, a dating quite irreconcilable with biblical chronology. Such a multilinear theory denies the claims of Judaism and Christianity to universality.[11]

Marsilio Ficino adopts the multilinear model in most of his works, but sometimes tries to relate them to the Christian revelation, by saying that *one* truth can be transmitted in various ways. Under the influence of Pletho, Ficino introduced a chain of authorities, in which Mosaic sources play no role: Zoroaster, Hermes Trismegistus, Orpheus, Aglaophemus (a putative Orphic teacher of Pythagoras), Pythagoras and Plato. In his commentary on *Philebus* Ficino wrote:

> Through the liberation of their souls [these sages] came as near as possible to the divine beams, and by investigating all things in the light of these beams by combining and separating the One and the Many, they were able themselves to share in the truth. (Ficino 2000: 246)

This explanation relates to the Neo-Platonic and theurgical traditions of late antiquity, as formulated in the *Chaldæan Oracles*: the sages of antiquity and their successors up to the present can make contact with universal truth through the ascent of their soul into the divine spheres. This account clearly expresses the self-empowerment of the understanding subject, so recurrent in the esoteric tradition. In other writings, especially in his apology for the Christian faith *De Christiana religione*, Ficino grants biblical personalities a certain influence on the *prisca theologia*, but in his concurrently written *Theologia Platonica* he again asserts the pagan tradition of the pure theology. Unlike Pletho, Ficino did not contend the superiority of pagan over Christian theology, but rather their independence and equality.

10. The medieval interest in the *Chaldæan Oracles* was not limited to Psellos. The patriarch Michael Cerularius (c. 1000–1059), the famous Michael Italicus (first half of the twelfth century), celebrated as 'the second Plato', later the politician and scholar Theodor Metochites (c. 1260–1332) and his pupil Nikephoros Gregoras (c. 1295–1359/60) demonstrate the enormous attraction of this ancient source for philosophers and theologians of the period; see Woodhouse 1986: 50, and Stausberg 1998: 51-54.

11. Michael Stausberg establishes two aspects of the ensuing European reception of Zoroaster: '[a] Zoroaster's doctrines are no singular and inconsequent construction in the history of ideas, because they accord with the philosophy of the Pythagoreans and the Platonists, among whom Pletho counted himself. The reception of Zoroaster thus became an act of self-identification; [b] Zoroaster derives from an unimaginably distant past, and this...appears to have considerably enhanced Zoroaster's importance in Pletho's eyes' (Stausberg 1998: 61). This act of self-identification was consummated by Christian authors of the fifteenth century.

Giovanni Pico della Mirandola had a similar view. In his *Oratio de dignitate hominis* ('Oration on the Dignity of Man', on which see below) he described Orpheus as the primary source of philosophical and theological wisdom for Pythagoras and his successors. Kabbalistic traditions accorded with this tradition, but the first to formulate this independently was Orpheus. This is a somewhat divergent account from Pico by Piero Crinito:

> That divine philosophy of Pythagoras, which they called Magic, belonged to a great extent to the Mosaic tradition; since Pythagoras had managed to reach the Jews and their doctrines in Egypt, and achieved a knowledge of many of their sacred mysteries. For even the learning of Plato (as is established) comes quite near to Hebrew truth; hence many called him a genuine Moses, but speaking Greek. Zoroaster, the son of Oromasius, in practising magic, took that to be the cult of God and study of divinity; while engaged in this in Persia he most successfully investigated every virtue and power of nature, in order to know those sacred and sublime secrets of the divine intellect; which subject many people called theurgy, others Cabala or magic. (Quoted in Walker 1972: 50)

Here Pythagoras is described as independent of Mosaic theology, while Zoroaster's doctrines harmonize with the Kabbalah although they have developed independently of it. But if the Chaldaeans and Egyptians embodied the *prisca theologia* for Ficino, they do not fare so well with Pico. In his *Disputationes adversus astrologiam divinatricem* ('Refutation of Astrological Divination') he describes their religion as utter superstition with 'vain and superstitious ceremonies', their character is 'completely coarse', they are not receptive to the arguments of wisdom and so on. The supposed sages of religion became 'unwiser' the more one promoted them as sages.

Such differences cannot hide the fact that the multilinear model of esoteric transmission posed a great challenge for Christians and Jews of the fifteenth and sixteenth centuries. By seeking genealogies of knowledge beyond Christianity, the esoteric authors of the Renaissance had an important influence on the thought and science of the succeeding period. Through recourse to the *prisca theologia*, scientific research increasingly emancipated itself from the certainties of Christian revelation. Jewish thinkers, especially in kabbalistic circles, usually reacted by clinging fast to unilinear conceptions portraying Zoroaster, Orpheus, Plato and other representatives of the *prisca theologia* as students of the Jewish doctrine. They thereby simultaneously protested the adaptation of the Jewish Kabbalah to Christian tradition, which often betrayed an anti-Jewish undertone. Not until the seventeenth century did Jewish authors such as Abraham Yagel, Asaria de' Rossi or Menasseh ben Israel give consideration to individual pagan authorities, which may be attributed to the increasing influence of Neo-Platonic ideas and the writings of Ficino and Pico. Yet even such prominently pure Neo-Platonic works like those of Leone Ebreo, whose *Dialoghi d'amore* ('Dialogue on Love') belongs to the most important treatises of Renaissance Platonism, exhibit unmistakeable features of kabbalistic thought and thereby seek to defend an ultimately unilinear interpretation.

GIOVANNI PICO DELLA MIRANDOLA

Giovanni Pico della Mirandola (1463–1494) is numbered alongside Ficino among the most influential esoteric thinkers of the fifteenth century. This was not only due to his multilinear conception of the *prisca theologia*, because the Count of Mirandola left extensive works at his early death dealing with all the relevant philosophical and religious themes of his age. He caused uproar with his plan to debate in Rome with experts from all over Europe his 900 theses, in which he defended the compatibility of Platonism, magic, Kabbalah and Christianity. In the event Pope Innocence VIII forbade the debate, so that Pico had to restrict himself to the printing of his theses on 7 December 1486 (see Farmer 1998). The speech he had written to open the debate was to become famous as the *Oratio de dignitate hominis* ('Oration on the Dignity of Man').

To succeeding generations Pico was the embodiment of wisdom and education. He had studied law at Bologna (1477–78), then rhetoric, philosophy, theology and related disciplines at Ferrara (1479), at Florence (1479 or 1480), Padua (1480–82), Pavia (1482–83), again in Florence (1484) and in Paris (1485–86), but he never completed his studies by taking an academic degree. His private library was one of the largest of his age. There is no doubt that Pico is a particularly interesting personality of the Renaissance. However, his reputation as a 'symbol of his time', a precursor of modernity, who strove to assert human freedom against the ecclesiastical suppression of the truth, had to await the representations of modern historians (see Craven 1981). But leaving aside any possible exaggeration of his distinction, his works are highly significant in several ways for esotericism. His most important contributions include the 'Christianization' of the Jewish Kabbalah, which he directly applied as a weapon of Christian argument, and his representation of the human being as the central point of cosmic perception.

I will deal with Pico's impact on Christian Kabbalah more fully below (see pp. 71-72). We must first cast an eye at Pico's philosophy to understand his estimate of the role of man. The crux of his writings is the description of the human being as *magnum miraculum* and *copula mundi*, that is, a 'great miracle' and an 'intermediary' between the worlds. Here man is no longer a mere part of the world, but an autonomous and marvellous ruler of realities. His freedom therefore signifies a simultaneous break with the cosmos. Pico makes a radical distinction between rational explanation and myth, which enables him to open human reason to all areas of knowledge and purge them of the residues of faith. His 'Oration on the Dignity of Man' clearly expresses the freedom of the understanding subject, which leads effortlessly to self-empowerment. With reference to the *Corpus Hermeticum* Pico has the Creator God say to man: 'Thou, constrained by no limits, in accordance with thine own free will, in whose hand I have placed thee, shalt ordain for thyself the limits of thy nature', with the result that man is removed from nature and effectively deified: 'Let us disdain earthly things, despise heavenly things, and finally, esteeming less whatever is of the world, hasten to that court which is beyond the world and nearest to the Godhead'. Elsewhere one reads:

I have set thee at the world's centre that thou mayest from thence more easily observe whatever is in the world. I have made thee neither of heaven nor of earth, neither mortal nor immortal, so that with freedom of choice and with honour, as though the maker and molder of thyself, thou mayest fashion thyself in whatever shape thou shalt prefer. Thou shalt have the power to degenerate into the lower forms of life, which are brutish. Thou shalt have the power, out of thy soul's judgement, to be reborn into the higher forms, which are divine.[12]

The undertone of this new role of man can still be heard today.

12. Sentences such as these have caused Michael Pauen to rank Pico among the influential representatives of Gnostic-esoteric thought: 'A direct line leads from the Gnostics' insistence on the divine status of the subject via Pico's theory of human dignity to the apotheosis of the subject in Ernst Bloch' (Pauen 1994: 64).

5

ESOTERICISM IN THE CONFESSIONAL AGE

Alternative Renaissance models of interpretation were accompanied by internal processes of pluralisation and the emergence of various Christian denominations. With its onset long before Martin Luther (1483–1546), the Reformation is important far beyond the horizons of ecclesiastical history. Criticism of the institutional Catholic Church and an emphasis on the 'original' Christian gospel was linked to claims of knowledge that fostered a pietistic and spiritualistic interiority peculiar to esotericism and mysticism. In addition, it is important to address the relationship between empirical natural science, which followed in the wake of the 'scientific revolution' of this period, and esoteric models of explanation that favoured a holistic interpretation and strove to transcend the boundaries of materialistic science. This confrontation is frequently described as a conflict between 'science' and 'magic', between 'rationality' and 'Hermetism', or between 'Enlightenment' and 'esotericism'. A closer examination of the relevant sources shows how complex the matter is in reality. Magic and irrationalism are not the 'opposite' of science and enlightenment, which we should keep at a distance, but are indissolubly interwoven with our culture.[1]

The Mysteries of Nature: *Magia naturalis*

Magic has always had a very close relationship with esotericism, since magic shares a similar world-view based on an animated cosmos permeated with dynamic correspondences. Magic seeks to intervene in the energetic field of reality through rituals, visualisation or the mental concentration of one's own will. Magic thus creates an operational realm for esotericism.[2]

1. The terms 'modern age' and 'modernity' are indebted to the self-regard of the present which considers itself 'enlightened' and 'rational'. However, one can just as easily arrive at a negative estimate with Bruno Latour: 'We have never been modern' (1993); or examine the survival of magic in modern societies (Meyer and Pels 2003). The point is made even more strongly by Zika 2003: 4.

2. The concept of 'magic' has been and still is hotly debated in religious studies. As no theoretical consensus has been reached and its usage has continually changed since Graeco-Roman antiquity, many scholars have suggested dropping the term to avoid misunderstandings. This is

MARSILIO FICINO AND THE ANIMATION OF STATUES

Christian orthodoxy has always regarded magic as disreputable. On the one hand, magic was linked to the demonic and satanic realms, and on the other, the magician aimed to meddle in God's creation and claim dominion over nature. Christian theology did not dispute the existence of demonic powers, to which it attributed magic, but the conscious use of magical knowledge for the attainment of individual goals was seen as exceeding human competence. This argument was highly fragile, for it excluded Holy Communion, which could be regarded as a magical act, and classified Jesus' magical acts as 'miracles'. However, this negative view of magic has remained influential right up to the present. Whereas medieval Christians tried to distinguish a 'white' healing magic from a 'black' harmful magic, the Renaissance invoked the idea of *magia naturalis* to evade Christian censure. This 'natural magic' assumes that the cosmos is permeated with an energy integral to nature itself. As human beings are embedded in the energetic field of the universe, they can investigate this energy and use it to understand God's dominion. The idea of *magia naturalis* thereby arose on the interface between religion and natural science.[3]

Marsilio Ficino's contributions on this subject illustrate this well. First, one should recall that the *Asclepius*, that Hermetic treatise already known to the medieval world, gave a detailed account of the magical animation and movement of statues (*Asclepius* 23-24 and 37-38). These human artefacts are awoken to become divine intermediaries by appropriate rituals, so that they give prophecies and do other important things. 'Drawing down' divine energy into terrestrial spheres and its concentration in objects was highly attractive to Ficino and his successors. We are indebted to Ficino's pupil Francesco Cattani da Diacceto for this beautiful description of such a ritual:

> If for example he wishes to acquire solar gifts, first he sees that the Sun is ascending in Leo or Aries, on the day and in the hour of the Sun. Then, robed in a solar mantle of a solar colour, such as gold, and crowned with a mitre of laurel, on the altar, itself made of solar material, he burns myrrh and frankincense, the Sun's own fumigations, having strewn the ground with heliotrope and suchlike flowers. Also he has an image of the Sun in gold or chrysolite or carbuncle, that is, of the kind they think corresponds to each of the Sun's gifts. If, for example, he wishes to cure diseases, he has an image of the Sun enthroned, crowned, and wearing a saffron cloak, likewise a raven

hardly practicable given the significance and polemic value of the concept of magic right across the centuries. One should rather describe these changes and their relation to historical contexts.

3. See Goldammer 1991. In her influential book *Giordano Bruno and the Hermetic Tradition* (2002) Frances A. Yates has advanced the thesis that Marsilio Ficino marks a crucial transformation in the history of magic. The 'vulgar' and 'primitive' magic of the Middle Ages, really no more than popular sorcery, gave way to a 'Hermetic magic', which served to investigate the cosmos, which it also mysteriously permeated. Her view is countered by three arguments. First, as a classic Renaissance scholar, Yates failed to appreciate the fact that all elements of fifteenth-century ritual magic had already developed in the Middle Ages (see Klaassen 2003). Second, she described Ficino one-sidedly as a Hermetic esotericist, overlooking his Neo-Platonic Christian context and attempts to reconcile his Hermetism with Christianity. Last, Yates considered that the Renaissance authors were solely fascinated by the magical elements of the *Corpus Hermeticum*.

and the figure of the Sun, which are to be engraved on gold when the Sun is ascending in the first face of Leo. Then, anointed with unguents made, under the same celestial aspect, from saffron, balsam, yellow honey and anything else of that kind, and not forgetting the cock and the goat, he sings the Sun's own hymn, such as Orpheus thought should be sung. For here is the force, and as it were the life, of the conciliation of the planet's favour. He sings, I say, first to the divine Henad of the Sun, then he sings to the Mind, and lastly he sings to the Soul; since One, Mind, Soul, are the three principles of all things. Also he uses a threefold harmony, of voice, of cithara, and of the whole body, of the kind he has discovered belongs to the Sun. [...] To all these he adds what he believes to be the most important: a strongly emotional disposition of the imagination, by which, as with pregnant women, the spirit is stamped with this kind of imprint, and flying out through the channels of the body, especially through the eyes, ferments and solidifies, like rennet, the corresponding power of the heavens.[4]

These sorts of rituals are often described as 'astral magic', because astrology provides the symbols cumulatively ascribed to material objects and the magician must concentrate on these symbols. In his work *De vita coelitus comparanda* ('On Making Your Life Agree with the Heavens', 1489), his most widely read text alongside *Pimander*, Marsilio Ficino similarly describes how the positive powers of the heavenly bodies are 'drawn down'. Nevertheless, Ficino was rather reserved in his interpretation and tried to persuade the reader that this was a matter of purely natural forces, namely a *magia naturalis*. However, when one refers to Plotinus, whose *Ennead* IV.3.11 Ficino simply claims to be commenting on in *De vita coelitus comparanda*, one discovers that Plotinus had the animation of statues in mind. Hence Ficino's text can be understood as a reference to the incriminating sections of the *Asclepius*, while taking refuge behind the Neo-Platonic authority of Plotinus.

Ficino knew exactly how his more orthodox contemporaries would respond to such a ritual: as clear evidence of a pagan Sun cult. But this contradicted his own interpretation that he was not paying homage to the Sun, but simply using its power to perform pious works.

HERMETIC MAGIC AND PIOUS CHRISTIANITY: LODOVICO LAZZARELLI

Hermetism was not the sole focus of Marsilio Ficino's work but woven into a Neo-Platonic philosophy and theology. However, one of his contemporaries clearly deserves the appellation 'Hermetic Christian' or 'Christian Hermetist'. The Hermetic writings were absolutely central to the thought of Lodovico Lazzarelli (1447–1500).[5] Lazzarelli was the pupil of a certain Giovanni da Correggio, who even called himself 'Mercurio'. Correggio was an extraordinary personality. On Palm Sunday 1484, thirteen years after Ficino's publication of the *Pimander*, Correggio caused a stir by riding, dressed like Christ, upon a white ass through the streets of Rome, followed by mounted servants. Above the crown of thorns upon his head he bore a disc in the form of a waxing Moon inscribed with the words:

4.   Diaccetto, *De pulchro* ('Oh Beauty'), in *Opera omnia* (1563), pp. 45f.
5.   For the following, see the exhaustive introduction in Hanegraaff and Bouthoorn 2005.

> This is my Servant Pimander, whom I have chosen. This Pimander is my supreme
> and waxing child, in whom I am well pleased, to cast out demons and proclaim my
> judgement and truth to the heathen. Do not hinder him, but hear and obey him with
> all fear and veneration; thus speaks the Lord your God and Father of every talisman
> of all the world, Jesus of Nazareth. (*Epistola Enoch* 6.2.2, quoted in Hanegraaf and
> Bouthoorn 2005: 28)

Correggio believed the 'great Being', revealed to Hermes Trismegistus in the first treatise of the *Corpus Hermeticum* as Poimandres is none other than Christ himself, who later incarnated in Jesus of Nazareth. Giovanni da Correggio considered himself the returning Christ, who as the 'Hermetic Christ' combined Hermetism and Christianity in his own person. His ride to the Vatican in Rome was intended to prepare the public for the Day of Judgement.

Lodovico Lazzarelli had already become acquainted with Correggio several years before this incident and became his pupil. It is possible that the master learned of the Hermetic texts through his pupil, for Lazzarelli translated the last three treatises of the *Corpus Hermeticum* (CH XVI-XVIII) into Latin, using a different Greek manuscript from that utilised by Ficino for his translation, which contained only the first fourteen treatises. Dedicated to Correggio, Lazzarelli's translation was published several years after his death by the French scholar Symphorien Champier (1471–1537).

Between 1492 and 1494 Lazzarelli composed his *Crater Hermetis* ('Bowl of Hermes'), a work composed wholly in the Hermetic spirit, in which he assumes the role of the sage comparable to Hermes Trismegistus or similar authorities. His students are two historical personalities, namely King Ferdinand I of Aragon, king of Naples and Sicily, and his prime minister, the renowned poet Giovanni Pontano. The students are instructed in the path to true happiness, only attainable through true knowledge of oneself and God ('Gnosis'). Lazzarelli quotes from the Bible, and from Jewish and Christian authorities such as Philo of Alexandria and Pseudo-Dionysius Areopagita, and from the *Corpus Hermeticum*, as well as various texts of Jewish mysticism like the *Sefer Yetzirah*. From the very outset Lazzarelli leaves us in no doubt that Pimander (*Poimandres*) and Christ are one and the same person: 'It pleased Pimander, who was in the mind of Hermes, to take up his abode in me as Jesus Christ, and he comforted me by illuminating me with the light of wisdom, which is the eternal comforter'. When Pontano asks whether he is now a Christ or a Hermetist, he answers: 'I am a Christ, Pontanus, but I am not ashamed to be a Hermetist at the same time'. While instructing his students on the path of self-knowledge and happiness, he refers to the Gospels and the teachings of Hermes in equal measure.

Like most Hermetic texts, the *Crater Hermetis* opens with theoretical reflections supplemented with detailed biblical expositions on topics such as the symbolic meaning of the trees of paradise. But through their instruction the students soon approach a state of mystical ecstasy, whereupon Lazzarelli announces the revelation of the 'absolute mystery', consisting in the 'creation of souls'. Interestingly, the author succeeds in re-interpreting the most controversial sections of the *Asclepius*,

namely the passages concerning the creation of the gods, as a pious Christian text. First, he repeats the common assumption that the Egyptians lived in a state of error and were therefore not in a position to create souls. The only thing they could achieve was to fashion images, idols and statues, and then awaken these to life with already existing souls and demons. Lazzarelli concedes that Hermes Trismegistus had made himself guilty of idolatry by describing these practices, but this is only logical because he lived long before Jesus of Nazareth and therefore remained a pagan despite his wisdom. He was not able to understand the true meaning of *Poimandres* (CH I). Only *after* the incarnation of Poimandres in Jesus Christ did it become possible to bridge the gulf between God and human beings and to gain a perfect knowledge of God. This was the very knowledge preached by Giovanni 'Mercurio' da Correggio. Only after Poimandres had become flesh in Jesus were Christians able to attain 'Gnosis'. According to Lazzarelli, Christians attaining such knowledge became a part of the divine power in a natural way and were in a position to create life, just like God. For this reason they no longer needed to 'draw down' souls, but could create them through their own powers.

With this interpretation Lazzarelli could defend the passages relating to the 'creation of gods' and elegantly evade the charge of idolatry. Although unknown to the Egyptians and Hermes, the revelation of Poimandres was not truly about idolatry or astral magic, but a mystical perception enabling man to share in the creative power of God. This mystery stood at the heart of Correggio's teachings to the Christians.

Simple attributions such as 'magic' and 'Hermetism' do not evidently function as opposites to 'Christianity' in an esoteric field of discourse. New connections are constantly being made according to changing contexts, and these in turn produce their own arguments and identities.

Magic and Science: Agrippa of Nettesheim

The Hermetic disciplines revived in Italy soon became extremely popular in other parts of Europe. A number of Italian physicians and astrologers moved to France, where King Louis XI (1461–1483) had a particular interest in the occult sciences. Germany during the late fifteenth and early sixteenth centuries also lent further momentum to esotericism in various disciplines. Agrippa of Nettesheim (1486–1535) and Paracelsus (Theophrastus Bombastus of Hohenheim, 1493–1541) deserve special mention in relation to *magia naturalis* and medicine, for they demonstrate how closely related Hermeticism, nature-philosophy and science were in the early modern period (Bonelli and Shea 1975 offers a good introduction to this subject).

The turbulent life of Agrippa, whose actual name was Heinrich Cornelius, clearly shows the connection between Hermeticism and natural science. The Cologne thinker became known through his work *De occulta philosophia libri tres* ('Three Books of Occult Philosophy'), written in 1510 and published in 1531, which testifies to his astonishing familiarity despite his youth with all philosophical and Hermetic traditions. Inspired by Johannes Trithemius and also dedicated to him (see below, p. 74-75), this book is widely considered one of the most important books of Renaissance esotericism. The work again and again led to charges that Agrippa was a 'black magician'. Such reproaches subsequently denied the book the attention it deserved.

In *De occulta philosophia* Agrippa distinguishes in a Neo-Platonic manner the three worlds of the elementary, celestial and divine spheres, corresponding to the human trinity of body, soul and spirit. Besides the four terrestrial elements he describes the *quinta essentia* ('fifth essence', from which our word 'quintessence' derives) as a mediator in the stratified realm of nature, which operates as a geometric principle of formation in the mineral kingdom, as vegetative power in the plant kingdom, as instinct and sensation in the animal kingdom, and finally in human beings as reason. Aided by magic, humans may succeed in linking what is above with what is below, and thereby approach God, much as Marsilio Ficino described it. Corresponding to the three worlds, there are three kinds of magic, namely a natural, sidereal and divine magic. Agrippa described magic as the perfect and supreme science, the most sacred and sublime philosophy, comprising for him natural philosophy, mathematical philosophy and divine theology. Book I treats the elements, their occult powers, the heavenly bodies and various theoretical and practical instructions for magical operations, as well as the relationship between magic and language. Book II is concerned with numerology, mathematical symbolism, harmony in music, man as the microcosm and astrology. Book III is based on the Christian Kabbalah and describes the links between magic and religion, the need for secrecy, faith and neighbourly love, the Holy Trinity, the holy names (the *Sefirot* and the powerful name 'Jesus'), the world of angels and demons, the gift of prophecy and much else. Agrippa repeatedly stresses the necessity of a firm faith and trust in God. He was influenced by Lazzarelli's *Crater Hermetis*, evident in his emphasis on mystical ecstasy, which enables man to look at the world from a divine perspective, a self-empowerment and experience of 'Gnosis' otherwise denied to him.

After writing his book, Agrippa made his way through the world as a physician, lawyer, philosopher, as a captain in the Imperial Army and as a diplomat with more or less success. He was directly involved in the troubles of the first decades of the sixteenth century. His attitude towards the occult sciences was very nuanced. The magician displayed his critical faculties in his long essay *De incertitudine et vanitate scientiarum atque artium et de excellentia verbi Dei* ('On the Uncertainty and Vanity of the Sciences and Arts and the Excellence of God's Word', 1530), which he composed in 1527 as a settling of accounts with contemporary science. This 'recantation' is often interpreted as a break with his 'youthful' enthusiasm for the occult philosophy, but the matter is not that simple, because *De occulta philosophia* was finally published in the year following *De incertitudine*. Agrippa followed the strict Neo-Platonic separation of faith and rational explanation, using this as a weapon against scholastic ideas relating to the rational penetration of the divine. He offers an example of the complexity of 'esoteric' authors of this period, for he was simultaneously a magician, a humanistic theologian, and a sceptical philosopher. The target of his attack in *De incertitudine* is thus not only magic and astrology, but science itself. In the very first chapter, devoted to 'the sciences in general', he does not conceal his abhorrence for the view that science would bring humans closer to the divine. On the contrary, he wants 'to see the matter the other way round with different eyes, not praising the sciences but quashing much of them with contempt'. It is not science but goodwill that can unite humans with God. 'Moreover', continues Agrippa, 'all arts and sciences are nothing but human precepts and similar pretensions, harmful rather than useful, both poisonous and healing, good and evil, but never complete, always ambiguous and full of errors and bickering'. He basically argues that certainty can never be achieved in a scientific procedure and all assertions to this effect involve a grotesque degree of vanity. In Chapter 42 Agrippa speaks of 'natural magic', sharing the view of contemporary magicians,

> that it is nothing but the supreme authority of natural sciences and thus called the climax and most perfect use of natural philosophy. It is in fact a part of natural philosophy which through the help of natural effects and their clever application can produce such miracles as to astonish all men. The Africans and the Indians have mostly studied this art, because they have best access to the herbs, stones and other things, which serve this purpose.

Later he writes:

> For the magi, as the most precise investigators of nature, borrow that which comes from nature and apply it to their own purposes, and moreover in such a way, that they often anticipate an effect of nature, which the common man then considers a miracle, but these are all natural events, save that one has taken advantage in time.

Agrippa constantly recruits the chain of initiates who have preserved and developed this form of magic. Using a multilinear model, he favours Zoroaster, Orpheus, Plato and the Neo-Platonists in this role. This is an important aspect of his dispute with the vanity of contemporary scientists but also a clear division between what can be known through reason, and what can be glimpsed through a mystical link with the divine. Once again we find magic on the borderline between science and religion.

ALCHEMIST, PHYSICIAN, NATURE-PHILOSOPHER: PARACELSUS

Paracelsus was one of the greatest doctors and nature-philosophers of the German Renaissance. His alchemical and magical insights, contained within a massive opus, are composed in a spirit reminiscent of Marsilio Ficino, but which is primarily directed towards medicine (see Müller-Jahncke 1985; Grell 1998; Williams and Gunnoe 2002). Paracelsus also proceeds from the threefold Neo-Platonic division of the cosmos and the correspondence between the microcosm and the macrocosm. The formless primal matter (Iliaster) is organised according to three principles, which he characterises as Salt, Sulphur and Mercury in accordance with alchemical tradition. That which Agrippa defined as *quinta essentia*, Paracelsus calls the *archeus*, an organising and formative energy operating on all three realms of nature. The sidereal or astral body in man—a kind of aura—stands in a reciprocal relationship with the planets and, like a magnet, is able to draw down their corresponding astral energies and so influence the body.

Whenever the planets produce diseases or distinguishing marks, this is not simply a causal connection. Paracelsus maintains that the human body and the cosmos should be regarded as a unity, mutually reflecting each other. In the second treatise of his *Buch Paragranum* he states: 'The Sun and Moon and all planets are in man, similarly all the stars and the whole chaos'. Precise astrological knowledge is needed in order to diagnose and treat diseases, as Paracelsus declares in his inimitable fashion:

> [A]ll planets have the same aspect and signature and their children in man, and heaven is their father. Man is made according to heaven and the earth, for he is composed of them… The physician must know this, if he wishes to address the fundamentals of medicine. If he does not know it, he is nought but a cheat and practices medicine like a peasant, who hangs colocynth in wine as a cure for all.

However, it is not enough to know only the correspondences between the corporeal and astral planes. The physician must also know the exact time when a medicine is appropriate and how the course of a disease can be interpreted in relation to planetary movements. A remedy may be effective at one time but not at another, an occurrence which Paracelsus thought the average doctors of his era completely overlooked owing to their naïve fixation on empirics and the repeatability of trials.

As Paracelsus had already gathered a large following during his lifetime and many pseudo-Paracelsian works started to circulate after his death, the essence of his teachings is not always easy to determine. Paracelsians are rightly described as 'chemical philosophers' (see Debus 1975) due to the aforementioned medical and alchemical foundations of his thought. However, Paracelsus also offered an esoteric model of living nature furnished with magical powers ('Magic is natural, because nature itself is magical'). This was a pantheistic, or better, a panentheistic view, which recognises God in all things and all things in God, as well as a nuanced idea of correspondences, which assumes that man bears within himself an 'inner cosmos'. There is also his emphasis on the 'two lights' granted to man which mutually affirm each other, namely the 'light of grace' (the Bible) and the 'light of nature'. Paracelsus also promoted the idea of a 'star' or 'astrum' as an invisible, 'archetypal' double of the visible world and the doctrine that there was no soul without a body, nor a body without a soul.[6] He further imagined that a kind of 'astral residue' remained around the body after death, whose independent survival can lead to ghosts and similar phenomena. There was also the doctrine of elementary beings or nature spirits, which are assigned to the four basic elements

---

6. This doctrine was taken up by many authors, from Jacob Boehme to Friedrich Christoph Oetinger, who spoke of *Geistleiblichkeit* ('spiritual corporeality').

as gnomes, undines, sylphs and salamanders, though it is possible that this idea
does not actually derive from Paracelsus. He espoused a cosmogony in which
Creation proceeds from an original deity (*Mysterium Magnum*) to the primal matter
(the 'star'), whence come the three basic principles and the four elements to produce in their turn the multifarious material world. This account includes the fall of
Lucifer and his angels, whereby our world became 'cagastric', that is full of
suffering and death. Paracelsus also saw the whole of life as a form of alchemy. A
cosmic alchemical process of redemption and purification, in which Christ acts as
the Philosophers' Stone, led to the restoration of the primeval harmony, in a way
reminiscent of the kabbalistic doctrine of *Tiqqun*.[7]

Paracelsus' influence was enormous. Around 1700 even Arabic translations of
his writings were prepared and disseminated in Syria. A Paracelsian tradition
swiftly developed, especially directed towards a holistic medicine on the basis of
correspondences between the planets and parts of the body. Complementary
medical therapies like homeopathy and alchemical medicine (spagyrics) still refer
to his works today. Moreover, following Paracelsus' death, his followers initiated a
kind of 'Hermetisation' of alchemical medicine.[8] Paracelsus and the Paracelsian
tradition offer a particularly clear example of how esoteric discourses formulate
their own claims to knowledge against established authorities, which are then
legitimised with reference to the Hermetic tradition. One can only understand
Paracelsianism in relation to the institutionalised Christian church.

KABBALAH AND OCCULT PHILOSOPHY

All representatives of early modern esotericism were influenced by the Jewish
Kabbalah to a greater or lesser degree. This influence became more evident the
more Hebrew texts were available in Latin translation. In the sixteenth and seventeenth centuries partial translations of the Zohar, the works of Gikatilla, and other
'classical' texts were produced, so that Christian authors could make full use of
them. Many Christians regarded Hebrew as a sacred language that had been
spoken in the Garden of Eden, but this interest in Jewish sources should not be
seen as a neutral process of exchange or dialogue. More often it was marked by a
polemic tone with attempts to prove the 'truth' of Christianity with the aid of Jewish sources. Such concerns influenced the choice of passages considered worthy of

---

7.   For a full discussion of Paracelsus' thought, see Koyré 1971: 75-129.

8.   Wilhelm Kühlmann investigated the social and religio-political consequences of this
Hermeticisation, concluding: 'What becomes apparent is the scientific pluralisation of concepts of
knowledge and their respective integration in world-views, which are resolutely distanced from
the dogma of religious groups. This reflected the controversy raging within the church, whether a
Hermetic revelation, combining the old mysticism of the Logos with the alchemical symbolism of
an eschatological restoration of true universal knowledge, could offer alternatives to the existing
ecclesiastical scholasticism and its monopoly over knowledge and belief. The opponents of the
Paracelsians and Hermetists interpreted this legacy of the Renaissance correctly and always called
on the support of the authorities' (Wilhelm Kühlmann in Trepp and Lehmann 2001: 39).

translation, while others were deemed less interesting. The 'dialogue' was thus always an instrument for Christian missionary activity towards the Jews, while the Jews for their part usually regarded the Christian adaptation of their doctrines as expropriation and distortion.[9]

PICO ONCE AGAIN: KABBALAH AND POLEMICS

The beginnings of Christian Kabbalah inevitably lead us back to Pico della Mirandola. One hundred and eighteen of his '900 Theses' concern the Kabbalah in claiming the Jewish doctrine as a proof for the truth of Christianity. (Moreover, the kabbalistic theses were not among those thirteen rejected by the papacy.) Pico considered this subject so important that he explicitly referred to the 'divinely inspired' teachings of the Kabbalah, confirmed by 'famous authors', in his opening speech 'On the Dignity of Man'. These 'ancient mysteries of the Jews' were misunderstood by the Jews themselves and had been corrupted. In the fifth kabbalistic thesis of the *Conclusiones* he writes unambiguously:

> Every Hebrew Cabalist, following the principles and sayings of the science of the Cabala, is inevitably forced to concede, without addition, omission, or variation, precisely what the Catholic faith of Christians maintains concerning the Trinity and every divine Person, Father, Son, and Holy Spirit. (Farmer 1998: 523)

In order to learn the Jewish doctrine, Pico learnt Hebrew from a Jewish convert from Sicily who called himself Flavius Mithridates, from whom he also commissioned the translation of several kabbalistic treatises into Latin replete with anti-Jewish polemics. In his argument, Pico applied the kabbalistic interpretative techniques in various different ways. For example, he concurs with the Jewish emphasis on God's Name as a central part of the doctrine, but assigns a kabbalistic meaning to the name 'Jesus' (in Hebrew '*Yod Shin Waw*'). In his fourteenth kabbalistic *Conclusio* he writes:

> By the letter…*shin*, which mediates in the name Jesus, it is indicated to us Cabalistically that the world then rested perfectly, as though in its perfection, when *Yod* was conjoined with *Vav*—which happened in Christ, who was the true Son of God, and man. (Farmer 1998: 527)

---

9.   Steven M. Wasserstrom has coined the concept of 'interconfessional circles' in an earlier phase of the European history of religion to describe the processes of exchange between Jews and Muslims in medieval Spain. These intellectuals were 'interconfessional despite themselves', because they were chiefly interested in the other religion for purposes of polemical identification rather than real dialogue. Certain topics had equal interest for Jews and Muslims, but the others' traditions were adopted as their own. According to Wasserstrom, 'it was through their shared passion for specific intellectual subsystems—Sufi, Ismaili, Ishrâqî, Kabbalistic—that intercourse between Spanish Jews and Muslims flourished' (Wasserstrom 2000: 69). Even if Wasserstrom applies this model to the particular situation of Andalusia, I consider the term 'interconfessional circles' appropriate for both the Middle Ages and the early modern period. Wasserstrom's idea of 'intellectual subsystems' is comparable to my 'fields of discourse', in which there were exchanges of religious tradition, as well as in philosophical and scientific spheres. The interest in kabbalistic forms of interpretation is a particularly instructive example of this.

This project is ambivalent. On the one hand, Pico asserts the absolute sacredness of the Hebrew language and closes his kabbalistic theses with the famous
sentence, 'Just as the true astrology teaches us to read in the book of God, so the
Kabbalah teaches us to read in the book of the law'. On the other hand, he
describes the Kabbalah, or more precisely, its scientific branch, as 'formal metaphysics and inferior theology'. But Pico does not regard this Kabbalah as Jewish—
rather he expropriates the Jews with the reproach that they had not understood the
true meaning of their own teachings.[10] Despite this harsh rebuff, Pico cultivated
friendly relations with Jews. The Jewish kabbalist Yohanan Alemanno encouraged
Pico to complete his commentary on the *Song of Songs* and otherwise had an
intensive intellectual exchange with him. Pico's library contained all relevant
kabbalistic works, many of them in the original Hebrew.[11] It is better to describe
such ambivalence as 'discursive transfer', rather than the upholding of a unitary
religious identity. This is clearly the case with Johannes Reuchlin, who represents
the blossoming of Christian Kabbalah.

JOHANNES REUCHLIN

Johannes Reuchlin (1455–1522) is indisputably the most important representative
of Christian Kabbalah at the beginning of the sixteenth century. Scholars such as
Joseph Blau and Gershom Scholem celebrate him as the first researcher of Kabbalah in history, who did more for Jewish literature than many a rabbi (see
Grözinger 1993 and also Schmidt-Biggemann 2003: 9-48). Both his major works,
De verbo mirifico ('The Wonder-Working Word', 1494) and especially *De arte
cabalistica* ('The Art of the Kabbalah', 1517), have been held in high regard by
Christian kabbalists. With his first Hebrew grammar, published in 1506, he laid
the basis of research into the Hebrew language and biblical studies. Writing also
under the pseudonym Capnion, Reuchlin was an ardent follower of Pico della
Mirandola and took up several of the Italian's kabbalistic theses in order to
elaborate them into a general theory. In *De verbo mirifico* it was primarily the
kabbalistic derivation of the name Jesus, which Reuchlin used and which provided
the book with its title. By inserting a *Shin* into the middle of the Tetragrammaton
YHWH, one obtains YHShWH, which is none else but *YeHoShUH*, that is
'Jesus'.[12] Reuchlin further explains that the letter *Shin* occurs in such significant
words as *shemen* ('oil') and *mashiah* ('anointed', 'Messiah'), and every individual can
experience the supreme knowledge of the sciences and ultimately the deification of

    10.   For the most bitter reaction on the part of Jewish scholars, especially Moses Cordovero,
see Idel 2002.
    11.   Kibre 1966; see also the relevant study by Wirszubski 1989.
    12.   Pico did not take this step. However, Nicholas of Cusa offered a precedent for Reuchlin
in his sermon *Dies sanctificatus* (1445): see Schmidt-Biggemann 2003: 19. The unutterable Jewish
Tetragrammaton becomes pronounceable for Reuchlin as a Pentagram (i.e. a word with five
letters); this utterability is once again interpreted as a symbol of the incarnation of the Divine in
Jesus.

human nature once he has been anointed by Jesus Christ. Both this interpretation and his emphasis of the wonder-working word demonstrate how strongly Reuchlin wished to integrate magical traditions into Christianity.[13]

Reuchlin's knowledge of the Kabbalah was relatively superficial in his first work. For example, he could not list the ten *Sefirot* in their correct sequence. But this soon changed as a result of his intensive engagement with the Jewish sources. *De arte cabalistica* is also the first complete account of a kabbalistic system written by a non-Jew. Like *De verbo mirifico*, Reuchlin's second major work is composed in the form of a discussion between three persons: Marranus, a circumcised and baptised Muslim, Simon as a Jewish kabbalist, and Philolaus, a Christian and Pythagorean. In the idiom of his age, Reuchlin describes the Kabbalah as a precursor of Pythagoreanism, but he names only Plato and Aristotle among the other *prisci theologi*. The Kabbalah is an original form of philosophical wisdom-teaching, which must now be made accessible once again. For this reason, the magical elements of the doctrine, which still loomed large in *De verbo mirifico*, played a relatively minor role twenty years later. This is not to say that he is no longer interested in the practical aspect of the Kabbalah, but his chief concern is with 'winging' the soul upwards to God, rather than 'drawing down' the divine.

Reuchlin developed his own kabbalistic system through his eclectic selection of Jewish sources (which was common practice with Jewish authors as well). His emphasis on the divine *language* is interesting, because this similarly represented a key to the mystery of the world for many other esotericists (see Coudert [ed.] 1999). 'Through thought', says Reuchlin's Jew Simon, '[man can attain], so far as nature allows this, that divine-like state (*deificatio*), which is the supreme blessing'. Here one detects the influence of that Aristotelian conception of Kabbalah found in Abulafia and (early) Gikatilla, for with the aid of his intellect man scales the ladder of knowledge. At the end of the first dialogue Simon summarises this as follows: through the kabbalistic contemplation of the Torah, 'we gain the power to raise ourselves above gloomy confusion to simple things, and from the simple to the most simple of all, from the caused to the causes and finally from the lower world to the higher, and from the higher world to the Messiah, who is the highest goal of our thought'. The path to the Messiah leads through the understanding of the letters in the name of the Messiah, which contains the hidden name of God. 'Through the Messiah we reach the unrecognisable God. We reach that goal through these holy letters as upon Jacob's ladder…'. With this reasoning, Reuchlin opens the way to his Christian conception of the Kabbalah.

Owing to his highly positive portrayal of Jewish wisdom-teachings, Johannes Reuchlin was enmeshed in the coils of the acrimonious Jewish–Christian debate. Johannes Josef Pfefferkorn, a Jewish convert to Christianity and spokesman of a

---

13. The magical aspect of his doctrines and their clear traces of Jewish and Muslim tradition—for example the *Picatrix* or the magic of 'Abramelin of Worms'—have been more fully discussed than heretofore in recent research; see Bernd Roling in Bremmer and Veenstra 2002: 231-66.

large anti-Jewish movement, asked Reuchlin in 1510 for an affidavit for Emperor Maximilian relating to the question of whether all Hebrew books opposed to Christianity should be burnt. But Reuchlin recommended that this should not be done: even if the Jews adhered to a false religion and were rightly criticised by Christians because they had not accepted the Messiah, they must be granted the same rights as Christians. No one had the right to expropriate them. At the most one should burn those books which spoke openly against Jesus, but spare the rest. Instead of destroying the property of the Jews, Christians should seek to persuade the Jews. Moreover, the intellectual and literary quest for the highest knowledge demanded that one make a detailed study of the writings of the Jews (see Grözinger 1993: 181).

As one might expect, Pfefferkorn was not satisfied with this recommendation and launched a violent attack against Reuchlin. This resulted in the Inquisitor, Jakob van Hoogstraten (Hochstraten), opening an ecclesiastic trial against Reuchlin in 1513 and even entering the debate himself with publications against the Kabbalah. After an initially favourable verdict for Reuchlin at Speyer in 1514, the trial ended in 1520 with his condemnation by the Pope. Reuchlin submitted and taught as Professor for Greek and Hebrew in 1520–21 at the University of Ingolstadt and then at Tübingen until his death in 1522. There were already further disputes during the trial, in which Reuchlin published his learned correspondence in his defence. In 1516–17 a group of young critical humanists published the so-called *Dunkelmännerbriefe*, in which the hostility towards the Jews was made into a grotesque, thus mocking scholastic theology at the University of Cologne. Intended as support for Reuchlin, these letters were ultimately to his disadvantage.

Attitudes towards the Kabbalah were already long influenced by the confessional tensions at the beginning of the sixteenth century. One should not forget that in the same year *De arte cabalistica* appeared, Luther went public with his theses and so stoked the smouldering conflict. The need to take up a clear position in order not to endanger one's own identity was even greater than previously. Reuchlin's work shows how far esoteric motifs entered the internal Christian conflict. One example may suffice: whenever kabbalists and advocates of *magia naturalis* talk about magical names and words conjuring specific effects on spiritual and material planes, they were touching upon one of the fiercest debates of the Reformation, namely, the transubstantiation of the body and blood of Christ in the Eucharist. While Catholics assumed that the 'Blessed Sacrament' was actually transformed into a communal benefit in the Eucharist, many Protestants insisted on the 'purely symbolic' character of this ritual. This dispute still divides the denominations today.

JOHANNES TRITHEMIUS

The Benedictine abbot Johannes Trithemius (1462–1516) also worked on the interface of Christian Kabbalah, *magia naturalis* and the humanistic sciences. Born Johann Heidenberg in Trittenheim (hence his later name Trithemius), he already dreamed at the age of fifteen of devoting his life to study. By the age of twenty he had completed the relevant studies at Heidelberg University. During a journey he found shelter from a snow storm at Sponheim Abbey near Mainz and saw this as a divine sign that he should become a monk. He remained at Sponheim for twenty-three years, creating an important library there, and corresponded with numerous scholars of his time, including Johannes Reuchlin, who taught him Greek and Hebrew. Trithemius may also have developed his great interest in the Kabbalah thanks to Reuchlin. In the winter of 1509–10 Trithemius had already taken up his appointment at Würzburg, where the young Agrippa of Nettesheim visited him, and they conversed about the need to put research into *magia naturalis* on a professional footing. Agrippa's *De occulta philosophia* is the fruit of this meeting and exchange and Agrippa dedicated it to his elder colleague.

Trithemius initially voiced his criticism of the magical arts and 'witchcraft'. At this point one might recall that the infamous *Malleus Maleficarum* ('Hammer of the Witches') by Heinrich Kramer (Institoris) and Jakob Sprenger was published in 1486 and reprinted thirteen times up to 1520. However, in 1499 Trithemius suddenly turned out to be a practitioner of the occult arts. In a confidential letter to the Carmelite monk Arnold Bostius, he enlarged on steganography, namely the art of composing secret messages and communicating them over great distances with the aid of angels. However, as Bostius had just died, the letter fell into the hands of a brother monk, who was aghast and made the matter public. Henceforth, many regarded Trithemius as the typical Renaissance magician. There was a famous legend that Trithemius had invoked the spirit of Emperor Maximilian's dead consort Mary of Burgundy in 1482. Such rumours further increased interest in the numerous writings of the abbot: the first printed edition of *Steganographia* (1606) was reissued seven times by 1721. In view of his example, one may well ask today how many ecclesiastical authorities belonged to what Richard Kieckhefer calls 'the clerical underworld', which arose in the Middle Ages and was active into the early modern period (Kieckhefer 1990: 151-75).

Several years later the French scholar Carolus Bovillus visited Trithemius at his monastery and was asked his opinion about steganography. But this colleague was also appalled and immediately wrote a letter about Trithemius' 'demonic magic', so the abbot kept quiet about such subjects in future. The relationship with his brother monks was however troubled, not just on account of their differences over magic, and in 1506 Trithemius took up a new position as abbot of St Jacob's abbey at Würzburg, where he remained until his death.

Trithemius' supposed ambivalence between the rejection and practice of the magical arts has been hotly debated. According to Noel L. Brann, Trithemius' 'Janus face' is not so surprising. First, like Ficino and others, he describes 'white' magic as compatible with Christian doctrine and simply rejects 'black' magic, the *Goeteia*, as demonic. Second, he intended his warning to be taken seriously concerning the dangers of magical operations with angels and demons (which as is well known are not always easy to distinguish) (Brann 1999).

GIORDANO BRUNO

With Giordano Bruno (1548–1600) we encounter one of the most controversial personalities of the early modern period. He was more embroiled than almost anyone else in the scientific and religious debates of his time and ultimately became their victim. He stood up for his convictions and, instead of recanting the Copernican world-view and his religious ideas, paid with his life by being burnt at the stake. For this reason he is regarded, perhaps rather one-sidedly, as the herald of modernity, who upheld the freedom of thought and enquiry above all else.[14]

Giordano Bruno led an extremely turbulent life and travelled throughout Europe. Born at Nola near Naples, Bruno joined the Dominican order at the age of twenty-four and studied theology. After four years his wilful notions of Christian dogma caused trouble and he fled first to Rome, travelling in northern Italy (with a detour to Calvinistic Geneva), before arriving at Paris in 1581. There he devoted himself to the 'art of memory', a topic which played an important role in modern esotericism, which combines logic, imagination and magic.[15] We will encounter this subject again with John Dee.

In 1583 Bruno travelled to England, in order to defend the heliocentric world-view of Copernicus at the University of Oxford. This unleashed a violent debate, further increasing Bruno's reputation. He now distinguished himself as a highly versatile author, initially with his *Sigillus Sigillorum* ('Seal of Seals'), and then with several of his most famous works in the Italian language. In 1585 he returned to Paris and wrote among other works his 120 articles against the Aristotelians. After staying at Wittenberg, where he enjoyed a friendly reception from the Lutherans, he composed several works on the so-called *Ars magna* ('Great Art') of Raimundus Lullus (1232–1316). After travelling to Prague and Helmstedt, he published *De rerum principiis* ('The Principles of Things') as well as his most important contributions to magic: *De magia*, *Theses de magia*, *De magia mathematica* and *De vinculis in genere* ('On Linkages in General') in 1588. In 1590, in Frankfurt, he published three closely related books, *De minimo*, *De monade* and *De immenso*, in which he presented the fundamentals of a theory of monads, which would later play such an important part in the work of Franciscus Mercurius van Helmont and Gottfried Wilhelm Leibniz.

In 1591 Bruno made the great mistake of accepting the invitation of the Venetian patriarch Giovanni Mocenigo to speak on the art of memory. Mocenigo handed him over to the Inquisition, which arrested him and charged him with heresy. After being transferred to Rome in 1593, the trial lasted many years, during which Bruno worsened the situation with his utterances. On 21 December 1599,

---

14.   In *Giordano Bruno and the Hermetic Tradition* (2002), Frances A. Yates draws quite a different portrait of this man. In her account, Bruno becomes a thinker firmly anchored in the Hermetic tradition, with which he significantly influenced modern science (see above, p. 3). Forty years on, research had adopted a more modest position, neither seeing Bruno as a hero of modernity, nor regarding Hermeticism as the central characteristic of his work.

15.   Besides the contributions of Frances A. Yates see Rossi 2000.

after he had refused to recant his doctrines, he was condemned to death by Pope Clement VII. His chief offences were his rejection of transubstantiation (the Catholic doctrine of the real presence and 'transformation' of the body of Christ in the sacrament), his doctrine of reincarnation, the boundlessness and eternity of the universe, his view that Moses and Christ were magicians and that there were men before Adam. Giordano Bruno was burnt alive on 17 February 1600 on the Campo de' Fiori in Rome.

Bruno's significance for modern esotericism is more than that of a 'Hermeticist'. He was a representative of an *occulta philosophia*, which inquired into the cosmos as a 'whole' and saw man within a network of forces upon which he could act through appropriate measures. His doctrines deal with a *magia naturalis*, which also recognises an empirical science. In this respect, Giordano Bruno stands with one foot in the tradition of the fifteenth and sixteenth centuries, and the other already in the scientific outlook of the seventeenth century, as it would be formulated in Sulzbach (see below) and elsewhere.

It should not be forgotten that the heliocentric view of the cosmos, which won the upper hand in the scientific revolution, represented a challenge for the esoteric disciplines.[16] Magicians like Agrippa of Nettesheim, at home in the Ptolemaic world-view, could look 'upwards', in order to reach through the planetary spheres to God. However, if one did not subscribe to a pantheism, which found God everywhere, the question arose of where God was, if the Earth was just one planet among many. The same applied to the boundlessness of the universe, which made it difficult to localise the deity, the angels and other intermediary beings. As Blaise Pascal (1623–1662) would later put it, man had become a 'stranger in the universe'.

SULZBACH: AN ESOTERIC CROSSROADS

The seventeenth and eighteenth centuries were marked by crucial upheavals. The Thirty Years War, grounded in the conflict of confessions and formally concluded by the Peace of Westphalia in 1648, had destroyed large areas of Europe and killed a considerable proportion of the population, with major consequences for politics, religion and philosophy. In the face of this devastating experience, many philosophers thought that the influence of religion should be restricted and men should be united in a 'religion of reason'. The idea of the separation of state and religion, now the hallmark of modern Western states to a greater or lesser degree, henceforth developed from Thomas Hobbes (1588–1679) to Jean-Jacques Rousseau (1712–1778) and Immanuel Kant (1724–1804). But the esoteric tradition with its ideas of *prisca theologia* and *philosophia perennis* also held the potential for defining religion beyond confessional boundaries. Moreover, the seventeenth-century scientific revolutions based on the primacy of empiricism were by no means averse to esoteric interpretations, as is often supposed. On the contrary, many investigators of nature knew how to combine their interest in a holistic interpretation of the cosmos with empirical research.

16. On astrology see von Stuckrad 2003b: 252-74.

The small Bavarian town of Sulzbach provides a fascinating example of all these connections. In the seventeenth century the Count Palatine Christian August von Sulzbach pursued a religious policy oriented towards integration rather than confrontation. Upon the recommendation of his friend Franciscus Mercurius van Helmont (1614–1698), son of the famous Paracelsian Johannes (Jan) Baptista van Helmont (1579–1644), Christian August gathered renowned philosophers, theologians, linguists, scientists, craftsmen and artists at his court in the 1660s, in order to promote science and culture. In 1666 Christian Knorr von Rosenroth (d. 1689) was appointed chancellor of Sulzbach, and in the succeeding years the court developed into an important centre of esoteric and scientific research in Europe. Poetry and music, philology and Hebrew studies flourished alongside an ecumenical religious policy and empirical scientific research. There were new developments in the treatment of timber, the art of weaving, iron foundries and agriculture. Two printing presses were set up, one under Abraham Lichtenthaler and another under Moses Bloch, which specialised in the printing of Hebrew, Aramaic and Syriac texts. Like many other princes, for example, Landgrave Moritz von Hessen (1572–1632) (see Moran 1991), Christian August was extremely interested in the occult disciplines and promoted them in the context of his programme of integration. In Sulzbach 'it was perfectly possible to subscribe to an esoteric, animistic philosophy while adhering to a genuine scientific methodology involving a sceptical, empirical, and mathematical approach to scientific knowledge' (Coudert 2001: 29f.).

Christian Knorr von Rosenroth was a key figure at the court of Sulzbach. Besides his activities as chancellor, he found time to write several works, including a book on religious hymns, a commentary on the book of Revelation, a numismatic treatise, a book on 'German statecraft', an alchemical masque play and an interpretation of the comet of 1680. His various translations had a major influence. From Boethius' *Consolations of Philosophy* to three of the most important texts on natural magic—Gianbaptista della Porta's *Magia naturalis*, Thomas Browne's *Pseudodoxia epidemica* and Johannes Baptista van Helmont's *Ortus medicinae*—to his Latin translations of Hebrew kabbalistic works, Knorr von Rosenroth gave a crucial impetus to the esoteric discourse of his time.

However disparate these works may appear at first glance, they are closely linked from the perspective of seventeenth-century esoteric research. They all share the conception of a living nature containing a hidden knowledge accessible to man. The kabbalistic traditions supplied an historical and salvific model for the restoration of religious concord or even the culmination of world history, which possessed a particular attraction in the Christian context of that time. The notion of *Tiqqun*, with its central importance in the Lurianic Kabbalah, was interpreted as a restoration of the *prisca theologia* by Knorr von Rosenroth and his colleagues. Furthermore, inspired by the Jewish Kabbalah, which assumed the linguistic constitution of the cosmos, seventeenth-century researchers hit upon the idea of a 'primal language', identical with the language of God and nature (see Coudert [ed.] 1999).

Illustration 3. The symbolical engraving of the 'Unveiled Kabbalah' from Knorr von Rosenroth's *Kabbala denudata* (1677) represents the quest for perfect knowledge, linking the Jewish and Christian revelations while also transcending them. (Knorr von Rosenroth, *Kabbala denudata* [1677], frontispiece, BPH)

Christian August encouraged the settlement of Jews and Christians of various denominations within his principality. With the support of Jewish scholars, Knorr von Rosenroth prepared a partial Latin translation of key sources of the Jewish Kabbalah, which was printed under the title *Kabbala denudata* ('The Kabbalah Unveiled') at Sulzbach in 1677. This encyclopaedic work contained portions of the *Sefer ha-Zohar*, extracts from Gikatilla's work and the treatise *De anima* ('On the Soul') by Moses Cordovero. One can justifiably say that not until *Kabbala denudata* was published did Christian Europe gain access to the Jewish Kabbalah, if only in a selection indebted to the Christian interests of the age. Right up to the twentieth century, esotericists unversed in Hebrew would essentially draw their knowledge of Kabbalah from this work, for example Samuel Liddell MacGregor Mathers (see below, p. 119), who prepared an English translation of the work.

It is worth looking closely at the frontispiece of *Kabbala denudata* (Illustration 3). Here one sees a female figure, supposedly the 'unveiled Kabbalah' herself, advancing towards the shining rays of the Sun. She is ascending from the confusion and chaos of the contemporary world, symbolised by ships in rough seas, as the Sun drives away clouds following a storm. With one foot, she is already standing on firm soil. The promise of her security and knowledge are symbolised by a chest, on which stands the inscription *palatium arcanorum* ('palace of mysteries'). The key to the palace hangs from her wrist, while in her right hand she carries the torch of knowledge and 'enlightenment' to drive away darkness. In her left hand she holds a scroll: one end displays the first sentence of the Hebrew Bible, so often interpreted by kabbalists, while the other end shows the beginning of the Gospel of John: 'In the beginning was the word'. This is a clear reference to the meaning of language in the communication of esoteric knowledge, which is further emphasised by the word *explicat* ('explained') on the edge of the scroll.

The metaphor of light and darkness is an important element of esoteric discourses in the early modern period but also plays a major role in representations in the Enlightenment and the modern period (see Adler 1990). For Knorr von Rosenroth, the 'dawn' or 'morning-glow', as it is called in one of his best known poems, symbolised the commencing new age of unity and knowledge of the truth. Jacob Boehme characterised this with the Latin word *Aurora*, and the idea of a dawning new age has continued to fascinate esotericism up to the twentieth century—one needs only to recall the 'Hermetic Order of the Golden Dawn' or the metaphors of the New Age movement. However, there is still more to it, for the frontispiece can also be understood as the symbolisation of the wisdom of the *Zohar*, since *Zohar* means 'splendour', and also points to the superior quality of esoteric knowledge, which as 'absolute knowledge' far exceeds mere mundane knowledge.

Knorr von Rosenroth and his Sulzbach circle regarded Kabbalah, occult philosophy and the empirical investigation of nature as legitimate instruments for the realisation of a political, religious and scientific programme of progress towards the unity of religious truth and the absolute knowledge of history and creation. This he described in his poem *New Helicon*:

> Search for everything that has ever been taught/
> Whatever heathen/and Jewry promised/
> And what one hears among Christians/
> Consider diligently in all respects.
> Here nothing matters to the large crowds
> Who rush on their wild courses.

INFLUENCES UP TO THE NINETEENTH CENTURY

Kabbalistic ideas are a recurrent theme in European philosophy between the seventeenth and nineteenth centuries. Like Pico della Mirandola, Johannes Reuchlin and Christian Knorr von Rosenroth before them, Jacob Boehme, Franciscus Mercurius van Helmont, Paulus Ricius (d. 1541) and Gottfried Wilhelm Leibniz (1646–1716), with regard to the Luria critique of Henry More (1614–1687), would also assimilate the Kabbalah into their own theories (see Coudert 1999; Schmidt-Biggemann 1999; Coudert 1995).

In the eighteenth and nineteenth centuries Kabbalah had a notable influence on Christian philosophy and theology, while, as Gershom Scholem maintains, 'the world of Kabbalah [was] closed to the rationalism prevailing in the Judaism of the nineteenth century' (Scholem 1991 [1957]: 2). The esoteric and speculative aspect of Judaism was neglected by emancipated Jewish scholars. Here Kabbalah stood for heresy, for Sabbatianism, or for regression and the spiritual pre-modernity of the *stetl*.[17] The Christian Romantics saw things quite differently. Kabbalah constantly proved a useful tool for elaborating nature-philosophical, magical, mythological or pantheistic world-views, whether this was Schelling making the kabbalistic *tzim-tzum*, the 'contraction' of God into himself—the basis of his philosophy of a living God—or the 'immanent *En-Sôf*' entering the Spinozism of Jacobi, Herder and Schelling (see Goodman-Thau *et al.* 1994; Goodman-Thau 1999).

Even Georg Wilhelm Friedrich Hegel (1770–1831), whose work many besides himself regarded as the climax of Western philosophy, has been classified as a Hermetic-esoteric thinker in recent studies. Glenn Alexander Magee offers the following provocative argument:

> Hegel is not a philosopher. He is no lover or seeker of wisdom—he believes he has found it. […] By the end of the *Phenomenonology*, Hegel claims to have arrived at Absolute Knowledge, which he identifies with wisdom. Hegel's claim to have attained wisdom is completely contrary to the original Greek conception of philosophy as the love of wisdom, that is, the ongoing pursuit rather than the final possession of wisdom. His claim is, however, fully consistent with the ambitions of the Hermetic tradition. […] Hegel is a Hermetic thinker. (Magee 2001: 1; see also Desmond 2003)

Many a historian of philosophy will find such a portrait one-sided and simplistic, perhaps with justification. But doubtless Magee has hit the mark where philosophy produces esotericism: the claim to *absolute* knowledge, which is accessible to man from a transcendent source—in Hegel's case the Absolute. When Hegel equates absolute knowledge, namely his perfection of philosophy, with the 'self-consciousness of God' in man, and conceives of the essence of God as the 'thinking of thought', because God is 'mind', he has entered an esoteric field of discourse, with a clearly discernible prehistory in Europe.

But let us return to the sixteenth century.

COMPLEX IDENTITIES

JOHN DEE AND THE ANGELS

John Dee (1527–1608), variously described as a natural scientist, mathematician, magician, astrologer, kabbalist, philosopher and theologian, counts among the leading personalities of the sixteenth century. He went up to St John's College, Cambridge at the age of fifteen. After completing traditional studies in Aristotelian logic, natural philosophy, humanistic dialectics, Greek and mathematics, Dee

---

17. Examples are Moses Mendelssohn's *Jerusalem* (1783) and *Salomon Maimons Lebensgeschichte* (1792–93).

became increasingly interested in the 'occult' philosophy and tried to combine it with his mathematical and scientific inclinations. With his master's degree and a fellowship at Trinity College, he travelled frequently from 1548 onwards to Antwerp, Brussels, Paris and especially Louvain, where he refined his mathematical and astrological knowledge. He corresponded with scientists on the subject of navigation, in which he would soon make a great name for himself. From 1562 to 1564 Dee lived in the Netherlands, there publishing his work *Monas Hieroglyphica, mathematice, magice, cabbalistice et onagogice, explicata* (1564), which is dedicated to the interpretation of an alchemical symbol conceived by Dee (Illustration 4).

Illustration 4. John Dee conceived his 'hieroglyphic monad' as the focal point of all powers, elements and energies. (John Dee, *Monas Hieroglyphica* [1564], BPH/Photo: Wim Dingemans)

This 'hieroglyphic Monad' symbolised for Dee the unity of the created world and all knowledge, into which the knowing person can be initiated. The book may elude a definitive interpretation, but it certainly shows the strong influence of alchemical, magical and kabbalistic ideas that Dee had increasingly absorbed. His private library was one of the largest in Europe and contained practically everything that could be collected in its specialist fields. Its holdings of Hebrew literature exceeded that of the Universities of Oxford and Cambridge combined. However, as his interest in the Hebrew language was that of a kabbalist rather than a Hebraist, Dee himself never attained the linguistic facility of Reuchlin or Trithemius, whose works he greatly respected.

In 1570 Dee wrote his 'Mathematicall Praeface' to the English translation of Euclid's *Elements*, thereby confirming his reputation as a distinguished mathematician. Maybe this work also shows how Dee regarded mathematics as a connecting link between the divine and the created world, rather like the 'heavenly' world of Agrippa (see Clulee 1988). In 1583 Dee travelled to Prague, where Emperor Rudolf II was gathering a circle of renowned scholars immersed in Hermetic, magical, kabbalistic, and alchemical studies. Dee showed the emperor his 'magic mirror' and several alchemical experiments, an art in which he had gained experience. The 'magical mirror' served to make contact with the angels and ask them specific questions, which were translated by a medium. The *Libri mysteriorum* ('Books of the Mysteries'), which John Dee wrote on this theme between 1583 and 1589, were never intended for publication but laid the basis of his dubious reputation as a typical Renaissance *magus*. At the instigation of the papal nuncio, Dee was soon forced to leave the court of Rudolf II. He had once calculated the favourable date for the coronation of Queen Elizabeth I and in 1595 she appointed him warden of Manchester College, where he remained until her death in 1603. He found less favour with her successor King James I, and retired to his home at Mortlake, where he died at the age of 81.

What is the importance of these 'conversations with angels'? Do they prove that John Dee had somehow gone mad, or at least no longer rationally pursued his own scientific research? Or do they portray the 'true' Hermetic Dee, who intellectually anticipated the Rosicrucian manifestoes, as Frances A. Yates supposed? Neither. The angelic conversations are rather a 'pursuit of science by other means' and evidence of a personal and a socio-religious crisis, during which John Dee came to the conclusion that the end of the world was at hand.[18]

The angelic conversations that John Dee conducted between 1581 and 1586 and again in 1607 on questions of natural philosophy and apocalyptic prophecy, but also on personal matters, had a truly experimental character and were scrupulously recorded by Dee in the so-called 'angelic diaries' (see Illustration 5). The experiments required a special crystal, known as a *showstone*, as well as a medium or *scryer*, who translated the messages. This role was usually undertaken by a certain Edward Kelley. Dee sought the correct astrological dates for the experiments, but apart from prayers no kind of ritual activity or consecration was required, so it would be wrong to assume that these operations were founded on Hermeticism or natural magic. The angels even informed Dee that the 'art of the Egyptian magicians' was of no importance whatsoever (see Harkness 1999a: 122). One must instead con-

18.   This is the conclusion of the study by Harkness 1999a.

sider the holistic scientific interpretation of light rays and optical studies, in which
Dee was a proven expert. In his book *De radiis (stellarum)* ('The Rays of the Stars')
the medieval Muslim scholar al-Kindī had already applied the Stoical concept of
sympathy between material objects and explained that the rays of the planets and
all other things were connected with each other in mysterious ways (see Travaglia
1999). Medieval scientists like Roger Bacon had taken up such ideas, and John Dee
was experimenting further with them.

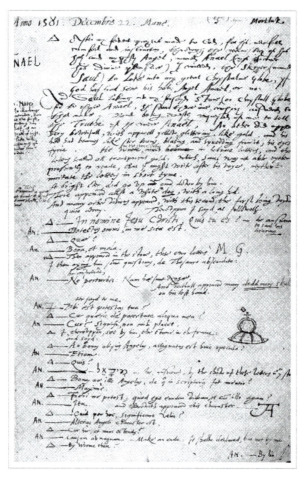

Illustration 5. The first page of John Dee's angelic diaries. Barnabas Saul acted as the scryer for this
angelic conversation on 22 December 1581. On the right side Dee drew his crystal supported by a stand.
The Greek delta symbol signifies Dee's questions, while the remarks of the angel, in this case Anael, is
indicated by 'An'. (The first page of John Dee's angelic diaries, from 22 December 1581. British Library,
Sloane MS 3188f 8r [from Harkness 1999, p. 18]) John Dee conceived his 'hieroglyphic monad' as the
focal point of all powers, elements and energies. (John Dee, *Monas Hieroglyphica* [1564], BPH/Photo:
Wim Dingemans)

Angels are not a simple species. In return for their promise to reveal absolute knowledge and information about the end of the world, the angels demanded complete obedience from the scryer and Dee. It appears to have been worthwhile for Dee, because he not only learnt about the mysteries of nature, inaccessible to him by normal means, and the details of the approaching apocalypse, but he also learned *Enochian*, the language of the angels, which has since entered the history of modern esotericism.[19] John Dee's quest for a universal language is an expression of contemporary kabbalistic ideas, that the cosmos can be comprehended linguistically. For this reason, the Enochian language was regarded as having an even higher degree of purity than Hebrew or Arabic.

GUILLAUME POSTEL, INHABITANT OF SEVERAL WORLDS

Guillaume Postel (1510–1581) is one of the most interesting and brilliant figures of the sixteenth century. His journeys throughout Europe and the Middle East, his extensive scientific and linguistic studies, and his highly opinionated publications earned him both admiration and contempt. His admirers included the Austrian humanist Johann von Widmanstadt, the famous Protestant scholar Joseph J. Scaliger and the French geographer André Thevet. However, some of his work displeased the ecclesiastical authorities, Calvinists rejected him, and his own Roman Catholic church imprisoned him for four years. Regarded as insane, Postel was banished to a monastery, where he spent the last eighteen years of his life. This fate only enhanced his prestigious mystique and many regarded him as a scholar, whose wisdom bordered on the miraculous.

Who was Guillaume Postel and what is his significance for the history of religion in the early modern period? Thanks to extensive research we are now in a position to separate truth from fiction in Postel's life, revealing the career of a scholar at home in various cultural and religious worlds. In the words of Homi Bhabha, one could say that Guillaume Postel was a self-conscious inhabitant of the 'third room'. This is well expressed in the Hebrew inscription of a copper engraving by Léonard Gaultier:

> A language in this head speaks to the Gentiles,
> This figure is a soul, which travels to all places,
> And the intellect of this man is marvellous in all studies,
> He loved and was beloved of all those, who recognised the *one* God. (Quoted in Bobzin 1995: 364)

Postel was born in 1510 in Normandy, where he soon had to fend for himself, as both his parents died of the plague when he was eight years old. Thanks to his enormous appetite for knowledge he was at the age of thirteen already a village schoolteacher at Sagy. After the failure of his first attempt to study in Paris, when a gang of robbers stole his savings and he was hospitalized for eighteen months, he

---

19. Aleister Crowley, who considered himself the reincarnation of Edward Kelley, produced tables for the translation of Enochian.

joined the Collège de Sainte Barbe, where he found an appointment with the
Spanish Aristotelian Juan de Gelida (Johannes Gelidius). Soon he was so proficient
in Greek that he could translate Aristotle for Juan de Gelida. Within several months
he could also speak Spanish and Portuguese. Equipped with a Hebrew alphabet, a
Hebrew–Latin psalter and a grammar from a neighbouring Jew, Postel learned
Hebrew and was soon able to give instruction in this language. He was renowned
for more than just his talent in languages, and his expertise in mathematics and
philosophy led his fellow students to regard him as a second Pico della Mirandola.
Although he worked for a living alongside his studies, Postel had already achieved
his Master of Arts degree at the age of twenty in 1530, and shortly afterwards
graduated as a Bachelor of medicine.

In 1529 Ignatius of Loyola arrived at the Collège de Sainte Barbe and gathered a
nucleus of followers—including Postel—which would become his Society of
Jesus. This encounter certainly reinforced Postel's own tendency to mystical and
ascetic piety and his advocacy of church reform. The missionary idea was also an
important stimulus for Postel to learn Arabic, beginning in 1531 at the latest. His
further progress in this respect was greatly helped by his journey with the embassy
of Jean de la Forêt to Istanbul, during which he became acquainted with the
Muslim societies in Tunis, Istanbul, Syria and Egypt. According to Postel, it was
not easy to find a good Arabic teacher in Istanbul. The Turk whom he finally
found to teach him later turned out to be a Christian. However, he made good
progress in learning Arabic, and also learned Turkish. It was in Istanbul that a
Jewish doctor pressed a book into his hands bearing the title *Cabala*. Postel's great
interest in Jewish mysticism must date at least from this time.

During his stay in Istanbul Postel stocked up with Arabic literature, both on
behalf of the French king's library and for his own collection. On his return
journey to Paris (1537) he met the printer Daniel Bomberg at Venice, who had
already published a series of important works of Jewish literature. He soon became
close friends with Bomberg, who encouraged him to work on linguistic publications and an Arabic grammar, which were soon published. In 1538 Postel was
appointed by King Francis I as *mathematium et linguarum peregrinarum professor regius*
at the Collège de France. However, owing to hostile political circumstances, Postel
soon fell into disfavour, gave up his professorial chair and concentrated wholly on
writing his 'universal missionary handbook' in the winter of 1542–43. Rejected by
the Sorbonne, the work was published in Basle under the title *De orbis terrae concordia libri quatuor* ('Four Books on the Harmony of the Terrestrial Globe') and contains translations of important sections of the Qur'an (see Bobzin 1995: 461-97).

As the situation in Paris was deteriorating, Postel went to Rome and joined the
Jesuits, whom he already knew from his student years. However, there were soon
differences with the order, since Postel doubted the authority of the pope and
regarded the French king as an instrument of God in the realisation of world
harmony (*concordia mundi*). At the end of 1545 Postel broke with the Jesuit order.
For ten years he wandered through Europe, while further deepening his knowledge of Islam and Judaism. From an Ethiopian priest he received an Ethiopian

version of the *Book of Enoch*, a work of fundamental importance for Jewish and Muslim mysticism. An even more important station on his life's path was his meeting with 'Mother Johanna' (Madre Zuana), who had founded a small hospital in Venice where Postel worked as a priest (see Kuntz 1981: 72-93). Postel was fascinated by the piety, charitableness, asceticism and mystical talent of this woman, then about fifty years old. Mother Johanna could for example explain to him difficult passages from the *Sefer ha-Zohar*, which he was studying intensively at this time. On account of her mysterious abilities, Postel regarded Johanna as the 'world mother' (*mater mundi*) and 'new Eve', even as the Shekhinah of kabbalistic speculation. In the following years Postel promoted the idea of the rebirth of the Shekhinah, which he took from the *Bahîr* and *Zohar*, in several publications in Basle and Venice, including a Hebrew leaflet entitled 'The Candlelight of the Menorah', translated by Konrad Pellikan into Latin. Pellikan later played a major part in Postel's translation of the *Zohar*.

In the summer of 1549 Postel departed on a second journey to the East, which was financed by his friend Daniel Bomberg, for whom he collected Arabic literature. In Jerusalem he immersed himself in the history and sources of the Samaritans, Maronites and Druzes, to whose secret teachings his own writings may have been indebted (according to Bouwsma 1957: 143f.). After an extended stay in Anatolia and Istanbul, w here he was researching for his book *De la République de Turcs* (1560), Postel returned around 1551 to Venice. As Mother Johanna had died in the meantime, Postel tried again to establish himself in France and was initially successful thanks to changed political circumstances. However, instead of politics a profound mystical experience around the turn of the year 1551–52 now interrupted his career. According to his own account, the 'spiritual body' of Johanna had taken up its abode in him and henceforth Postel felt he was called to be the prophet of the approaching new age of restoration (*restitutio*), as well as its firstborn (*primogenitus*), and even a second Messiah. Once again one sees how the kabbalistic concept of the restoration of the original cosmic order (Luria's *Tiqqun*) was linked with apocalyptic ideas then current in contemporary Christian discourse.

Postel now broadcast the 'hermeneutics of the world's end' in an extended series of sermons and publications, with some 29 works appearing between 1551 and 1553. His books and lectures were extremely successful, but in 1553 his licence to teach was withdrawn, chiefly because one of his books, *Les très merveilleuses victoires des femmes du nouveau monde* ('The Most Wonderful Victories of the Women of the New World'), celebrated the ascendancy of women and was considered scandalous. Postel left Paris and in 1553 went again to Basle, where many religious dissidents found refuge at that time. Here he made contact with moderate Protestants, but soon he travelled on to Venice, in order to realise his plan of editing a Syriac edition of the New Testament on the basis of his collected manuscripts. He then completed this project in Vienna, where he enjoyed a high reputation and was offered a professorship. However, he fled from Vienna a year later—whether due to hostilities or because his books were placed on the index by the Inquisition is unknown. He travelled to Venice, where he again publicly promoted his ideas concerning the Venetian virgin and the dawning age of *restitutio*. At his own request Postel defended his ideas before the Inquisition in Venice, but he was ready to recant some of his teachings, so that he was finally declared 'confused'.

Almost devoid of means, Postel decided to sell fifteen valuable manuscripts to the Count Palatine Ottheinrich who resided at Neuburg on the Danube and had a great interest in oriental books. Shortly afterwards he met a swordsmith in the Hebrew printing works of Cornelius Adelkind in Sabionetta, who was able to cut Arabic fonts for him. He was finally in a position to publish an Arabic–Latin lexicon, edit the writings of Johannes Damascenus and print the Gospels in Arabic, and so fulfil a dream of many years. However, this was not to be, because the Inquisition began to harass him anew. This time he was imprisoned and only just escaped with his life. He was not released until 1559. The year 1556, which he had prognosticated as a year of destiny, remained uneventful, but Postel clung to his vision of an imminent renewal of the world order. After various wanderings through Europe he was brought by the king's command to the Abbey of Saint Martin des Champs, where he was able to work on several scholarly projects until his death in 1581.

The life of Guillaume Postel is interesting on two counts. First, on account of the major influence of his writings, and second, because his career exemplifies the process of exchange between the religions in the age of denominational conflict. Postel, Pico della Mirandola and Knorr von Rosenroth are the most important mediators of Jewish mysticism into Christianity. His translation of the *Zohar* and his own kabbalistic writings show that typically Jewish speculations about history were hungrily consumed under a Christian label specifically charged with apocalyptic expectation. It is also noteworthy that Postel placed the study of Arabic sources in the centre of his attempt to restore the unity of the Christian world and to motivate Jews and Muslims (whom he described as *semichristiani*) to Christian conversion on grounds of reason. Postel is thereby one of the most important precursors of Islamic scholarship, and his translation of the Qur'an is a crucial contribution to inter-faith dialogue.

Guillaume Postel is exemplary, because he shows the ways and means through which dialogue between the three scriptural religions proceeded in the early modern period. Naturally the study of another religious tradition was interest-led, but nevertheless religious interpretations passed to and fro between the scriptural religions, because Muslims, Jews and Christians had a *common* interest in certain questions. This included, for example, the question of interpreting the signs of the times, as to whether a new age was imminent, in what manner the deity would reveal himself to the world, what status the revelatory texts possess and much else. The answers were naturally diverse, but the methods with which they could be found could be exchanged. With regard to the signs of the times it was astrology in general, and the doctrine of Great Conjunctions and cycles in particular, which were regarded as compelling by Europeans of all religions. With regard to questions of divine revelation, the Jewish Kabbalah provided a highly developed model of explanation of inestimable value, for Christians and for Muslims.

COPERNICUS, KEPLER, GALILEO AND NEWTON: SCIENTIFIC REVOLUTION?

The connections between esotericism, religion and science can only be understood in the context of the so-called scientific revolutions of the late sixteenth and early seventeenth centuries. Twentieth-century historians characterise as a 'revolution' that radical and complete restructuring of the knowledge of nature, which superseded the medieval and Renaissance models of the cosmos, making 'objective science' possible for the first time, and thereby opening the way to modernity and our own times. However, historiography today is no longer so sure about the unique status of this supposed revolution. From the perspective of cultural and social history, talk about the revolutionary breakthrough to modernity is a mythologization of one's own origins, which ignores the complexity and contradictions of the process as well as the continuities and precursors in medieval and early modern science.[20]

As almost all the scientific innovations attributed to the seventeenth-century 'revolution' had been anticipated by Muslim researchers in the Middle Ages—for example their advanced study of optics—the innovation is not a matter of facts, but rather the question of how it could be reconciled with a dominant Christian cosmology and whether scientists rather than theologians would be granted authority to proclaim the facts. The Copernican Revolution was first and foremost a metaphysical transformation. This relativisation does not deny that decisive changes occurred in science and philosophy in seventeenth-century Europe. To be sure, these changes primarily concerned what was henceforth regarded as objective and scientifically tenable by a majority and also the procedure used to gain scientific knowledge. In this regard, the stimuli that had already been formulated in the Middle Ages, Renaissance and Reformation were now completed with pioneering observations in the realm of physics. This was not so much a revolution, but rather the establishment of method as a dominant culture.

Nicolas Copernicus (1473–1543) was one of the most important pioneers of the new thinking. His discovery of the Earth's movement around the Sun was considered an epochal transformation by his successors. In 1832 Goethe described this emotionally to Chancellor von Müller, as 'the greatest, most sublime and momentous discovery which man has ever made, more important than the whole Bible.' But in any case Copernicus could refer back to models of calculation that had been

20.   Instead of perpetuating the myth of the Scientific Revolution, one is now inclined to analyse the *cultural negotiation of collectively shared opinions* regarding reality, truth, man and nature. Such analysis should have regard for the social contexts that favour the dominance of a scientific or philosophical model.

developed before him, and especially to Ptolemy, just as the notion of the Earth as a globe had had its supporters since ancient times. Copernicus had first studied at Cracow with the famous astronomers and astrologers Johann von Glogau and Albert Brudzewo, and then in Italy, where he graduated as a doctor of canon law at the University of Ferrara. However, his chief interest was still astronomy, which he combined with his Platonised Christian world-view, by assuming that God must have created a simple and elegant cosmological system and not the complicated model required to calculate the movement of the planets from a geocentric perspective. Like many scholars before him Copernicus found that the remarkable disappearances and reappearances of Venus and Mercury could be explained much more easily if they orbited around the Sun and not around the Earth. Once he had been appointed chancellor of the cathedral chapter at Frauenberg in 1510, he entirely devoted himself to work on his heliocentric model. The fruit of his labour was the work *De revolutionibus orbium coelestium* ('On the Revolutions of the Heavenly Bodies'), whose first printed edition was handed to the author on 25 May 1543, the day of his death. Between 1510 and 1514 Copernicus had already sent a first draft of his theory to renowned mathematicians and astronomers, but the contemptuous reaction of the scholars was so crushing that he bitterly withdrew and was only finally convinced by the advice of friends to publish the work. Interestingly it was primarily astrologers who urged the master towards publication, among them Georg Joachim Rheticus (1514–1574), who had published a preliminary report on Copernicus' theory at Danzig in 1539 and now obtained the royal permission of the King of Poland and Saxony for Copernicus' extensive manuscript and helped finance its printing. The new theory, which gained force only slowly due to ecclesiastical opposition, essentially stated that the Earth performed three movements: one about its own axis, one around the Sun, and a rocking movement of the Earth's axis around the ecliptic pole, which produced the precession of the equinoxes. This model was an affront to the Christian church, both Catholic and Protestant. The unique position of the Earth and man as the focal point and final goal of divine creation was usurped by this model. Although the conflict of the Bible and science was not as great for Copernicus and his followers as is often supposed (see Howell 2002), the real revolution lay in the altered position of mankind, which would not meet its equal until the nineteenth century when Charles Darwin dethroned man once again by asserting their descent from the apes. However, the challenge was far less for esoteric views, especially astrology, and this was understood by Copernicus as well as by his colleagues Galileo and Kepler. All three held fast to the legitimacy of astrology. Galileo and Kepler were also practising astrologers, and in the tenth chapter of *De revolutionibus* Copernicus expressed himself in an astrological manner by making reference to Hermes Trismegistus.

Copernicus may well have had the same views as Johannes Kepler (1571–1630). As a mathematician and astronomer Kepler elaborated Copernicus' ideas underpinning them with a coherent geometric explanation. In this endeavour he profited significantly from the notes that the great astronomer Tycho Brahe had bequeathed to him. With his discovery of the three planetary laws, Kepler succeeded in sub-stantiating the plausibility of the Copernican model. He proved that the planetary orbits around the Sun are not circular but elliptical in form. His further fascinating discovery was that the distances of the five planets from the Sun correspond to the five Platonic solids, namely the cube, tetrahedron, dodecahedron, icosahedron and octahedron. This led him to conclude that exactly five planets must exist, because the Creator God had conceived a mathematically perfect cosmos.

Kepler wanted to reconcile the Neo-Platonic view of universal world harmony with the laws of geometry and thus describe the rational structure of the God-ordained cosmos in all its simple beauty. He presented his findings in his two major works *Astronomia nova* ('A New Astronomy', 1619) and *Harmonices mundi* ('The Harmonies of the World', 1619). The speculations of natural philosophers since Pythagoras were now a scientifically established certainty: God was a mathe-matician and the logical application of mathematical principles would lead to the definitive knowledge of the divine order of creation. This rational model of the cosmos was later consolidated by Newton, Leibniz and others, who envisaged nature as a machine functioning according to mathematical laws.

Kepler did not regard his new astronomical models as a problem for astrology. It was obvious to him as for most of his contemporaries that heavenly signs indicated and foretold terrestrial events. The observation of a supernova (the 'birth' of a star) on 10 October 1604 led him to write about the messianic star. In two works, *De Stella Nova in pede Serpentarii* ('The New Star in the Constellation of Serpentarius ', 1606) and *De anno natali Christi* ('The Year of the Nativity', 1614), he developed his theory that, because the supernova of 1604 was preceded by a Jupiter–Saturn conjunction, the same event in ancient times had been a cosmic signal for the advent of the Messiah. Kepler described the Star of Bethlehem as a supernova in the year 5 BCE. In this respect the astronomers of the early seven-teenth century were active participants in a discourse involving the interpretation of time, Christian salvation and new scientific models and methods. Naturally they had differing points of view but there was sufficient congruity in their outlook to invalidate any talk of a simple conflict between the 'new science' and 'Christian opponents'.

This is also true of Kepler's friend Galileo Galilei (1564–1642). Unlike Tycho Brahe, he agreed with Kepler that the Copernican system was the only correct one, but, as he wrote to Kepler on 5 August 1597, he had until now refrained from making his views public. However, ever more observations gave unanimous sup-port to the Copernican model: the supernova of 1604, the discovery of terrestrial magnetism by Gilbert in 1600 and above all his own discoveries with the aid of the newly invented telescope. These included the existence of Jupiter's four moons, which orbited around their planet just as the planets did around the Sun, the phases of Venus corresponding to the course of the Moon, the 'threefold' form of Saturn (later identified as its rings) and finally the discovery of sunspots unequivo-cally proving the rotation of the Sun. Faced with this mounting evidence, Galileo had to make a public stand for the Copernican doctrine in his *Nuncius sidereus* ('The Message from the Stars', 1610).

Even Galileo saw no conflict with the Catholic faith in these discoveries. But Popes Paul V and Urban VIII, with whom he discussed the matter, were of quite a different opinion. In 1616 Galileo received from Cardinal Bellarmin the instruction that 'the doctrine attributed to Copernicus is contrary to Holy Scripture and may therefore be neither defended nor held to be truthful'. To begin with, Galileo would not change his mind and in a hypothetical discussion of 1629 he declared the Copernican system to be superior. This led to his summons before the Inquisition in 1632 when he solemnly consented to abjure the heliocentric world-view. Unlike Giordano Bruno, who was burnt at the stake for his firm stance, Galileo decided on a compromise that saved his life, but at the price of being able to publish freely, as he was subject to the oversight of the Inquisition for the rest of his life.

Through his observations, especially his experiments with falling objects, the analysis of projectile paths, and hydrostatic scales, Galileo made a major contribution to planetary mechanics and the development of new methods of investigation in physics that no longer required occult forces but only the visible and quantifiable as a means of explanation. Like Kepler, Galileo saw no conflict with astrology, which he continued to practice and investigate. His diaries and letters contain a series of horoscopes and astrological calculations. When his pupil P. Dini was concerned that the new world-view threw doubt on the foundations of astrology, Galileo responded in a letter that his fears were quite groundless.

Although there was considerable resistance to physical and astronomical observations and their consequences, no critical contemporary could ignore the validity of the heliocentric world-view by the middle of the seventeenth century. However, yet another generation would have to pass before the new paradigm won the upper hand. As is well known, this was largely due to Isaac Newton (1643–1727), whose complex work appeared to his successors as supremely representative of the mechanistic world-view and was henceforth known as 'classical physics'. In 1666, his so-called *annus mirabilis*, Newton developed the foundations of the theories that would make him famous. First, infinitesimal calculus, whose discovery was claimed by Leibniz in 1690, because Newton's theorem was published subsequently. Second, his theory of 'universal gravitation', which proposed a single law governing events in the universe, and thereby served to explain the stability of the solar system, and the description of regular movements such as falling objects and the pendulum. Third, the discovery of the coloured nature of light, which Newton was able to prove by the spectrum produced through a prism.

He published these discoveries in his major work *Philosophiae naturalis principia mathematica* ('Mathematical Principles of Natural Philosophy', 1687),[21] which ensured his fame far beyond England's shores. An important factor in the success

---

21.   One should note that Newton speaks of 'natural philosophy' and not 'physics'.

of his ideas, which clearly competed with the natural philosophy of René Descartes (1596–1650), was the enormous political influence he wielded and continually increased. In 1669 he was appointed Professor of Mathematics at Cambridge; in 1672 he became a member of the Royal Society of London for the Improvement of Natural Knowledge; in 1696 he gained his first political office; in 1701 he became a Member of Parliament; in 1703 he was elected president of the Royal Society (an office he held until his death), and in 1705 he was knighted.

Newton's very personification of the 'new science' has led to much of his work lying outside the narrow limits of mathematics being forgotten. This impression is slowly beginning to be modified by the attention now focused on his contributions to Hermetism, alchemy and astrology (see Curry 1987; Dobbs 1991; Fauvel 1993). Towards the end of the seventeenth century he wrote a commentary on the Hermetic *Tabula Smaragdina*. In his theological writings Newton also combined his scientific views with an interpretation of religious history and of God's role in the universe. For example, between 1681 and 1705 he developed new cometary theories in collaboration with Edmond Halley, which for the first time predicted the movement of comets, and thereby contradicted the traditional astrological view that comets were unforeseeable omens. He took this opportunity to express his abhorrence at the power of the clergy. In his work *Theologiae gentilis origines philosophicae* ('The Philosophical Origins of Pagan Theology'), on which he began to work in 1683, he disclosed that an authentic natural philosophical religion had once existed, which recognised the true structure of the cosmos. He thought this had been formulated in a symbolical form in Pythagoreanism. Later this perfect knowledge had been corrupted by the idolatry of stars and the investment of the cosmos with souls. In Chapter 11 he went so far as to assert that the Christian religion was no less corrupt than its Oriental and Jewish precursors. In this respect he was in agreement with Thomas Hobbes. According to Newton, the cult of the stars was only the obverse side of the false cometary theory—just as the attribution of souls to stars and the worship of idols, saints and subordinate entities of Christianity had led away from the true philosophy of nature. Newton was convinced that the latter had recognised God as the single, absolute and legislating authority. Once again one glimpses how closely linked astronomy was with other cultural concerns, such as morality, theology and politics.

One result of the scientific changes was the universalisation of natural laws and the attempt to represent them in the form of mathematical calculation. As we have already seen, this was intimately linked to the esoteric quest for a primal language. Another result was the dispensability of theories involving the occult properties of objects. This excluded both the Aristotelian separation of matter and form as well as the view that there were hidden connections based, for example, on the attraction ('sympathy') between planets or on an inherent 'energy' in things. According to the now prevailing mechanical world-view, only physical explanations such as the gravity of particles were admissible. This threatened to disqualify the esoteric element in natural scientific discourses. Nevertheless, it had to be accepted that the mathematisation of natural laws could never be wholly complete. Moreover, the mechanistic and materialistic models of explanation also rested partly on *a priori* assumptions incapable of empirical verification. How, for example, can one show that the sensation of pleasant or unpleasant smells or tastes are caused by the coarse or smooth surface of the particles forming those 'bodies'? How can one explain magnetism, which is clearly an 'occult', hidden property but causes material effects? The latter would achieve renewed importance in the later debate about Mesmerism. Critical historians today suggest that this was more a matter of a gentlemen's agreement of what was acceptable as an explanation, rather than the rational proof of the facts.

Even the most radical advocates of the 'new thinking' could not make a strict distinction between scientific and Christian views nor between mathematically exact and esoteric–Hermetic approaches. The participants in this debate succeeded in combining both intellectual viewpoints in an amazingly casual fashion.

APOCALYPTICISM, ALCHEMY AND NATURAL SCIENCE IN PROTESTANTISM

ALCHEMISTS AND THEOLOGIANS

Religion and science continually interacted with one another. The scientific reflection of religious convictions and the religious cast of scientific interests are a basic characteristic of the European history of religion, especially prominent in the seventeenth century. It would be quite misleading to restrict science to the mathematical and empirical interests of that period, for much research focused on alchemy's quest for the 'basis of life' and the processes of formation inherent in history and nature. 'Creation *in vitro*' was a field of research that fascinated alchemists, particularly in the Protestant camp. I have already referred above (p. 7) to Pastor Johann Rist (1606–1667), who set up an alchemical laboratory in his vicarage at Wedel and had no problem with the idea that his experiments put man on a par with God. Rist was not alone in this. Even the polymath G.W. Leibniz, also an alchemist and a member of the alchemical society founded by the priest Daniel Wülfing at Nuremberg, wrote fifty years later in his *Essay on Theodicy*, 'Man is thus akin to a small god' (§147).

Neither Rist, nor Leibniz, nor Newton regarded such views, which actually deviated from Christian orthodoxy, as a reason to question their own Christianity. For them, alchemy was rather a tool to discover what God intended with the world and how his plan was working. The debates of the Reformation and the devastating experience of the Thirty Years War led to an apocalyptic climax that influenced all esoteric discourse and with it natural science.[22] This apocalyptic mood was so

22.   On the relationship between John Dee and Isaac Newton see Harkness 1999b. Anne-Charlott Trepp has suggested that one should not overlook the importance of lay-scientists like Johann Rist, who popularised contemporary knowledge, alongside the familiar 'giants' of research. 'In early modern Germany, and not only there, the religious interpretation of nature was not only inseparable from its investigation but its very substance' (Trepp 2001: 108). See also Barnes 1988.

widespread in the Protestant milieu, that many turned to the 'Book of Nature' in order to discover the 'last things' (*eschaton*).

Following the Reformation many feared that Lutheranism itself would become a rigid orthodoxy, which led to a renewed quest for the 'true Christianity' that could offer a way out of the catastrophes of the present. Hermeticism, alchemy and *prisca theologia* were important elements in this discourse, of which there are abundant examples, including the Paracelsian movement and the Rosicrucians (described in more detail in Chapter 7). The *Vier Bücher vom Wahren Christentum* ('Four Books on True Christianity', 1606) by Johann Arndt (1555–1622) offered a synthesis of esoteric–hermetic traditions with a Protestant view, which would have a lasting influence on pietistic and spiritualistic circles long after the seventeenth century.[23] Alchemists like Johann Rist turned to the study of nature to find 'proofs' of the Christian gospel when their faith was confronted with an existential challenge. In 1668 he wrote:

> It proves an excellent entertainment, when one resurrects all kinds of herbs and flowers from their own ashes so that they regain their former bloom and growth. This clearly represents and proves to us the resurrection of the dead, and one must be a stone and a clod to still doubt this most consoling article of faith in the face of such an excellent natural miracle.[24]

In this fashion Rist subjected traditional statements of faith to an empirical test.

The Protestant milieu had a great affinity for the esoteric habit of thinking in analogies between natural processes occurring in a test tube on the one hand and salvific processes on the other (see Schütt 2000: 429-37). The *prima materia*, the original matter which becomes the *ultima materia* and animates the 'Philosophers' Stone' was equated with Christ as the archetype of a 'purified' life principle being resurrected from death. This connection is graphically portrayed in the magnificently illustrated work *Atalanta fugiens* ('Fleeing Atalanta', 1618) of Michael Maier (c. 1569–1622). The stone is the *One* that connects everything and its preparation will coincide with the end of time and the Second Coming of Christ. The *opus magnum* ('Great Work') of alchemy is simultaneously the *restitutio* of the chaotic world. Heinrich Khunrath (1560–1605), an alchemist influenced by Paracelsus, expresses the same idea (see Illustration 6 [next page]). It is no surprise that alchemical books were in great demand in this time of crisis. After 1580 their production increased sharply, reaching its first peak after 1610 with some 130 new titles and 40 new editions, dipping because of the wars, and then rising again after 1660. The wave did not ebb until the eighteenth century, although in 1800 there was still an annual production of 30 new titles and a dozen reprints.

23.   For a full account see Geyer 2001.

24.   Quoted in Trepp 2001: 138. She states: 'Here he had clearly overstepped the critical boundary from the deduction of religious ideas from nature to the offering of experimental and inductive proof' (p. 140).

Illustration 6. Michael Maier's *Atalanta fugiens* and Heinrich Khunrath's *Amphitheatrum* are among the most richly illustrated alchemical texts of the early modern period. This plate from Khunrath's work shows how precisely the individual elements of alchemical practice must correspond with each other in order to perfect the 'Great Work'. Everything must relate to everything else in order to understand the significance of the 'Book of Nature'. (Heinrich Khunrath, *Amphitheatrum sapientae aeterna* [1608], BPH/Photo: Wim Dingemans)

CHRISTIAN THEOSOPHY: JACOB BOEHME

The confessional debates of the sixteenth century also greatly expanded another branch of esoteric discourse, namely Christian theosophy. This tradition is an elaboration of Jewish, Muslim and Christian mysticism, prevalent in various ways since late antiquity, and should not be confused with Madame Blavatsky's theosophy and the Theosophical Society (est. 1875). Kabbalah is a matter of the 'wisdom of God', and as this is the literal meaning of 'theosophy', both have much in common. The Protestant demand for sole reliance on the Bible and individual access to the divine led to the new elaboration of theosophical doctrines as an alternative to dry theology. Four phases of Protestant theosophy may be distinguished (according to Faivre 1999): (1) 'Classical' theosophy developed in the sixteenth and seventeenth century under the influence of Luther's theology. Alongside its most important figure Jacob Boehme, this movement also included Valentin Weigel, Heinrich Khunrath, Johann Arndt, Aegidius Gutmann, Caspar von Schwenckfeld,

Gerhard Dorn, Johann Georg Gichtel, Gottfried Arnold, John Pordage, Jane Leade, Pierre Poiret and Antoinette Bourignon. (2) In the first half of the eighteenth century there developed a theosophy which was more intellectual and less visionary in orientation. Its most important representative was Friedrich Christoph Oetinger, but William Law, Dionysius Andreas Freher, Douzetemps, Saint-Georges de Marsais, Georg von Welling, Sincerus Renatus and Hermann Fictuld also belonged to this current. (3) In the period of Pre-Romanticism and Romanticism Louis-Claude de Saint-Martin and Franz von Baader espoused a strongly speculative and less prophetic form of theosophy; in this regard one should also mention Martinez de Pasqually, Dutoit-Membrini, Karl von Eckartshausen, Heinrich Jung-Stilling, Novalis, Gotthilf Heinrich von Schubert, Carl Gustav Carus and, as a special case, Emanuel Swedenborg. (4) Theosophers of the nineteenth and twentieth centuries include Vladimir Soloviev, Sergei Bulgakov, Nicolas Berdyaev, Rudolf Steiner, Leopold Ziegler and Valentin Tomberg.

This form of esoteric thinking is well illustrated by the most influential Christian theosopher, namely Jacob Boehme (1575–1624). Boehme was born in Alt-Seidenberg near Görlitz and learnt the trade of a cobbler. At the age of twenty-five, after a profound crisis, he had a mystical vision, in which he looked into the heart of things (*Zentralschau*) and saw 'God's light'. In Chapter 19 of *Morgenröthe im Aufgang* ('Day-Spring, or Morning Rednesse in the Rising of the Sun', also known as *Aurora*, 1612), Boehme called this experience a 'triumphing in the spirit', which he could not express. 'Neither can it be compared to anything, but to that wherein the life is generated in the midst of death, and it is like the resurrection from the dead'. The manuscript of *Aurora* was circulated without the knowledge of its author and came into the hands of Gregor Richter, the chief pastor of Görlitz, who accused Boehme of heresy. He was briefly imprisoned, his writings were confiscated, and he was forbidden to publish any further works. Not until 1618, at the beginning of the Thirty Years War, did he yield to the encouragement of friends to start writing again and in 1619 he published *Die Beschreibung der drei Prinzipien göttlichen Wesens* ('Concerning the Three Principles of Divine Essence'). While Boehme worked as a travelling dealer, he composed several works, including a response to his critics, and *Theosophische Sendbriefe* ('Theosophic Epistles'), which were eagerly read by his growing number of followers. After *Der Weg zu Christo* ('The Way to Christ') and several shorter works had appeared in 1624, Gregor Richter again began to harass Boehme, but Richter died during the campaign. Even on his own deathbed Boehme was subject to cross-examination before he received final communion, and Richter's successor refused to hold a funeral service for the 'heretic'.

Boehme's doctrine was mostly written in a mystical, obscure and visionary language, and moreover in German, earning him the title of *philosophus teutonicus*. However, despite his highly personal style, the influence of the German mystical tradition (Meister Eckhart, Johannes Tauler) and the Paracelsian alchemical movement is clearly evident. Given his historical circumstances, it is not surprising that Boehme began with the problem of evil and sought to explain the nature of 'God's anger'. In his view, divine anger is not revenge for human excesses, but a fundamental attribute of the creation, or even prior to Creation. God is born out of this primary reality, which Boehme calls the *Ungrund*. The (re)birth of God must be accomplished in man, and this 'second birth' is the salvation of man.

The birth of God occurs in an alchemical process of seven stages, not so much an evolution—an 'unfolding' as Hegel influenced by Boehme understood it—but 'before time' comparable to the emanation of God in the *Sefirot*. The first principle of God in anger is followed by his second principle, which Boehme identified with love and the Son of God. A third principle is then important for salvation. Our material world came into being through the fall of Lucifer and must be restored to its original state of harmony. The 'reborn God' of the second principle can only be recognised by reborn human beings. For this to occur, man in the third principle must struggle with God like Jacob in the Hebrew Bible. Through a divine act of mercy, man will be redeemed from this struggle and granted absolute knowledge.

The Lutheran retreat from institutionalised theology is carried further in the work of Jacob Boehme. The 'letter' of the Bible should be awakened to life through personal experience, in order that God's work may be fulfilled in man. This summons to an inner vision and a strong bias towards the individual experience of truth fell on fertile soil among pietistic and spiritualistic Protestant circles. It therefore came about that the theosophical movement also flourished in the American colonies, where its doctrines mingled with an ascetic form of Protestantism. As a potent influence on the American history of religion, it can be regarded as a precursor of the New Age movement (see Hanegraaff 1996: 403-10; Fuller 2001; Versluis 1999).

6

ESOTERICISM, ENLIGHTENMENT AND SCIENCE

Far from being mutually exclusive, esotericism and science have many points of contact. The esoteric element surfaces in scientific discourse whenever scientists are not content with simply understanding the processes of nature but strive for an *absolute knowledge*, whenever they ask, as in Goethe's *Faust*, 'what holds the world ultimately together'. Such absolute claims to knowledge have an altogether different validity from the mechanical and empirical procedures of science as defined today. In this chapter I shall introduce scientists who valued empirical studies, but directed them towards a metaphysical goal, where knowledge was legitimated by reference to the revelatory tradition of *prisca theologia* or *prisca sapientia* ('original wisdom'). Alternatively, one could say that a scientific element consists in the recognition of empirical methods in esoteric discourse. Many of the previously discussed figures combined both empiricism and esotericism. There is plenty of evidence for esoteric ideas, often used polemically, even in the so-called Enlightenment which spread through Europe in the second half of the eighteenth century, leading to major revolutions and the foundation of modern nation states.

The background of this religious development is better understood in the context of the confessional debates of the early eighteenth century. In 1700 Gottfried Arnold (1666–1714) published his work *Unparteyische Kirchen- und Ketzer-Historien vom Anfang des Neuen Testaments bis auf das Jahr Christi 1688* ('Impartial History of Churches and Heretics from the New Testament until AD 1688'), marking an important turning-point in the history of religion and its writing. As an evangelical Protestant who soon joined the pietist movement, Arnold made a determined counterstatement to Martin Luther by referring to the Hermetic tradition, which he chiefly identified with Paracelsus. By separating theology and historiography, he presented an account of the numerous alternative Christian currents arising in the early modern period. Arnold notably rehabilitated the 'Gnosis' as a quest for 'original religiosity' in an age that usually equated this term with heresy. Arnold defined Gnosis in three respects, namely: '1) That one recognises things; 2) that one achieves what one knows; 3) and one describes what in truth is hidden in a divine way'. The gnostic quest for higher theosophical knowledge is thus

> A real perfection of the human being…through the knowledge of divine things, both
> in words as in deeds and in one's whole life, as they speak of these things. And thus
> the Christians have also called themselves *Gnosticos*, especially those who have consid-
> ered divine things in a contemplative life.[1]

This positive evaluation marked a temporary truce in the long-standing, bitter
dispute between Paracelsians, Behmenists and Rosicrucians on the one side, and
representatives of the Catholic and Lutheran camps on the other.[2]

The place of esotericism in public discourse also changed as the old social order
of the estates dissolved and institutions were criticised. As the social system altered,
so new bearers of esoteric tradition arose who were motivated by an individual
search for meaning. These people ultimately influenced the literature, art and
philosophy of the nineteenth century.

THE BATTLE FOR THE SPIRITUAL WORLD

Holistic or monistic concepts of the cosmos are basic assumptions of esoteric
thought. The existence of an invisible 'other' world alongside the visible material
world was claimed again and again in the European history of religion, and became
the basis of literary, philosophical and religious enquiry. Besides esoteric interpretations there also existed a genre of 'The other world' (*L'autre monde*), a significant
factor in art and literature from the Middle Ages until modernity. The esoteric
element in this literary genre consists in the other world harbouring knowledge
which must be fathomed or revealed with the aid of intermediaries.

The scientific revolution called into question the existence or rather the revelatory quality of the world beyond, excluding it together with the occult dimension
from serious discussion. The dispute between Emanuel Swedenborg and Immanuel Kant well illustrates this sharp debate and also shows the strong resistance to
secularism, which ultimately ensured that the quest for transcendental certainties
remained a part of modern culture.

SPIRIT-SEER AND ENLIGHTENED CRITIQUE: SWEDENBORG AND KANT

Emanuel Swedenborg (1688–1772) grew up as the son of a pietistically inclined
bishop in a Lutheran milieu (see Benz 2002). Chiefly interested in natural science,
Swedenborg gave no early indication that he would become one of the most
controversial and influential mystics of the Enlightenment era. He studied philology, mathematics and natural sciences and travelled in 1710 to England, where he
pursued his researches under the influence of the Cambridge Platonists (Henry
More) and the empirical philosophy of John Locke. Swedenborg later resided in

---

1.   Quoted from the edition, Schaffhausen 1740, vol. I: 70; partly printed in bold type in the
original.
2.   See Gilly 2000. Arnold's *Unparteyische Kirchen- und Ketzerhistorie* (1700) is also socially
important. From a pietistic point of view, Arnold suggested 'the possibility of living religious
subjectivity in a society, in which the slow development of functional systems in early modern
society gradually dissolved their prevalent hierarchical and sectional principles' (Schlögl 2001: 186).

Holland, Germany, France, Sweden, Denmark, Italy and England, and achieved renown through his scientific studies (crystallography, writings on the brain, the body-soul connection and much else). Like Newton, he sought a general theory of the cosmos using empirical and mechanistic methods. In this sense he stood with both feet firmly rooted in the critical science of the eighteenth century. However, he also acknowledged the limitations imposed by human perception subject to pure reason. The Cartesian separation between *res cogitans* and *res extensa* (see below, p. 107) preoccupied him greatly, because nature in its living entirety thus eluded comprehension.

In 1740–41, in Amsterdam, he published *Oeconomia regni animalis* ('The Economy of the Animal Kingdom'), in which he introduced a complex doctrine of correspondences. In 1743 he experienced a profound spiritual crisis, which he described and analysed in a dream diary. In 1744, while in Holland, Swedenborg had a vision of Christ, followed by a vision of vocation the following year in London, where he had links with the Moravian brethren. His new 'calling' to theology consequent on these visions prevailed over any further pursuit of science and Swedenborg devoted the rest of his life to a mystical quest for religious knowledge. He authored several voluminous books. His eight-volume *Arcana Coelestia* ('Heavenly Secrets', 1749–56), a theosophical interpretation of the first Books of Moses, established Swedenborg's reputation as a mystical visionary. In 1782 numerous congregations of the 'New Church' were formed, especially in England, Germany and the USA, to realise his plans for a universal religion.

It is not easy to classify Swedenborg's doctrine in the history of religion. The visionary was somewhat indebted to esoteric traditions, but these were creatively integrated into his own system insofar as he ultimately presented his mystical experiences as the sole source of revelation. Proceeding from a strict division of the material and spiritual world, Swedenborg's chief interest lay in the correspondences between the two. He believed that during their earthly life, humans live with their consciousness in this world, but with their unconscious in the world beyond. Only at death does the soul 'awaken' to its conscious spiritual existence. On the basis of their convictions in this life the souls join communities of the 'like-minded' in heaven or hell, which are simply mirror reflections of their life on Earth. In heavenly spheres the souls can develop further into angelic souls or into angels, because there is no fundamental difference between the human soul and the angelic world.

Swedenborg's theosophical system unleashed extreme reactions soon after its publication. Already in the 1760s the well-known theologian Johann August Ernesti asserted that Swedenborg was propagating a basically naturalistic and materialistic theology, barely concealed by its use of biblical metaphors. The most controversial critique, and the most effective, once its initially anonymous author was known, came from Immanuel Kant (1724–1804), who also had a pietist background, but who progressed with his *Critiques* to become the most important thinker of the Enlightenment. The Enlightenment was no longer prepared to tolerate the explanatory authority of the Church in matters relating to the world and regarded reason as the only pointer to the truth. To quote Kant's famous dictum, the Enlightenment represented man's liberation from self-imposed tutelage. In his 1781 preface to the first edition of the *Critique of Pure Reason*, Kant outlined his programme:

> Our age is the very age of criticism, which has to overthrow everything. Religion, on account of its holiness, and government, on account of its majesty, generally want to evade this criticism. But thereupon they arouse justified suspicion, and cannot rely upon genuine respect, which reason accords only to that which can withstand free and public enquiry.

The scientific revolutions and the court of 'free and public enquiry' did not only challenge the churches but clearly also the 'occult' disciplines. Under such auspices Kant was bound to reject Swedenborg's theosophical speculations. His work *Träume eines Geistersehers, erläutert durch Träume der Metaphysik* ('Dreams of a Spirit-Seer, Illustrated by Dreams of Metaphysics'), dating from 1766 and thus his precritical phase, polemically debates the mystical visions of Emanuel Swedenborg and his claim to be in active contact with the spiritual world. As one might expect from an Enlightenment author, Kant begins his investigation with the words: 'The realm of shadows is the paradise of the fantasist. Here they find a land without frontiers, where they can build according to their heart's desire. Hypochondriacal vapours, nurses' tales and monastic miracles leave no shortage of building materials' (A 3). To this fantasy world he assigns Swedenborg and other spirit-seers, who simply project inner experiences outwards (A 63), and then he addresses himself to the reader: 'Therefore I do not consider it amiss if the reader, instead of seeing the spirit-seers as denizens of the other world, loses no time in consigning them to an asylum, and spares himself all further research' (A 72).

Words like these have infuriated Swedenborgians as much as they have amused strict positivists. However, one would misunderstand Kant, if one left the matter there. Also playing the devil's advocate, Kant states that it is just as much 'stupid prejudice…, to believe without good cause *nothing* that is told with some semblance of truth, as to believe without examination *everything* that is just common rumour' (A 6). But this examination is extremely testing. Not only do we not know whether there are spirits, but we cannot even answer the question 'what a spirit means' (A 9). Swedenborg's assertions are not only unproveable, but so are assertions to the contrary. In his youth Kant had himself believed in reincarnation, but later concluded:

> Precisely due to this lack of certainty I would not dare to deny all truth in tales of spirits, except for the simple—if strange—proviso that each single one should be questioned, while granting some credibility to their entirety. (A 78)

With regard to the spirits, one can 'henceforth *believe* all sorts of things, but one can never *know* more' (A 79). By 'knowledge' Kant here means what he later defined as the statements of pure reason, something quite different from the 'absolute knowledge' of esoteric discourses. It follows that the question of whether spiritual entities actually exist or whether they are social constructions cannot be resolved within the bounds of rational discourse. Both assertions are subject to critical scepticism. What is scientifically interesting—and this is the prime target of the Kantian argument—are simply the *consequences* resulting from each premise. Kant is completely certain what the implications would be of recognising only a few spirit tales as true (A 5). The whole basis of the natural sciences would be called into question, because the great majority of scholars, including Kant, are united in their rejection. But that is not a *proof*.

The Enlightenment made Western thought immune to its encounter with the irrational, whose persistent fascination was displaced into other, non-intellectual fields of discourse. Friedrich Nietzsche's cogent challenge to the belief in reason at the end of the nineteenth century found but a faint echo.[3]

Swedenborg's movement proved astonishingly tenacious despite Kant's scathing polemics. While philosophers of nature and theosophers such as Friedrich Christoph Oetinger, Franz von Baader and Louis-Claude de Saint Martin criticised parts of his doctrine, others regarded his writings as a fount of inspiration. The American transcendentalist Ralph Waldo Emerson was as greatly impressed by Swedenborg as was the scholar of religion William James, the French author Honoré de Balzac, the artist Paul Gauguin and the composer Anton von Webern.

ANIMAL MAGNETISM: FRANZ ANTON MESMER

The German doctor Franz Anton Mesmer (1734–1815) straddles the border between rational science and the Romantic philosophy of nature. Mesmer became well known through his theory of 'animal magnetism', which he propagated from the 1770s onwards. This is based on the idea of an all-pervasive 'fluid', a magnetism, which the 'magnetiser' can sense, influence and direct. Such notions had always been at home in alchemy and in the esoteric philosophy of nature. There one spoke of 'ether', *spiritus* (with Marsilio Ficino), or a ray, which pervades the whole cosmos. A child of his time, Mesmer regarded magnetism primarily as a material product of this energy and developed instruments in order to concentrate the animal magnetism in its curative effects. These so-called *baquets* (French, 'buckets') in which patients experienced crises, ecstasy and trance, conquered Parisian society once Mesmer had opened his practice there. Reactions were naturally divided: some regarded Mesmer's researches as revolutionary, since they appeared to demonstrate scientifically the spiritual and mental forces of nature and man; while radical representatives of the Enlightenment, however, dismissed the whole affair as a freak of human superstition (see Schott 1985).

However, Mesmer had a significant influence on the history of modern esotericism. First, he formulated a theory placing hidden, 'occult' forces at human disposal, which interested many nineteenth-century occultists. Second, Mesmer

---

3.   The Enlightenment, described by Martin Pott as a 'battle community', still exists today: 'More than other movements of cultural history, the Enlightenment is a battle community, which achieves its consolidation not least by specific images of the enemy' (Pott 1992: 2).

had a strong impact on the 'metaphysical movement' which developed especially within American transcendentalism. Spiritualism aroused great interest in the middle of the nineteenth century (see below, pp. 124-25) and was also indebted to Swedenborg and Mesmer. Third, Mesmer stands at the beginning of research into depth psychology. The Romantic idea of the 'unconscious'—first introduced by Carl Gustav Carus—and in particular the American 'mind-cure' movement, emphasising man's self-healing potential through the active suggestion of 'positive thoughts', indicates a close relationship with Mesmerism (see Fuller 1982). These examples show how the so-called New Age movement of the twentieth century has its roots in the nineteenth century.

Although Mesmer ultimately followed a mechanistic model, he regarded the whole of nature as a texture of living energies. The notion that nature was not only living but also sacred would find increasing support in the nineteenth century. With this sacralisation of nature and the human self, the German philosophy of nature not only influenced American transcendentalism but played a leading part in twentieth-century esotericism.

NATURAL SCIENCE IN THE NINETEENTH CENTURY

'Nature' is a central point of reference both for esotericism and for science. The close relationship between esotericism and science is really neither here nor there, as the links between their respective fields of discourse have remained neither constant over time nor in their theoretical formulation and have often given rise to bitter antagonism. However, overlaps between esotericism and natural science have always existed in holistic notions of nature and the cosmos. The same is true of *pantheistic* and *animistic* descriptions of nature as a living being.

Not until the nineteenth century was any clear division drawn between the philosophy of nature and natural science in its present sense. Misunderstandings arise if we transpose our present views of 'exact empirical science' to earlier eras. 'Investigators of nature', as they still described themselves in the nineteenth century, saw the religious aspects of their study of nature, and this tendency can be seen in the personalities responding to the changes wrought by the Enlightenment and early industrialisation. The following figures are representative of many others, both in regard to the holistic and pantheistic implications of natural science and to the exchanges between the fields of art, literature, philosophy, science and religion.

PANTHEISM IN LITERATURE: GOETHE AND NOVALIS

Johann Wolfgang von Goethe (1749–1832) is indisputably one of the most pivotal figures on the interface between the philosophy of nature, science and art at the end of the eighteenth century. Much has been written about Goethe's Hermetic and esoteric interests, usually with reference to the figure of the magus in *Faust*, and the philosophy of nature espoused by this poet, statesman, and scientist (see Zimmermann 1969 and Sladek 1984). There is no doubt that Goethe received much inspiration from the esoteric traditions and also contributed to their further development.

The philosophy of nature anticipated Romantic and modern ecological discourses with its theological elevation and sacralisation of nature. Goethe's famous novella *Die Leiden des jungen Werthers* ('The Sorrows of Young Werther', 1774) offers an outstanding example. In his letter of 10 May 1771, Werther describes a 'wonderful serenity' that fills his soul; he feels the 'presence of the Almighty' and the 'breath of the All-Loving'. His soul is the 'mirror of the infinite God'. Goethe's works particularly show the combination of the sacralisation of nature, pantheism and animism, which arose in response to the opportunities and dangers of the European Enlightenment.

The same applies to other contemporaries, but especially to Novalis (Friedrich von Hardenberg, 1772–1801). His entire work ranging from poems to novellas and novels to philosophical treatises is permeated by a holistic and pantheistic conception of nature. Here I will confine myself to examples from his novels *Die Lehrlinge zu Saïs* ('The Disciples at Saïs') and *Heinrich von Ofterdingen* (both published in 1802).

Die Lehrlinge zu Saïs, a novel within the esoteric alchemical tradition, describes nature as a holy organism, whose secrets can only be deciphered by artistic empathy and universal love. Novalis relates how the 'contemplation' of ever-flowing nature leads the observer to

> a new revelation of the genius of love, a new bond between Thou and I. The careful description of this inner history of the world is the genuine theory of nature. A system of thought for the true representation and formula of the universe is spontaneously evoked through the internal harmony between the world of thought and the universe.[4]

Novalis stated that in its entirety, nature is 'only conceivable as an instrument and medium for the understanding of intelligent beings'. A little earlier he wrote: 'One could more easily imagine that [nature] were the product of an inconceivable understanding of endlessly differing beings, the wonderful bond between the world of spirits, the point of union and contact between countless worlds' (p. 222), for, according to Novalis, 'nature would not be nature, if it had no soul'.

Novalis maintained that it is the poets who stand on the intersection of these worlds, for only they 'can handle the flow', namely living nature; 'the workshops would be temples and people would honour their flame and currents and boast of them' (p. 229). For Novalis, the poet is the real mystagogue of nature, who understands the language of the universe. He calls this 'that holy language…, once the shining link of those royal human beings with heavenly regions and dwellers'. Only very few, specifically the disciples at Saïs, are still in possession of such secret knowledge.

---

4.   Quotations are taken from *Gesammelte Werke*, 3 vols, Darmstadt 1999; here I: 225.

> Their speech was a marvellous song, whose irresistible tones penetrated deep into the interior of every nature and set it asunder. Each of their names appeared to be the password for the soul of every natural body. With their creative energy, these vibrations aroused all the images of worldly manifestations, and one could rightly say of them that the life of the universe was an eternal conversation of a thousand voices; because all energies, all sorts of activity seemed to be united in the most inconceivable way in their speaking. (p. 230)

Nature as a communicating universe, in which man appears as one participant amongst many, leads Novalis to the dissolution of all boundaries between supposedly separate entities: 'Sometimes the stars were people to him, sometimes the people stars, the stones animals, the clouds plants' (p. 202).

In his posthumous novel *Heinrich von Ofterdingen* similar links are presented. But here the fusion of non-human entities is even more strongly evoked than in *Die Lehrlinge zu Saïs*, which cannot only be described as a *unio mystica* but as intercourse with other worlds. Novalis speaks of this already in the first chapter of *Heinrich von Ofterdingen*: 'I once heard talk of ancient times, when animals and trees and rocks held converse with men. Now I feel as if they all wanted to start talking and as if I could see from their appearance what they wanted to tell me' (p. 241). After this statement the narrator loses himself in his fantasy, falls asleep and has a remarkable dream: behind a meadow he discovers a cliff with a large opening leading into a deep passage. He goes through the passage deep into the rock, until he sees from afar a bright light, which he tries to reach. When he emerges from the tunnel, he finds himself in a new, mysterious world, from which he receives revelations, particularly from a 'tall, light blue flower' (p. 242). Here Novalis picks up on the alchemical motif of the 'blue flower of wisdom' related to a rite of initiation involving esoteric, alchemical and Masonic symbolism. The influence of this way of looking at nature can be traced from the North American transcendentalists and the European philosophy of nature as far as the current neo-shamanic scene (see von Stuckrad 2003c: 174-232).

Even if Novalis' *Heinrich von Ofterdingen* was influenced by Goethe's *Werther*, the role assigned to nature clearly surpasses the pantheistic theme in the latter work. Empathy and admiration lead to fusion:

> The plants are thus the most direct language of the soil. Each new leaf, each special flower is a mystery which forces up, and because it cannot move for love and pleasure and cannot speak, it becomes a mute, tranquil plant. If one finds such a plant in the solitude, it is as if everything around were transfigured and the small feathered notes preferred to keep it company. One would like to weep for joy, and separated from the world, stick one's hands and feet in the earth in order to take root and never leave this happy neighbourhood. This green, mysterious carpet of love is drawn over the whole arid world. (p. 377)

Novalis asserts that it is the 'memory of ancient flowerhood' which keeps the knowledge of the mysterious unity of all being alive in man. Because man himself is a part of the whole living universe, it is not surprising that the animals and plants can converse directly with him. When the 'pilgrim' Heinrich reflected on these things, 'the tree began to tremble. The rocks resounded in muffled tones, and as from a deep subterranean distance several clear little voices began to sing' (p. 369). They sang the song of universal love.

German Romanticism ontologised and spiritualised nature in a heightened fashion. Interpretative links were thereby forged, leading to the sentimental personification and sacralisation of the 'German forest' in general and the 'German oak' in particular. This topos has performed the function of creating national identity from the nineteenth century, and through both world wars, up to present times. Despite the prominent role of nature in nineteenth-century German thought, one must not overlook that similar ideas prevailed in other European countries, such as the esoteric tendencies of French Romanticism or the function of gardens, parks and landscapes for the English (see Schama 1996).

SCHELLING'S PHILOSOPHY OF NATURE

Friedrich Wilhelm Joseph Schelling (1775–1854) elaborated a philosophy of nature, which not only prevailed among the Romantics but which is still evident today. Even more: in the face of global ecological crisis, Schelling's concept of a living nature in which the knowing human subject is fully integrated finds widespread approval.

Like Leibniz before him, Schelling conceives of nature and the cosmos as a single large organism. In his work, *Erster Entwurf eines Systems der Naturphilosophie* ('First Sketch of a System of Philosophy of Nature', 1799), he calls the individual organism 'the concentrated, reduced image of the universal organism' (*Gesammelte Werke* [GW]: III, 198). Like Leibniz, he also concluded that this assumed there was no longer any difference between organic and inorganic life. The latter is rather simply an aspect of the former and merges into it. Schelling is convinced that the inorganic proceeded from the organic and thus still bears vitality within itself. Central to his philosophy is the distinction between the *product* of natural events and the underlying *process*, which he describes as the proper subject of the philosophy of nature. In order to understand nature in its reality, we should not ask about its products but about its 'absolute activity' or 'productivity'. Schelling defines it as follows: 'We call nature as a mere product (*natura naturata*) an object (which is the concern of all empiricism). We call nature as productivity (*natura naturans*) a subject (which concerns all theory)' (GW: III, 284).

The concept of *natura naturans*, which Schelling took from Aristotle and which was expounded in scholastic philosophy—first by Averroes, then by Albertus Magnus, Thomas Aquinas and Roger Bacon—describes the aspect of living Becoming prior to the study of dead Being. Created objects are only interesting insofar as they permit inferences about the fundamental principle of Becoming. Here Schelling contrasts his organic philosophy of life with the mechanistic conception of nature accepted by empiricism. This metaphysical and ontological concept also contrasts with Kant's conviction that the observing subject is the only competent authority to judge nature. In Schelling's view, nature appears as an independent and self-organised unity, recognised by man through their empathetic and open attitude of mind. His philosophy of nature succeeds in resolving the opposition between man and nature, between *res cogita* (the 'thinking') and *res extensa* (the 'extended' or 'material' thing), as well as between object and subject in a monistic system of spirit and matter, which both form part of absolute metaphysical Becoming.

With these kinds of considerations, Schelling anticipates challenges which arose not only in the Romantic period but are today a regular feature of the debate over the philosophy of nature, especially in questions regarding the self-organisation of nature (see Schmied-Kowarzik 1996). I am not claiming Schelling was an 'esotericist': the importance of his philosophy is that it represents an important element of nineteenth-century esoteric discourse, directed towards recognising the hidden qualities of nature in a holistic and animistic perspective. The undertone of this philosophy can still be heard in contemporary Deep Ecology, in biocentric ethics, and in the constructions of New Age science.

THE SACRALISATION OF NATURE IN ROMANTICISM
The influence of the young Schelling is a convenient starting-point for a survey of the Romantic philosophy of nature and its reception at the beginning of the twentieth century. The debate between Fichte, Hegel and Schelling at the beginning of the nineteenth century drew many young students to the University of Jena who later achieved renown as Romantic philosophers. However, it would be mistaken to classify Schelling as a Romantic philosopher; he was concerned with a *concept* of nature and the embedding of philosophy of nature in his whole system of a philosophy of identity, while the Romantic elaboration of his doctrine is best described as the *aetheticisation* and *emotionalisation* of nature (see Groh and Groh 1991). As a result of the increasing dominance of technical and mechanistic thought, coupled with the success of scientific research, Schelling's philosophy was eclipsed in the second half of the nineteenth century. However, between 1900 and 1930 many thinkers rediscovered the holistic theory of idealism and Romanticism owing to the doubts that were raised about the mechanistic and causal paradigm by the philosophy of life, the theory of relativity and quantum mechanics.

A number of important philosophers of nature attended Schelling's lectures at Jena around 1800, developing his ideas in various and sometimes contrary ways. These thinkers included Lorenz Oken (1779–1851), Friedrich Hufeland (1774–1839, Christoph Wilhelm's less famous brother), Dietrich Georg von Kiefer (1779–1862, appointed Professor of Medicine at Jena in 1812), Gotthilf Heinrich von Schubert (1780–1860) and Ignatius Paul Vital Troxler (1780–1866). All these philosophers were fascinated by Schelling's organic model of nature and they each elaborated the idea of the animated cosmos in their own fashion.

In his *Lehrbuch der Naturphilosophie* ('Handbook of the Philosophy of Nature', 1809 [a third edition appeared in 1853]), Lorenz Oken viewed the philosophy of nature as an essential precondition for a philosophy of mind (§15). The eternal or absolute forms a unity with the real and material, while the latter proceeds from the former: 'Whenever the ideal and the real are one, then everything is bound to be identical, and this identity not only prevails between the ideal and the real, but also between all individual members of the real' (§38). The emergence of the organic and real thus follows the principle of all Being, namely polarity, that is a formative dynamic of opposites (§§76-92). This dynamic is life itself, which has existed from the beginning of time, 'an idea, a moving thought of God, the original *fiat* with all its consequences' (§88). Because nothing exists without such dynamism or movement, Oken joins with Schelling in asserting: 'There is actually nothing dead in the world; the only thing that is dead is that which does not exist, just nothingness' (§90).

The constants in the philosophy of nature consist in the rhythm of the creative and life principles, whereby all Being is brought into life through a dynamic encounter with its opposite pole. 'The solar system did not arise mechanically but dynamically. It took its form not through a flick of God's hand, nor through shocks and aberrations, but through polarisation according to eternal laws, according to the laws of light' (§227).

The only difference between the organic and the inorganic is that the latter dispenses with motion and is thus mere mass. The organic is animated and ensouled, because 'motion is…the soul, through which the organic surpasses the inorganic' (§993). The organic world reflects nature in its totality upon all levels of development. However, it is man who embodies the supreme level and unites the animal and plant kingdoms within himself. 'The higher organism is a universe in miniature; in the most profound, truest sense it is *a little world, the microcosm*' (§1019).

Gotthilf Heinrich von Schubert provides a good illustration of the degree to which Romanticism embraced an aesthetic and emotional view of nature in contrast to Schelling's earlier analytical initiative. As Odo Marquard (see Marquard 1987) has suggested, this might even amount to a 'Romantic nature' prevailing over a 'controlling nature'. Schubert published his work *Die Symbolik des Traumes* ('The Symbolism of the Dream') in 1814 and in his *Geschichte der Seele* ('History of the Soul', 1830) he once more overstepped the narrower confines of the philosophy of nature. In this work he unmasks empiricism as an impression of the senses, making this a crucial element in the experience of nature. Whereas Schelling still tried to conceptualise the 'sense of the Absolute', Schubert foregoes such analysis and appeals to the feelings of his readers. Schubert calls nature 'an embodied dreamworld, a prophetic language in living hieroglyphs'. The esoteric factor of his thinking is explicit, when Schubert refers to 'the serving soul in the doctrine of the old kabbalists'.

The Romantic philosophy of nature ushered in a pantheistic outlook, which saw a revelation of transcendental divinity in nature. Art and poetry could link man emotionally with this sacralised nature. This was the view of Carl Gustav Carus (1789–1869), a Romantic doctor, thinker and artist well known for his medical, artistic and psychological theories. He was the first to launch the concept of the 'unconscious', which C.G. Jung later developed into his own theory. Carus worked in Leipzig and Dresden, where he was appointed Royal Physician in 1827, but he was also active as a philosopher of nature. At the founding conference of the *Gesellschaft deutscher Naturforscher und Ärzte* ('Society of German Investigators of Nature and Physicians') in 1822, he defined the philosophy of nature as 'the science of God's eternal metamorphosis into the world' and thereby pantheistically elevated Hegel's explanation of the Absolute Mind (see Gladigow 1989: 220f.).

FROM DARWINISM TO PANTHEISTIC MONISM

Using Max Weber's terminology, one might describe the Romantic philosophy of nature as a dialogue with the processes of rationalisation and disenchantment of the cosmos. It was also an attempt to 're-enchant' the world which still influences esoteric projects in the twentieth century (see von Stuckrad 2003c: 268-72). Although such a philosophy of nature came under increasing pressure owing to industrialisation and the advance of new natural sciences, holistic, monistic, vitalist and pantheistic ideas had always been current in the first half of the twentieth century as an 'antidote' to the mechanistic view of nature. Even scientists as Charles Darwin and Ernst Haeckel, later celebrated as protagonists of sober empirical science, can be cited as examples here.

In his fundamental work *On the Origin of Species by Means of Natural Selection* (1859), Darwin set out a view of nature brimming with life and fertility against the Judeo-Christian doctrine of creation. As Hans G. Kippenberg says, 'Darwin's travel valise helps us understand this metaphor'. Darwin took Lyell's *Principle of Geology* and, more importantly, Milton's *Paradise Lost* in his luggage on his world voyages. Milton's account of creation as an act of voluptuous love and fecundation brought Darwin to the idea of *natura naturans*, a notion having nothing to do with the war of all against all (Kippenberg 2002: 33; see also Wilson 2002). Although Darwin did not imagine nature as a huge sacred organism, as did many Romantics, he combined a religious sense of wonder at the abundance of nature with scientific empiricism. Ernst Haeckel (1834–1919) offers the strongest proof for the religious infiltration of Darwinism in the nineteenth century. His monism is far more than a radical realisation of the mechanistic model. In *Die Welträthsel* ('The World Riddles', 1899) Haeckel anticipates the ideas of Deep Ecology and biocentrism, advanced today by many pantheists, although he was also a staunch advocate of the mechanistic and deterministic world-view.

He makes it clear in his preface that he wants to overcome the regrettable separation between pure empiricism and metaphysical speculation prevailing in German universities. Only the reunion of both disciplines would be worthy of the term 'philosophy of nature'. Haeckel concedes that the doctrine of evolution is the major achievement of the nineteenth century, but he thinks Darwin should be seen alongside Jean Lamarck and Johann Wolfgang von Goethe as a trio of 'brilliant philosophers of nature, three stars of the greatest magnitude among all other men of our century' (Haeckel 1899: 8; cf. p. 14 and *passim*). Haeckel later added

Baruch Spinoza to his pantheon, as Spinoza cogently developed pantheistic thought, juxtaposing it with Judeo-Christian anthropomorphism. Haeckel sees the hypostatisation of man as the centre of the universe as the crucial problem facing contemporary philosophy and religion, a position which surpassed Darwin. Man cannot be regarded as 'the premeditated goal of organic creation nor as a creature similar to God' (p. 11), but as an organic component of the entire universe. Haeckel's monism excludes the existence of anthropomorphic deities and he never tired of polemicising against monotheistic religions, and even against polytheistic ones because these contradict monism. His monism leads him to a pantheism, which he conceives, contrary to the evolutionary models of comparative religion, as the overcoming of monotheistic religions rather than their archaic predecessor. Pantheism is the product of a 'civilised man's refined observation of nature', in contrast to theism, 'whose crudest forms were already evident among primitive peoples more than ten thousand years ago' (p. 116).

Like many natural scientists since his time, Ernst Haeckel finds his God in nature (see Gladigow 1989). Far from personifying nature, he seeks the solution of the 'world riddles' in the mystical unity of spirit and matter, which reveals itself in strict laws but without the evolutionary goal of perfecting man.[5] Creation always remains incomplete, because organic like inorganic nature is characterised only by 'a constant flow of development' (p. 107). Here Haeckel echoes the supreme principle described by Schelling, which would find later votaries in the philosophy of life. In his study *Kristallseelen* ('Crystal Souls'), published two years before his death, Haeckel sought to make this more concrete by combining crystallography and psychology. Haeckel regarded Goethe as the exemplar of a sensitive natural scientist—three Goethe quotations formed the motto of this book. Referring to Goethe, Haeckel saw the year 1904 as a crucial turning-point of science, because that year saw the publication of studies that realised Goethe's prophetic programme:

> The artificial boundaries previously erected between inorganic and organic nature, between death and life, between natural sciences and the humanities fall at a single blow. *All substance possesses life*, inorganic as well as organic; *all things are animated*, crystals as well as organisms. The ancient conviction in the inner, unified linkage of all events, in the unlimited dominion of generally valid laws of nature reasserts itself as an unshakeable truth. (Haeckel 1917: viii)

But Haeckel goes even further in his religious conception. In *Die Welträtsel* one finds a section entitled 'Monistic Churches':

> Modern man who possesses science, art and thus also religion, has no need of a particular church, no narrow, enclosed space. For everywhere in open nature where his eyes fall upon the infinite universe or a part of it, he finds the harsh 'battle for existence' but also 'the true, the beautiful, and the good'. Everywhere he finds his 'church' in magnificent *nature* itself. (Haeckel 1899: 138)

---

5.   This should not conceal the fact that Haeckel presented a theory of evolution extending to a racial theory, which played an important part in both the race doctrines and euthanasia programme of German National Socialism.

With such utterances Haeckel enters the same field of discourse mapped by Novalis and American transcendentalists like Henry David Thoreau, albeit coming from a different direction. He speaks with a voice we will later recognise as that of Deep Ecology.

7

INSTITUTIONALISED ESOTERICISM: SECRET SOCIETIES

Esoteric traditions passed into modernity through processes of institutionalisation, which had a wider effect on the political and cultural landscape of Europe between the seventeenth and nineteenth centuries. Rosicrucianism, Freemasonry and their successors acted as a reservoir for esoteric interests. The Rosicrucian movement is self-evidently esoteric, while the significance of Freemasonry, essentially an emancipatory bourgeois eighteenth-century movement, lies in its creation of institutions and hierarchies, which were adopted by the magical orders of the nineteenth and twentieth centuries. But let us begin our story with the Rosicrucians.

ROSICRUCIANS OR IN THE BEGINNING WAS A FICTION

THE FICTION

In the year 1614 a mysterious book was published at Cassel. The anonymous, 147-page text bore the title:

> Universal and General Reformation of the whole wide world; together with *Fama Fraternitatis* of the Laudable Order of the Rosy Cross, written to all the Learned and Rulers of Europe; also a short reply sent by Mr Haselmeyer, for which he was seized by the Jesuits and put in irons on a Galley. Now put forth in print and communicated to all true hearts. Printed in Cassel by Wilhelm Wessel, 1614.

The essence of this text, known henceforth as the *Fama Fraternitatis* ('Fame of the Fraternity') was the mysterious story of the life of a certain Christian Rosenkreutz and his followers, who had dedicated themselves to a 'General Reformation', seeking to combine the Christian reformations of the sixteenth century with a Paracelsian philosophy of nature. The inclusion of a 'reply' indicates the *Fama*'s hostility towards the activities of the Jesuit Order (est. 1540), a determined opponent of the Reformation.[1]

---

1. A survey of the history of the Rosicrucians appears in McIntosh 1987 and Edighoffer 1982.

The legend of Christian Rosenkreutz describes how he became acquainted with the science and wisdom of the East on an extended voyage via the Holy Land to Arabia and Egypt. He gained insight into the *Liber mundi* ('Book of the World'), which corresponded alchemically to the book of nature. Rosenkreutz experienced the deeper meaning of the Hermetic doctrine of the microcosm and macrocosm and the *Tabula Smaragdina* ('Emerald Table'). He recognised that his Christian faith harmonised with these esoteric teachings but that 'true religion' had been wholly corrupted by Christian dogmatism. On his return to Europe he tried to disseminate the original wisdom but encountered bitter opposition from the established Church. Following the example of the Arabian and African scholars, he decided to found a learned society in Europe. This community of scholars, who would place their wisdom in the service of princes, would herald a new era characterised by the revival of the old philosophy of nature in the spirit of Paracelsus. Following their reforms, underpinned by institutional rules, the members of the order would disperse and overturn the conventional ideas of the establishment.

Sensing his approaching death, Rosenkreutz erects a memorial to himself, which initially remains a secret. Following the death of the founder of the order, his followers go about their work in secret for a further 120 years. Only when the grave is discovered and the symbols, figures and books of the fraternity have been found, has the time come to go public. It is no coincidence that the discovery of Rosenkreutz's tomb recalls the rediscovery of the grave of Hermes Trismegistus familiar from Hermetic literature. According to the legend, the books found in Rosenkreutz's grave were the writings of Paracelsus, the biography of the founder, and other works, which would now be published, while the vault itself would be resealed.

THE FIRST ROSICRUCIANS...

The *Fama* is a confessional text, in which the brothers of the order declare themselves to be Lutherans seeking no political goals, but hoping the 'truth' will prevail on its own merits. They protest against a false alchemy, concerned only with 'ungodly and accursed gold-making' and summon the learned to declare their mind 'in print'. They announce that an answer will be given, even if the fraternity is not in a position to reveal their names or meeting places.

Further writings of the Rosicrucians soon started to circulate, and in 1615 the *Confessio* followed the *Fama*, in order to counter the many rumours and misunderstandings that had already arisen. This text gave further particulars concerning Christian Rosenkreutz: he was said to have been born in 1378, and died at the age of 106 in 1484. His grave was opened after 120 years, giving the year 1604 as the date when the Rosicrucians began their public activity.

Who stood behind these writings? The authors may be identified as a circle which formed in the early years of the seventeenth century at the University of Tübingen. The legal scholar and professor, Christoph Besold (1577–1638), the theology student, Johann Valentin Andreae (1586–1654), who took his master's degree in 1605, and the physician, theologian and jurist, Tobias Hess (1568–1614) are considered responsible for the early Rosicrucian manifestoes. Adam Haselmeyer, mentioned in the title of the *Fama*, also played an important role.[2] Besold and Hess were followers of the reputed 'enthusiast' Simon Studion (b. 1543), who also took his master's degree at Tübingen in 1565. Hess and Studion may have belonged to the secret society 'Milita Crucifera Evangelica', which surfaced at Lüneburg in 1586. In any case, Studion was well-known as the author of millenarian and anti-orthodox texts, in which he promoted the establishment of the inner and outer 'temple' (*naos*), corresponding to the perfection of the knowledge of nature, after the Second Coming of Christ. Studion predicted this for the year 1620, following the crucifixion of the last pope in 1612.

Johann Valentin Andreae is the primary figure in the actual composition of the manifestoes. His autobiography, written later as an orthodox Protestant, sought to draw a veil over his youthful enthusiasm for the Rosicrucians and only admitted authorship of a third important text, *Chymische Hochzeit Christiani Rosencreutz. Anno 1459* ('Chymical Wedding of Christian Rosencreutz, AD 1459'), that he claimed to have begun in 1603 and that was first published in 1616. This work relates the adventures of the aged Rosenkreutz in terms of alchemical symbolism. Andreae was also known for further works, including *Christianopolis* (1619), a utopia describing the ideal reformation of politics and religion.

However, although the manifestoes are attributable to a specific circle and no actual Rosicrucian order existed that one could join, the social and religious ramifications of the movement were quite extensive. This goes some way to explaining the astonishing resonance of the manifestoes in seventeenth-century Europe (see Bibliotheca Philosophica Hermetica 2002). The combination of Hermetic tradition, Paracelsian medicine and the philosophy of nature, alchemical symbolism, reformed Protestantism, apocalypticism and social utopianism matched the spirit of the age.

...AND THEIR IMPACT

People interested in alchemy and esotericism were the first to take up and spread the ideas disseminated by the original Tübingen circle. The most important sympathisers included Michael Maier, alchemist and personal physician of Emperor Rudolf II (see above, p. 83), as well as his friend, the English doctor and philosopher of nature, Robert Fludd (1574–1637), whose own writings made a significant contribution to Rosicrucian literature in England. Besides this more alchemical tradition, another more theosophical current combined—with the following of Valentin Weigel, Jacob Boehme and Christian mysticism via Abraham von Franckenberg (1593–1652)—to influence pietism. Both movements led to the formation of real Rosicrucian groups in the eighteenth century, often with a close link to lodges of Freemasonry. Various initiatory and thus secret associations arose, which

2.   Carlos Gilly has written the standard works on the origins of the Rosicrucians.

acted as a foil to the Christian Church in the age of absolutism and the Enlightenment (see Reinalter 1983).

Rosicrucian groups also appeared later as modern occult societies. These
included the *Societas Rosicruciana in Anglia* (est. 1865), the Hermetic Order of the
Golden Dawn (est. 1888, see below, p. 119), the O.T.O. (*Ordo Templi Orientis*),
which perpetuated Egyptian high-grade Freemasonry, the *Lectorium Rosicrucianum*
founded at Haarlem in 1924 by Jan Leene alias Jan van Rijckenborgh (1896–1968)
and finally the influential AMORC (*Antiquus Mysticus Ordo Rosae Crucis*), which
was founded in 1915 by Harvey Spencer Lewis (1883–1936) and counted several
million members at the time of his death.

FREEMASONS OR THE POWER OF MYSTERY

Besides the Rosicrucian movement, the traditions of Freemasonry have been a
significant factor in the institutionalisation of esotericism over the past three hundred years. One must speak of traditions in the plural, for no single type of Freemasonry actually exists. The movement is marked by so many internal and external
rifts and divisions that one must always be on one's guard with respect to what
kind of Freemasonry one is actually dealing with. Here I will confine myself to
a general description relating to issues raised by esotericism (see Ridley 1999;
Reinalter 2002).

THE MYTH OF ORIGIN

The Freemasons dearly like to invoke ancient traditions concerning their own
origins. Their founding legend usually invokes a mystical notion of architecture,
beginning with King Solomon and his building of the First Temple at Jerusalem,
via the masons' and carvers' guilds that built the medieval cathedrals, to the later
Masonic lodges. Alongside this craft tradition are mentioned the most varied initiatory societies, including Brahmins, priests of Osiris, Pythagoreans, ancient mystery
cults, the Sabaeans of late antiquity, medieval Knights Templar, druids and many
others.

All these derivations are subsequent inventions, which cannot be verified by
recourse to history. That does not mean that the doctrines, practices and symbols
so important to Freemasonry have no precedent in the history of religion. It is their
combination and institutional form that is modern.

The historical precursors of the Freemasons may be found in the craft fraterni-
ties and lodges that formed around the cathedral building sites. Their customs have
left many marks upon Freemasonry. Thus the craft legends of the Freemasons,
first recorded in the so-called Regius poem (c. 1390) and Cooke manuscript
(c. 1430–40), and their oldest constitutions dating from the mid-fifteenth century,
hark back to the ancient master builders from Enoch to Solomon. Hermes appears
here as the adviser of Isis and inventor of geometry. The two pillars of Solomon's
temple, *Yachin* and *Boaz*, play a major role in the symbolism of both Kabbalah and

Freemasonry. The Cooke manuscript relates how Hermes Trismegistus found the first of these pillars after the flood, while Pythagoras found the second, and together they began to teach the sciences inscribed upon them. These sciences primarily serve to purify, transmute and refine men. In many later lodges of so-called Hermetic masonry, based in France and German-speaking countries, this more theosophical tendency was coupled with the practical preparation of the 'Philosophers' Stone' or a universal elixir of life.

After the English guilds had begun in the seventeenth century to admit non-masons into their ranks, a precedent existed to establish masonry independently from its craft traditions. On 24 June 1717 five London lodges joined to found a Grand Lodge, which soon became the centre of an internationally oriented Free-masonry, thereby justifying this date as the actual beginning of Freemasonry.

ENLIGHTENMENT, ESOTERICISM, POLITICS

By the second half of the eighteenth century the Freemasons had become a crucial factor in the Enlightenment and the new political order of Europe (see Neuge-bauer-Wölk 1995). Their lodges were variously involved with Enlightenment societies, in which the emergent middle classes sought to realise their ideals of universal education, tolerance and human progress. Once adopted by the educated elite, the craft motif of the dressed stone became a symbol for the education of the new human being, while the lodge hierarchy of novice, apprentice and master represented degrees of individual progress. The esoteric aspect of these ideals concerned the 'higher knowledge' frequently sought by Enlightenment societies. The esoteric motif is also obvious in the idea, often expressed in alchemical symbolism, of transforming and refining the individual into a perfect human being.

Given this supposition it is not surprising that Freemasonry would also play an active political role. Many Freemasons supported the ideals of the French Revolution and were engaged in the struggle for bourgeois rights against the absolutist state, though most lodges refrained from taking an official position on religion and politics. Reinhart Koselleck has suggested that the middle classes found a form of sanctuary in Masonic lodges beyond the reach of the administrative state. The very secrecy of Freemasonry (arcanum) served as a protection against the absolutist state and ultimately helped to undermine it.[3]

The secret league of the Illuminati, founded at Ingolstadt in 1776, represents a radical political wing of Freemasonry. This order was started by Adam Weishaupt (1748–1830), professor of natural and ecclesiastical law, and has nothing to do with the Illuminism of Suhrawardī or the Christian mystics, or even Theodor Reuß's 'resurrected' Order of the Illuminati a century later. Clearly demarcated from the Rosicrucian infiltration of Freemasonry, the Order of the Illuminati seemed to have pursued a radical realisation of rational French Enlightenment philosophy.

---

3. Koselleck 1973; see also Agethen 1984. This approach was recently critically adopted by Linda Simonis and applied to the 'esoteric communication'—I use the term 'discursive transfer'—between religion, art and literature (Simonis 2002).

Almost anarchically oriented, it imagined a political order without kings, priests and private property. Weishaupt assigned ancient cover-names to members, who could rise through three grades to become 'Minerval illuminatus'. The Freemason Adolf Freiherr von Knigge, who had joined the Illuminati under the name 'Philo', gave the order a new constitution but it failed to flourish. The Illuminati made few friends among moderate Freemasons or politicians and mutual denunciations led to the official suppression of the order. It only survived until 1785, and Weishaupt was forced to flee Bavaria, settling at Gotha, where he lived until his death.

Higher Degrees and Rosicrucians

Freemasonry is a highly pluralistic institution. Many Freemasons were simultaneously members of other secret societies (Illuminati, 'Asian Brothers', Rosicrucians), and many competing groups formed in the course of time. The standardised forms of the English and Rectified Scottish rites were not universally followed and thus developed the so-called high-degree Freemasonry which added further degrees to the original three-craft degrees. In 1782 at the international Wilhelmsbad Convention attempts were made to establish a new binding constitution, but unity could not be achieved owing to the gulf between lodges guided by Enlightenment values and Rosicrucian lodges interested in alchemy and esotericism.

The Rosicrucians adopted the first three-craft degrees of Freemasonry, adding a further series up to seven, nine or more degrees. A representative example is the Order of the Gold and Rosy Cross, which after its reform in 1777 invested the highest ninth degree (*Magus*) with the omniscient wisdom of ancient authorities: 'Nothing is concealed from them, they are the masters of everything, like Moses, Aaron, Hermes and Hiram Abif'. The Rosicrucian groups and 'irregular' high-degree masonry, in the sense of 'unaccepted' by the English Grand Lodge, created a basis for the secret societies and magical orders of the nineteenth century, which are so important in the history of modern esotericism.

Magical Orders or Egypt in England

Towards the end of the nineteenth century a stream of initiatory societies and magical orders arose from the milieu of Freemasonry, Rosicrucianism, the Romantic philosophy of nature and occultism. The esoteric fascination with ancient Greece and the 'East', with Persia and Egypt as the cradle of 'the true religion' (see Hornung 2001), was now supported by theological, philological and historical studies in universities. The foundation of the Theosophical Society in 1875 was the most important fruit of these developments and will be discussed in the next chapter. Here I will briefly mention several groups that had a significant influence on twentieth-century esotericism.[4]

---

4.   For all groups and persons mentioned here, the reader will find entries and extensive information in Hanegraaff et al. 2005.

THE HERMETIC ORDER OF THE GOLDEN DAWN

Almost all the following orders were founded by persons who were members of the Theosophical Society or in close contact with it. Samuel Liddell MacGregor Mathers (1854–1918) was the driving force behind the foundation of the Hermetic Order of the Golden Dawn in 1888 (see Howe 1972). The name of the order combines Hermetic authority with the notion of 'dawn', by which Paracelsus, Boehme and others had signified a new spiritual era. Here one might only recall the title of a work published by the pseudonymous Dominicus Gnosius (!) in 1610 and reprinted in 1700: *Hermes Trismegisti Regis Graecorum, ex aurora* [= Dawn, Sunrise] *consurgente Tractatus vere aureus de Lapidis philosophici secreto…*

Besides Hermes-Thoth, the Order of the Golden Dawn adopted a wide variety of mainly Egyptian deities for its magical and theosophical teachings. The mixture of Egyptophilia, Christian Kabbalah and Rosicrucian ritualism is evident in the initiation to the degree of Adeptus Minor, which deploys all these traditions. The temple is constructed as a replica of the vault (*pastos*) of Christian Rosenkreutz and the directions for the ritual reflect the original discovery of the founder in the *Fama*:

> The Chief Adept lies inside the Pastos on his back to represent C.R.C. [Christian Rosenkreutz]. He is clothed in full Regalia; on his breast is the complete Symbol of the Rosy Cross suspended from the double Phoenix Collar. His arms are crossed on breast [representing Osiris], and he holds Crook and Scourge; between them lies Book T. Lid of the Pastos closed and Circular Altar stands over it. Other Adepti outside Tomb as before. On the Altar are replaced Rose Cross, Cup of Wine, Chain and Dagger. (Quoted in Regardie 2000: 233)

ALEISTER CROWLEY, MAGUS AND PROPHET OF A NEW RELIGION

Aleister Crowley (1875–1947) was a leading figure besides MacGregor Mathers in the Golden Dawn. Crowley was the most important magician of the twentieth century (see Kaczynski 2002). He experienced a series of visions after 1900 and proclaimed himself the prophet of a new religion, 'Thelema', for the coming era. He caused a split in the Golden Dawn and founded his own order *Argentum astrum* (A∴A∴, 'Silver Star').[5] Crowley had a major influence on a further twentieth-century order, the *Ordo Templi Orientis* (O.T.O.), founded by Theodor Reuß and other German occultists, which largely through Crowley increasingly focused on sex-magic (see Möller and Howe 1986). Crowley combined Egyptian and Graeco-Roman deities with kabbalistic symbolism to create his own form of ritual magic (see Illustration 7 [next page]).

This combination of neo-pagan religiosity, traditions of Freemasonry and Rosicrucianism, and magical practice helps one to understand the rise of twentieth-century neo-paganism. Even the modern witchcraft movement, particularly the widely known Wicca cult, would scarcely exist but for the influence of these

---

5.   Other interpretations as to the meaning of A∴A∴ are possible, though.

groups. In his history of modern pagan witchcraft Ronald Hutton (1999: vii) states that 'it is the only religion which England has ever given the world'.

Illustration 7. Aleister Crowley with the headdress of Horus has raised his hands in the sign of Pan. Before him stands the book of Abramelin talismans; below left lies a cross decorated with a topaz. The photograph dates from 1910. (Aleister Crowley, *Magick. Buch Vier* [Liber ABA], translated into German by Michael DeWitt, vol. 2, Edition Ananael, Bad Ischl 1996)

HERMES AS A UNIVERSAL KEY

Let us return from magic to Hermetism and the fascination with Egypt. No lesser personage than Rudolf Steiner (1861–1925), who left the Theosophical Society in 1913 to found his own Anthroposophical Society, was actively engaged in this discourse. In September 1908 he gave eight lectures in Leipzig explaining the 'mystical truth' of the ancient mysteries of Egypt. Here one again encounters Hermes Trismegistus as the great initiator, Moses as a student of Egyptian mysteries, and Isis and Osiris as eternally vital spiritual beings. Steiner also dramatised their initiation rituals in his own mystery dramas. The fourth and last drama, *Der Seelen Erwachen* ('The Souls' Awakening', 1913), sets the seventh and eighth scene in 'an Egyptian temple. The location of an ancient initiation. Third cultural era of the Earth'. The external action reflects the transmutation of the initiate's soul from its submergence in the darkness of death to its rebirth in spiritual worlds.

Hermetic constructions are still very much with us today, as can be seen at a glance from the 'Emerald Tablets of Thoth the Atlantean' written by 'Doreal' in 1998 on behalf of the *Brotherhood of the White Temple*, obtainable in any good esoteric bookshop. In the foreword one reads:

> You are holding in your hands one of the oldest and most secret works of ancient wisdom, compiled by the great spiritual teacher Thoth. Many of today's incarnated workers of light personally studied with him in their earlier Atlantean and Egyptian incarnations, eventually receiving their initiation at his hands. Many readers today will therefore discover in these texts a renewed acquaintance with their own ancient knowledge.

These promises take us deep into the mysticism of the 'New Age' movement. The influence of the Theosophical Society and other factors have transformed the Hermetic-esoteric discourse of the twentieth century, although much older traditions are still evident in the palimpsest of its rich and varied heritage.

8

PIONEER OF MODERN ESOTERICISM: THE THEOSOPHICAL SOCIETY

Many scholars of religion regard 1875 as the birth of modern Western esotericism. That year witnessed the foundation of the Theosophical Society, without whose influence twentieth-century esotericism might scarcely have existed. There are several reasons why the Theosophical Society was the most important recurrent stimulus of esoteric discourses into the twentieth century. First, the modern esoteric traditions were mustered and repackaged in the writings of Helena Petrovna Blavatsky (1831–1891). Second, Eastern doctrines were assimilated in a Romantic view of the 'Orient', whereby the purest form of 'ancient wisdom' was rumoured to lie in India and Tibet. Third, Blavatsky's charismatic personality ensured her writings widespread acknowledgment as a revelation. Fourth, Blavatsky's 'Esoteric School' became the model for many other initiatory societies and magical orders in the Rosicrucian and Masonic tradition. Last, the Theosophical Society offers an outstanding example of the mixture of religious and scientific thought in modern Western societies, as the Theosophists had a lively dialogue with leading contemporary philologists and religious scholars, and so popularised their academic theories and knowledge.

HELENA PETROVNA BLAVATSKY: THE SPHINX OF THE WEST

THE EARLY YEARS

So many rumours and myths have gathered around the biography of Helena P. Blavatsky—or HPB, as she liked to be called—that a description of her character and life very much depends on the individual viewpoint.[1] She was born on 12 August 1831 as Helena Petrovna von Hahn in Ekaterinoslav in the Ukraine and spent her childhood surrounded by Russian nobility. Her father Peter Alexeyevich von Hahn was descended from a noble German family and served in the army,

---

1.   Meade 1980 is a good biography; Cranston 1995 also contains abundant material; see also Godwin 1994: 277-331. Goodrick-Clarke 2004a provides a very good introduction to the works of Blavatsky; see also his 'Introduction' (2004a: 1-20).

while her mother Helena Andreyevna de Fadeyev achieved renown as a novelist but died young, so that HPB grew up with her aristocratic maternal grandparents. In 1849 she married the vice-governor of Erevan, Nikifor Blavatsky, but their union was unhappy and brief. She soon left her husband and embarked on an adventurous life of travels which are still not fully documented. She visited Turkey, Greece, Egypt and France, arriving in London in 1851, the year of the Great Exhibition.

According to her own account, it was in Hyde Park that HPB met her 'Master', whom she had known in dreams since her childhood. He came towards her in the company of an Indian delegation. Later she wrote to A.P. Sinnett: 'Saw him twice. Once he came out of the crowd, then he ordered me to meet him in Hyde Park. I *cannot*, I *must not* speak of this. I would not publish it for the world' (quoted in Cranston 1995: 45). Henceforth Madame Blavatsky claimed to live in continuous contact with these 'Masters'. Who they exactly were is not easy to establish, even within the Theosophical Society. Sometimes they are simply distinguished individuals who can materialise and incarnate at various places, sometimes they are subtle forces of energy, who only assume corporeal form in order to appear visibly to humans.

The first model was Blavatsky's choice, for she described her teachers as Indian gurus, namely Mahatma Morya—known as 'Master M'—born in the Punjab, and Mahatma Koot Hoomi ('Master KH') from Kashmir. *The Theosophist* of October 1907 printed Blavatsky's following account:

> There is beyond the Himalayas a nucleus of Adepts, of various nationalities, and the Teshu [Panchen] Lama knows them, and they act together, and some of them are with him and yet remain unknown in their true character even to the average lamas— who are ignorant fools mostly. My Master and KH and several others I know personally are there, coming and going, and they are all in communication with Adepts in Egypt and Syria, and even Europe. (Quoted in Cranston 1995: 83)

The idea of a 'White Brotherhood', long current in Europe, merges here with mystical notions of the 'Orient' (see Johnson 1994). The notion of a mysterious community of sages has recurred in esoteric discourse ever since Plato's 'philosopher-kings' gave rise to utopias with an ideal and sometimes transcendent government. The Renaissance conceived of a succession of distinguished world teachers bearing the *prisca theologia*, an idea further elaborated by the Rosicrucians as a secret society. This tradition was now supplemented by European fantasies concerning 'sages of the Orient', the Mahatmas ('Great Souls') who, either from the mythical paradise of Shamballa or from spheres beyond the material world, mysteriously directed the destinies of men.

This idea was taken up by many writers at the end of the nineteenth century. In his book *The Great Initiates* (1889) Edouard Schuré (1841–1929) presented a tradition that replaced Persia with India, as might be expected at this time, giving the lineage Rama, Krishna, Hermes, Moses, Orpheus, Pythagoras, Plato, Jesus. Schuré was friendly with Rudolf Steiner and his wife Marie Steiner-von Sivers, who not only translated the book from French into German, but also produced Schuré's mystery-dramas on the stage. The German edition of *The Great Initiates* with a foreword by Rudolf Steiner appeared in its twentieth edition in 1992. The idea of a transcendent world of sages, who safeguard the memory of the ancient wisdom, has cardinal importance for twentieth-century esotericism. It can be seen in the Anthroposophical discourse of 'Christ impulses' or in the many 'channelled' messages of those 'entities', which make their knowledge available to selected individuals (see below, pp. 141-43).

After the first contact with her Master, HPB led an extremely turbulent life, which led her on journeys to Canada, Mexico, South America, the West Indies, Ceylon and India. In 1854 she allegedly crossed the Rocky Mountains with settlers in covered wagons. Many biographers accept her account of journeys to India, Kashmir, Russia, the Caucasus, France, Germany, Egypt and Italy, but her alleged visit to Tibet, where she claimed to study secret documents in Lamaist monasteries, is not confirmed by scholarship. Whatever one's view, these extensive journeys to mythically charged places in the history of mankind represent an important instrument for the legitimation of esoteric knowledge (see Hammer 2001). Even if HPB had undertaken only half of these journeys, it would have been a clear indication of her extraordinary character and her driving ambition to abandon bourgeois mores and to achieve an education and self-emancipation denied to most women of her generation. Her whole life was a provocation to the guardians of Victorian etiquette.

From Spiritualism to the Theosophical Society

Blavatsky's public career really began in 1872 with her attempt to found a magical club or a *société spirite* in Cairo and her arrival in New York in 1873. By this time HPB was already an experienced medium and she soon made contact with the spiritualist scene, increasingly popular in America since the 1850s. The development of American spiritualism is usually reckoned to date from the events which occurred at Hydesville, New York, in 1847. Soon after John D. Fox, his wife and six children had moved into their new house in Hydesville, they began to hear mysterious rapping sounds. These rappings were attributed to the ghost of a murdered pedlar, whose body had been buried in the cellar of the house. Two of the daughters, Margaret and Kate, developed a form of communication with the ghost, and more importantly, they discovered the commercial success of such conversations with spirits. The novelty spread like wildfire in the United States, and the Fox sisters became national celebrities, who could charge for their performances.

Other 'mediums' lost no time in jumping onto the bandwagon. In 1855 two million Americans were said to be convinced of the truth of the observed phenomena, which were now reported from many farms. Research groups were founded in order to study the matter scientifically, and the famous Society for Psychical Research, which became even better known for its clash with Madame Blavatsky, owed its origin to these enquiries. Many of the alleged spirit communications were unmasked as hoaxes, and when Margaret Fox, some forty years after the Hydesville rappings, publicly confessed that she and her sister had staged the whole affair, the movement suffered a severe blow (see Jenkins 2000: 39-41).

In point of fact 'spiritualism' did not begin with the events at Hydesville. The only novelty in these circumstances was their becoming an object of public debate (Godwin 1994: 187f.; cf. Chapter 10, *passim*). Communication with 'ascended beings'—whether the souls of the deceased or with other spirits—has a long history, in which the mysticism of Emanuel Swedenborg is an important chapter (see Hanegraaff 1996: 435-41). But spiritualism was significant for the history of American religion, as it influenced many Christian denominations and led to a series of new religions. Under the name of Allen Kardec, Hyppolyte Leon Denizard Rivail (1804–1869), well versed in magnetism, Mesmerism and esoteric traditions, founded an important new religion, after the 'Druid spirit source' had revealed messages to him. His work, *Le livre des esprits* ('The Book of Spirits', 1857), became a fundamental text of the colourful spiritualist movement, which according to conservative estimates today numbers over one hundred million followers worldwide, with the majority in South America. Spiritualism was also an important factor for religious seekers outside the institutional churches, which Robert C. Fuller calls 'the emergence of unchurched America' (Fuller 2001: 38-44).

Helena Blavatsky was in any case very interested in the spiritualist debates of her time. In October 1874 she met Colonel Henry Steel Olcott (1832–1907), who was at that moment publishing a series of newspaper articles on spiritualist phenomena taking place at a farm in Vermont. For all their differences of personality, a close relationship developed between Blavatsky and her 'Theosophical twin'. Olcott was an advocate with a flourishing practice specialising in commercial law, and had earlier undertaken the public enquiry into the assassination of Abraham Lincoln. He had long been interested in esoteric subjects and was close to the Freemasons. He became Blavatsky's principal partner and was chiefly responsible for organising what would become the Theosophical Society.

On 9 March 1875 Colonel Olcott received a mysterious letter, written in golden ink and addressed to the 'Neophytos Olcott'. The sender identified himself as a certain 'Tuitit Bey, Grand Master of the mystical Brotherhood of Luxor'. Further letters followed from the 'Masters', in which Olcott was summoned to publish various articles in a New York newspaper about occultism and similar topics. Later he was encouraged to concern himself with HPB and her public influence.

In May 1875 Olcott founded the Miracle Club, without knowing that a group of that name already existed in London. Blavatsky was probably not a member of this club, but wrote in her scrapbook in July 1875: 'Orders received from India direct to establish a philosophico-religious Society and choose a name for it—also to choose Olcott' (quoted in Cranston 1995: 143). This commission was shortly fulfilled, for at a lecture by the architect and engineer George H. Felt on 'The lost canon of proportion of the Egyptians, Greeks and Romans', held on 7 September 1875 in Blavatsky's apartment before an audience of seventeen persons, Olcott had the idea of founding a new society. At successive meetings Olcott was elected president and after some leafing through a dictionary it was decided to call it the Theosophical Society.

The goals of the organisation were later defined as follows: (1) To form the nucleus of a universal brotherhood of humanity, without distinction of race, creed, sex, caste or colour; (2) The study of ancient and modern religions, philosophies and sciences; (3) The investigation of the unexplained laws of nature and psychical powers latent in man. These very goals demonstrate that the Theosophical Society bridged esotericism, the comparative study of philology and religion and the heritage of the Enlightenment.

THE 'CANONICAL' WORKS

Shortly after the foundation of the Theosophical Society, Madame Blavatsky, now sharing an apartment with Olcott, began working feverishly on her first major book. Many myths of doubtful truth have gathered around the composition of *Isis Unveiled*. Frequently dozens of pages of good English in a neat hand, as if written by a spirit, were discovered in the morning on her writing desk. Olcott claimed that the work was entirely written in the 'astral light' and that the Mahatmas rather than Blavatsky were its real authors.

On the one hand, HPB was indisputably possessed of mediumistic powers, which could have played a certain role in the creation of her major works. Even Blavatsky's account that she almost daily felt the presence of her Master, who was within her body and communicated knowledge otherwise inaccessible to her, describes a widespread phenomenon known today as channelling. On the other hand, there is little in *Isis Unveiled* that could not have been gathered from contemporary literature. Critics of the Theosophical Society close to the Society for Psychical Research took much trouble to prove that Blavatsky's works offered gleanings from about a hundred books, which were mostly available in Olcott's library. One might thereby suppose that Olcott also had a share in the composition of the extensive works of his 'Theosophical twin'.

These questions did not harm the book's success, which was published as *Isis Unveiled: A Master Key to the Mysteries of Ancient and Modern Science and Theology* in 1877. The first edition of one thousand copies had sold out within ten days, and some 500,000 copies have been sold up to the present day. The next year HPB travelled to India and settled in Bombay, where the Theosophical Society enjoyed an extremely positive response. Its construction of an 'Oriental spirituality' as the 'ancient wisdom' of mankind significantly contributed to the strengthening of an anti-colonial identity in India. In 1882 the headquarters of the Society were moved to Adyar near Madras. The wave of sympathy which embraced the Theosophists in India and Ceylon had strong political implications. One may cite the example of S. Radhakrishnan, the philosopher and President of India, who stated:

> When, with all kinds of political failures and economic breakdowns we (Indians) were suspecting the values and vitality of our culture, when everything round about us and secular education happened to discredit the value of Indian culture, the Theosophical Movement rendered great service by vindicating those values and ideas. The influence of the Theosophical Movement on general Indian society is incalculable. (Quoted in Cranston 1995: 192)

The most prominent example of this influence is Mahatma Gandhi, who became acquainted with the Theosophical Society during his law studies at London in 1889. In his autobiography he describes how, like many other intellectuals of his time, he first gained access to his own culture through his encounter with the Theosophical Society. For the first time he read the *Bhagavad Gita*, which later became a central reference point in his philosophy and politics.[2]

Illustration 8. The official emblem of the Theosophical Society, developed from the personal seal of Madame Blavatsky, consists of the Gnostic symbol of the serpent biting its own tail (*Ouroboros*), the left-rotating swastika from Hindu tradition, the Star of David as the 'Seal of Solomon' as well as the Egyptian 'ankh' cross. This combination expresses the idea that all wisdom-traditions share in a common truth. (Theosophical Society in England)

During their time in India the Theosophists would also experience serious setbacks. There were increasing accusations of fraud, whereby the Mahatma letters were alleged to be forgeries, and Blavatsky was supposed to have supplemented her 'mediumistic powers' with all sorts of tricks, which led to a loss of prestige for the Theosophical Society in Europe and North America. Space does not permit a detailed account here of how the relationship between Blavatsky and Olcott deteriorated. More important is the major work of Blavatsky, which she wrote as if possessed in the last years of her life. Following her return to Europe, she published *The Secret Doctrine: The Synthesis of Science, Religion and Philosophy* in the autumn of 1888. The first volume was entitled 'Cosmogenesis', the second

2. The Theosophical Society is thus a decisive factor in the twentieth-century discourse of 'Orientalism'; see Kippenberg and von Stuckrad 2003: 37-48.

'Anthropogenesis', while a third volume 'Esotericism' was published posthumously in 1897. Here Blavatsky elaborated the foundations of her complex Theosophical theory of the creation of man, the structure of the universe, and the ancient truth of all the religions which derived from a single common source. She referred particularly to notions drawn from Hindu and Buddhist religion, which she fashioned into the embodiment of the (Aryan) religion. She was by no means alone in this enterprise, as we know from scholarly debate at the end of the nineteenth century.

In the foreword to the first edition, the author (referred to rather as the 'scribe') emphasises that the 'truths contained in the book are in no sense presented as a *revelation*'. Blavatsky claims instead that she is presenting the translation of an ancient document of Asian occult literature, which only she has been allowed to read. Originally transmitted only orally as the 'Book of Dzyan' and 'hinted at in the almost countless volumes of Brahminical, Chinese and Tibetan temple-literature' (Volume I: xxiii), the original text written in an unknown language is in the safe-keeping of initiated adepts in the East. Subsequently, many philologists felt challenged to investigate the oracular language of the Book of Dzyan, but apart from an echo of Sanskrit and other languages they could give no definite explanation. If one cannot accept the Theosophical view, one would have to say that the 'Stanzas' within *The Secret Doctrine* are an extremely creative production of their ingenious authoress.

As a document in the history of twentieth-century religion the significance of *The Secret Doctrine* can scarcely be overstated. On the one hand, it simultaneously summarises and popularises the basic assumptions of major esoteric currents, on the other it introduced the trend towards 'Eastern spirituality' which is still very influential on today's esoteric scene.

ASCENDED MASTERS AND MUNDANE SQUABBLES

Blavatsky's final years were marked by conflict, and even after her death the Theosophical Society was riven by disputes over succession. Moreover, the 'ascended masters' were by no means free of such earthbound emotions. The 'Mahatma letters', which had been sent since 1880 to leading members of the Society, chiefly A.P. Sinnett and A.O. Hume, reflected the 'only too human'. The Masters complain about a lack of paper, take sideswipes at other rival Masters, deprecate human weakness and evince a misogyny, which seems astonishing given Blavatsky's role (e.g. women are described as 'a terrible calamity in this fifth race', as they lack all male powers of concentration).

After her move to London in 1887, Blavatsky's activities demonstrate the increasing tension between individual wings of the Theosophical Society, but also between herself and Olcott. She was still busy writing in her final years. In 1889 she published *The Key to Theosophy* and *The Voice of Silence* (for which the Dalai Lama wrote a warm acknowledgement in 1993), but much of her energy was directed towards securing her own position. The power struggle between Olcott and HPB was initially defused by Blavatsky founding her own Esoteric Section (or Esoteric School) in England, whose members were chiefly drawn from the previously formed Blavatsky Lodge, while Olcott was responsible for the affairs of the Indian Section (Adyar). The Esoteric School effectively acted as an inner circle of Blavatsky's closest male and female followers, and its teachings, initiations, and courses of instruction remained largely secret. By re-founding a British Section, HPB claimed yet more authority for herself, which Olcott, as president of the Society, would no longer tolerate. Blavatsky therefore declared her own British lodges independent of Adyar in 1890, simultaneously claiming to represent all of Europe. The break was thereby complete and would continue to influence the later history of the Theosophical Society, after Blavatsky's death on 8 May 1891.

The Wars of Succession and Schisms

After Blavatsky's death the Theosophical Society continued to be led by Olcott and other disputants. At this time Annie Besant (1847–1933) came to the fore. Besant had first joined the Society after writing a review of *The Secret Doctrine*. This discovery marked the close of a painful time in her life, when the quest for religious fulfilment had led her to break away from her marriage to an Anglican clergyman. Parallels with the life of Blavatsky will be evident. Besant strengthened the orientation towards India during the whole period of her leadership of the Society, which led to further schisms. Katherine Tingley (1847–1929) pursued a clearly different agenda by placing practical and social interests at the heart of her teachings. Supported by W.Q. Judge, a co-founder of the Theosophical Society, Tingley sought to give this movement an institutional basis by founding her own centre in 1897 at Pasadena near San Diego. Its guiding principle was the foundation of a new global society with new educational systems, new forms of horticulture and provision for theatre and the arts. Many ideas of the later 'New Age' movement are borrowed especially in their political aspect from Tingley's brand of Theosophy (see below). The Pasadena centre still publishes the magazine *Sunrise*, and according to its own report there are almost fifty centres with approximately one hundred groups worldwide.

Before returning to Annie Besant, a further Theosophist played an important role in the esoteric history of the twentieth century. In 1902 Rudolf Steiner (1861–1925) joined the Theosophical Society and became, together with his later wife Marie von Sivers, the first General Secretary of the Theosophical Society in Germany. Steiner was also a member of the Esoteric Section, founded by Blavatsky, and led its German section. His later claim that he was the first to establish such a section is clearly false. Indeed, his account of events is strongly slanted to suggest that his 'Theosophical phase', which lasted for more than ten years, was a completely independent gestation period for the foundation of his own Anthroposophical Society in 1913. However, if one examines his lectures prior to 1910, the close relationship between their contents and the writings of Blavatsky are quite obvious. Even the borrowing of the magazine title *Luzifer* ('Light Bringer'), from HPB's London journal founded in September 1887, demonstrates Steiner's proximity to Theosophy. Even in this case, Steiner advertised the idea as his own.

Steiner's involvement in the philosophical and intellectual debates of Germany, however, represented an important difference between his interests and the British–Indian brand of Theosophy. His book *Die Philosophie der Freiheit* ('The Philosophy of Freedom', 1894) clearly demonstrates the influences of Max Stirner and Friedrich Nietzsche. Later on he found himself at odds with the Theosophical emphasis on 'Oriental wisdom-teachings'. He opposed this with his own Christian world-view, which interpreted the development of human history as the product of so-called 'Christ impulses', a scheme which combined the doctrine of successive world-teachers with Christian mystical tradition.

Annie Besant had no time for his ideas, as her expectation of a new world-teacher was quite different. 'The climax of all this [Mrs Besant's activities] came when it was asserted that Christ would appear in a new earth-life within a certain Hindu boy. For the propagation of this absurdity a special society, *The Star of the East*, was founded within the Theosophical Society' (Steiner 1980: 362). When Steiner split off with his Anthroposophical Society from the Theosophical Society, most of the German Theosophists followed him, and the Theosophical Society in Germany became a shadow of its former self.

Yet another schism should be mentioned, which became particularly important in the United States because of its strongly Christian tendency. Born into a Christian fundamentalist milieu, Alice Ann Bailey (1880–1949) joined the Theosophical Society in 1915 but was expelled in 1923 on account of her Christian creed, whereupon she founded the 'Arcane School', still internationally active today. The objective of Arcane School Theosophy, which only admits adults according to strict criteria, is the recognition of the individual balance of karma. At the heart of its teachings lies the 'Great Invocation', a sort of mantra or magical formula, which should be recited as often as possible by the adepts. This serves to restore cosmic harmony and prepare for the Second Coming of Christ. As the idea of the transformation of the world into a new era, a common theme in the millenarian discourses of Christianity, is relevant for broad sections of twentieth-century esotericism, the 'Great Invocation' is quoted here:

> From the point of Light within the Mind of God
> Let light stream forth into the minds of men.
> Let Light descend on Earth.

> From the point of Love within the Heart of God
> Let love stream forth into the hearts of men.
> May Christ return to Earth.

> From the centre where the Will of God is known
> Let purpose guide the little wills of men—
> The purpose which the masters know and serve.

From the centre which we call the race of men
Let the Plan of Love and Light work out
And may it seal the door where evil dwells.

Let Light and Love and Power restore the Plan on Earth.

Like Blavatsky before her, Bailey also claimed that her writings had been written by an 'ascended Master' (in her case the Tibetan Dhwal Khul) and only received by her. Bailey also practised a form of astrology mystically influenced by Theosophy. She published a five-volume work under the title *A Treatise on the Seven Rays*, whose third volume *Esoteric Astrology* was devoted entirely to this mystical astrology. Even if there are few readers who have worked right through this extensive and often impenetrable book, the influence of esoteric astrology was immense. The work has the power of revelation for many spiritually minded astrologers and it is still available in esoteric bookshops.

The impact of Bailey's Arcane School upon esotericism in the second half of the twentieth century can be deduced from the fact that it maintains centres in New York, London, Geneva and Buenos Aires. A leaflet entitled 'What is an esoteric school?' and published around 1998 by the Lucis Trust in Geneva reads as follows:

> Today there exists no esoteric school which prepares individuals for initiation. Those that claim this are deceiving the public. One can teach followers in an academic sense, but by contrast initiation is always an individual goal, which each person can reach only by contact with the world of spiritual being. (p. 12, quoted from the German edition)

An esoteric school comes into existence, the leaflet continues, as 'advanced disciples' recognise their task in the world. The life of the disciple thereby becomes 'magnetic, radiant and dynamic, whereby he attracts and gathers those whom he can help. He thereby becomes *the living centre of a vital organism, but not the leader of an organisation.*' In New Age jargon such disciples are frequently called 'light workers'. This reflects the notion that the world will be transformed into light by a group of specially elect persons playing a key role:

> These followers, who have the difficult task of founding new schools, are known as 'world-disciples'. They extend their influence in all directions, upset the old schools, attracting students from them who are ready for the new teachings. They found new schools, which represent a staging-post between the old and the future schools. They influence the consciousness of human beings everywhere in the world, extending the horizon of the public, and giving humanity new ideas and new opportunities for development. This is the present situation. Seekers must therefore be able to distinguish between the well-meaning aspirant, who founds a school for beginners, the follower who is learning to be a teacher, and the world-disciple, who rejects the old teaching methods and teaches occult truths in a way suited to the times. The Arcane School is a part of this worldwide movement. (p. 16f.)

A final schism from the parent Adyar movement should be mentioned here. The United Lodge of Theosophists, founded in 1919 by Robert Crosby (1849–1919) as a reaction to the disputes between the various theosophical splinter groups, is still active today. In the United Lodge an attempt is made to avoid any kind of personality cult and the tendency towards bureaucracy: there is no membership and lectures and publications are largely anonymous. One might describe this as the 'anarchistic section' of the Theosophical Society.

There are a whole range of further groups close to the Theosophical Society, but as institutionalised associations they have little significance. Today the total membership of the Adyar Society is estimated at 40,000, the Pasadena Society deriving from Tingley at 2,000, and the United Lodge at 1,000 persons worldwide.

THE STAR IN THE EAST

Let us return to Annie Besant and her expectation of the coming of a world-teacher, which so amused Steiner. Helena Blavatsky had already alluded to the possibility of such a coming in her writings, but not in the concrete form now propagated at Adyar, where its chief advocates were Annie Besant and Charles W. Leadbeater (1847–1934), who had been a member of the Theosophical Society since 1883 and contributed greatly to the popularity of the movement through his publications. When Leadbeater observed a Hindu boy at play in 1909, he immediately recognised in him the reincarnation of the Buddha Maitreya and thus the future world-teacher. His name was Jiddu Krishnamurti (1895–1986). Krishnamurti was henceforth groomed for his great role at Adyar, received an English education and was supported in his contact with the Great Brotherhood especially by Besant. A year after his first initiation the Order of the Star in the East was founded in 1911. Without going into its complex history, I would point out that the prophecy of the world-teacher was fulfilled but not in the way that the Theosophists expected. Highly aware of his special spiritual vocation, Krishnamurti increasingly distanced himself from the authoritarian structure of the Theosophical Society, to which he opposed his ideal of the free individual who may depend on no authorities whatsoever. The death of his brother provided the trigger for his separation from Theosophy. On 3 August 1929 Krishnamurti renounced his role of Messiah and world-teacher in front of 3,000 members of the Order of the Star in the East and, as its president, dissolved the order itself. The speech he made on this occasion contains the essence of his teaching, which he would reiterate until his death:

> I maintain that Truth is a pathless land, and you cannot approach it by any path whatsoever, by any religion, by any sect. That is my point of view, and I adhere to that absolutely and unconditionally. Truth, being limitless, unconditioned, unapproachable by any path whatsoever, cannot be organised; nor should any organisation be formed to lead or coerce people along any particular path. (Jayakar 1988: 86)

Krishnamurti's teachings have been taken up in an eclectic fashion. For many in the New Age movement he has become an iconic spiritual authority, who renounced his role in consideration for his disciples.

9

ESOTERICISM AND MODERNITY

The years between the Enlightenment and the Romantic movement witnessed many debates which were highly influential on the development of modern esotericism. There was an increasing process of differentiation in social systems in modernity. At the same time, the individual acquired increasing personal responsibility for his or her religious and cultural identity. The sociologist Anthony Giddens has described this as a form of 'disembedding' from a safe, comforting order. The critical attitude to religion of the Enlightenment and the increasing rationalisation of the cosmos and life had not only produced gains. There was also a sense of loss, leading to a renewed search for meaning and a desire for the 're-enchantment' of the world. Far from introducing secularisation, natural science can also serve to produce 'meaning', as can the academic study of religion, by the popular reception of more scholarship on non-European cultures. These processes cannot be accommodated in a single narrative. There are rather *multiple modernities*, a multiplicity of reactions to the challenges of modernity.

MODERNITY AND ITS DISCONTENTS

DISENCHANTMENT AND RE-ENCHANTMENT

A major characteristic of the 'modern' in industrialised societies consists in the increasing separation of the sacred and profane spheres of existence. By contrast, pre-industrial societies tend towards a more symbolical way of thinking. In their 'sacramental view', the various aspects of reality are not considered as separate realms, but as a relatively unified whole and thus accessible to control in numerous ways. In modern Europe this unified way of thinking was subjected to a process of disintegration. 'The differentiation of domains…made it in the long run impossible, or at least illegitimate, to engage in activities that mingled the increasingly distinct religious and material realms.' But this is only half the story, because 'it is necessary to emphasize that the extrication of religion from the material world was, and still is, a contested process' (Benavides 1998: 198). On the one hand, there was the increasing rationalisation of nature, which expelled modern man from the entire framework of natural events, and on the other, a counter-reaction which sought the renewed sacralisation of nature, the cosmos and material reality.

Max Weber's analysis of religion is helpful in explaining this dynamic. There are many explanatory models bearing on modern esotericism and the philosophy of nature in his work, *Wirtschaftsethik der Weltreligionen* ('Economic Ethics of the World Religions'). Here Weber described the modern tendency towards a theoretical and practical rationalisation of the world and the conduct of life as a major turning-point in culture and society. He is quite certain that this process of *disenchantment of the world* has produced an irreversible breach of fundamental importance for modernity (see Weber 1988: 254; 1992: 87 and 68). Mankind could still lose its belief in the predictability of all things, and its confidence in comprehending the universe. Whenever science is itself the product of a specific history of religion—the biblical account of creation anticipated the de-spiritualisation of the cosmos—then the rejection of this religious tradition by the educated elite could also jeopardise this precondition for rational science. Disenchantment is thus no completed event but brings other challenges in its wake.

> The more intellectualism suppresses the belief in magic and thus 'disenchants' worldly events, so that they lose their magical meaning, the more urgent becomes the demand for the world and the conduct of life to appear significant and meaningful as a whole. (Weber 2001: 273)

This formulation makes it clear that disenchantment is not a secure accomplishment, but produces deficits which demand new solutions.

Modern esotericism may be understood as an example of the dialectic of the rationalisation of religion and life on the one hand, and the quest for individual salvation and resacralisation of an indivisible cosmos on the other. Tendencies towards the secularisation of the material world have been present since antiquity, but they were greatly reinforced in the nineteenth and early twentieth centuries, especially in enlightened intellectual circles, which no longer subscribed to the Christian interpretation of the world. Pantheism became the religion of the intellectuals, and since the Romantic era the philosophy of nature has combined with a specific reverence for nature (Gladigow 1989). In Chapter 6 I have already shown how the interaction between natural science and religion led to a pantheistic discourse. However, it was not only the discursive transfers between natural science and religion that became crucial to modern esotericism. The academic study of religion, and literary and artistic responses to the contemporary world, should not be underestimated in their effects on popular religious culture.

The interweavings of esoteric and political agendas in the twentieth century are important in this context. Claims to truth and knowledge sought outside the Judaeo-Christian tradition could easily be linked with *völkisch* or Germanic racialist ideas. The alliance of anti-Semitic and anti-Christian currents with racialist theories, which could in turn refer back to Theosophical ideas, led in German National Socialism to a political ideology, which made extensive use of esoteric and occult themes. National Socialism has been rightly described as a political religion, in which esoteric hermeneutics—for instance, the 'gnostic' symbolism of light—and individual occult groups have played a significant role.[1]

AHISTORICAL APPROACHES

Three scholars occupy a prominent position among today's heroes of esoteric literature: Carl Gustav Jung, Mircea Eliade and Joseph Campbell. In his four-volume work *The Masks of God* (1960–68) Campbell presented a psychological interpretation of myths, whose generalised discourse about universal symbols also appeared in many self-descriptions of esoteric provenance. He referred to the theory of 'archetypes', which C.G. Jung had developed and which was soon assimilated into the standard repertoire of psychological and religious interpretation in a New Age context. I will come back to this theory and its influence in the next section. First, I want to outline the influence of the historian of religion, Mircea Eliade (1907–86).

In all his writings, Eliade is motivated to discover the timeless centre of 'religion' which is always changing its external form, an idea that recalls features of *prisca theologia* (see von Stuckrad 2003c: 123-35). Of course there are no pure, original phenomena, but aided by the phenomenological method, one may deduce the main themes and constants of religious life. By personalising 'history', Eliade casts it as the effective counterpart of true religiosity. For Eliade, religion becomes a longing for an era before the 'fall into history', while archaic man becomes the religious exemplar. This *homo religiosus* is the ideal type for contact with the sacred, which Eliade contrasts with a mankind that has fallen into history.[2] The gospel of Eliade states that although we are increasingly severed from our mythical origins and religious source by the dominion of history, and in this sense the history of religion is a process of decadence, we have under certain circumstances the opportunity of approaching the sacred. Modern man is oblivious to myths but still receptive to their music.

Eliade thereby made an important contribution to the esoteric discourse of the twentieth century and its influence was felt in both academic circles and even more strongly in popular discourse.

SACRALISATION OF THE PSYCHE

The decision to seek the 'true centre' of the personality in the soul, and the idea of separating body and soul are by no means self-evident, but the result of an

---

1. See Ley and Schoeps 1997. For the standard works on the role of esoteric groups in German National Socialism see Goodrick-Clarke 2002 and 2004b. Today there are a range of societies in the neopagan milieu, describing themselves as 'neo-Teutons' or 'neo-pagans', which subscribe to such ideologies. These are extremist minorities, whose anti-Semitic and anti-Christian beliefs predominate over their esoteric interests.

2. Here there are clear parallels with Hermann Hesse, who described working on his novel *Das Glasperlenspiel* ('The Glass Bead Game', 1943) an intellectual antidote to the tragic circumstances of the present, namely the 1930s and the Second World War.

historical development already initiated by Platonism in the ancient world (see above, pp. 13-15). For many contemporary psychologists the assertion that the soul has a history is still somewhat controversial. It is much too firmly accepted that psychology and psychiatry are dealing with transhistorical mechanisms and symbols, so that their own conceptual framework is seldom challenged. One reason for this is the traditional orientation of psychology towards medicine with its modern mechanistic-scientific assumptions, which deprecates metaphysical speculations about the soul as irreconcilable with its own aspiration to scientific status.

Recent studies from the psychological camp have questioned this perspective. Cultural studies have embraced psychology, suggesting that scientific views are not dependent on a given 'reality', but that science itself is subject to social constructions, as are ideas about transhistorically valid truths. Psychoanalysis has naturally always been interested in cultural contexts, but has seldom given attention to the conditionality of its own investigative procedure. Today there is a range of psychotherapeutic models, which try to manage without normative statements concerning the spiritual life. The last two decades have simultaneously witnessed the discipline of historical psychology, which has now produced a crop of remarkable studies (see Jüttemann et al. 1991). It is increasingly evident that the boundaries of Western self-understanding are the product of historical constructions, all with their own philosophical and religious assumptions.

What is special about esoteric traditions is their tendency, not only to regard the human soul in a Neo-Platonic sense as the 'true centre' of man, but to grant this effectively divine status. The combination of the individual soul and the world-soul in Renaissance thinkers such as Ficino has already been discussed. It was Giovanni Pico della Mirandola who took up the notion of man as the bridge between transcendence and immanence, but then promoted man to the 'chain of supreme beings' and effectively deified him (see above, pp. 60-61). This revaluation of the concept of personhood by Renaissance thinkers like Ficino and Pico and their institutionalisation of esoteric study in learned academies made an important contribution to the idea of 'higher' or 'absolute knowledge' in the eighteenth century. Indeed, 'the divine man of the Renaissance is the basis of modern thought about human autonomy' (Neugebauer-Wölk 1999: 201). The human being no longer needs a mediator with God, but can now redeem himself.

This image of the human being is ubiquitous in twentieth-century esotericism. Transpersonal psychology, for instance, stands squarely within this tradition. By relating the human soul to cosmic dimensions and seeing the highest task of man—his individuation—as his absorption in transcendent universal spheres, transpersonal psychology perpetuates ideas from the Renaissance and early modern period. These involve a holism of the human soul and a sacred world soul, which are not characterised by an act of divine grace, but through man's own absorption in his own divinity. Corresponding anthropological assumptions may also be found in modern esotericism. Unlike the anthropology of many non-Western cultures, the esoteric concept of personhood places a high value on the individual, who perfects himself through harmony with cosmic forces.[3]

Carl Gustav Jung (1875–1961) played a major role in elaborating the modern esoteric concept of the soul. Besides psychology, Jung was always interested in the history of religion, conducted an intensive exchange of ideas with its leading scholars,[4] and developed a theory of universal symbols pertaining to the soul. According to Jung, these 'archetypes' could be identified through an analysis of the history of religion. Jung made an extensive study of alchemical symbols, which could thus be regarded as a key to understanding elementary transformations of the human soul. Astrological symbols once again acquired a universal status on the basis of psychological astrology. Largely through Jung's influence there arose a new way of reading the history of alchemy and astrology which placed the inner transformation of the adept at the centre of esoteric operations, an idea hardly supported by the actual sources (see Principe and Newman 2001).

Jung's importance in modern esotericism goes far beyond this. Because Jung interpreted the human Self as the spiritual Sun, he provided a foundation for the sacralization of the human soul, which led directly to a new religion. A movement reflecting a 'cult of the inner Sun' (with evident borrowings from *völkisch* ideas in the nineteenth and twentieth centuries) grew up around the mystified figure of Jung (Noll 1997). Jung's work thus represents a direct link between the German Romantic philosophy of nature and the present-day 'New Age' movement, in that he sacralised the psyche and simultaneously psychologised the sacred (Hanegraaff 1996: 513; for this whole subject see Heelas 1996).

THE SOUL AS A LANDSCAPE

By positing a transcendent, timeless, true reality and the sacralisation of the 'inner centre' of man, Eliade, Campbell and Jung offered an esoteric discourse which devalued modernity and the present age. A few examples, perhaps surprising ones, will suffice to show that this was a broad intellectual movement and not just restricted to a few representatives of the 'New Age' movement.

Parallel to the idea that the soul is the 'true centre' of the personality there arose the equally influential notion of the 'soul as landscape' (see Gladigow 1993: 121-30; von Stuckrad 2003c: 257-63). Following on from Plato's idea of the world soul, developed in turn by Renaissance authors, the period between Enlightenment and Romanticism produced the idea that the journey into the interior of the soul can be compared with a voyage of discovery to unknown regions of the world. Novalis'

---

3.   Once again, the individual is by no means a self-evident fact in anthropological discourse. 'Individuality might not be an "essence of man", but the historical and specific result of contemporary discourses and practice', writes Michael Sonntag in his *Geschichte der Individualität* (Sonntag 1999: 19). Likewise, there is a close relationship between esoteric concepts of the soul and person, with the central role accorded to individuality in the modern West.

4.   As in the Eranos Conferences, in which scholars from various disciplines regularly exchanged their views; see Wasserstrom 1999 and Hakl 2001.

work, already discussed, certainly belongs in this context. However, the connection between inner and outer journeys was already the object of literary endeavour before Novalis (Guthke 1983: 250-71). A glance at the work of Hermann Hesse and science fiction once again shows how this idea is picked up and extended in the current esoteric scene.

In Hermann Hesse's novel *Steppenwolf* (1927), Harry Haller (H.H. are the author's initials) finds the truth of the world in the interior of his soul. Despite his longing for death and contempt for all 'superficiality' he must learn this truth in order to attain the perfection and immortality of his spirit. Hermine, who like him has 'one dimension too many' (Hesse 1974: 165), becomes the mirror of his own soul, whose depths he must plumb in full consciousness, before he can reintegrate the many parts of his personality and enter into eternity. Concerning this knowledge he says:

> Once more my soul breathed, my eye had vision, and for some moments I had a burning suspicion that I only needed to gather the scattered images of my life as the Steppenwolf in order to enter the world of the images and become immortal. Was not this the goal towards which every human life tends and is directed? (Hesse 1974: 155)

The home of the soul—Hesse writes in a Platonic sense—lies beyond time and space. Hermine makes the point:

> It is the realm beyond time and illusion. We belong there, there is our home, that is where our heart tends, Steppenwolf, and that is why we long for death… Oh, Harry, we have to grope through so much muck and nonsense in order to reach home! And we have no one to lead us, our only guide is homesickness. (Hesse 1974: 168)

Thus Hermine, the mirror, conjures before Harry Haller 'the sacred world beyond, the timeless realm, the world of eternal worth and divine substance' (Hesse 1974: 169), the goal of all his striving, which he may only reach by recognising the evil of the world as his own and learning to laugh at it. The 'laughter of the immortals', the laughter of Goethe and Mozart, become for him a symbol of the soul's homecoming to eternity. 'And "eternity" was nothing but the redemption of time, was so to speak its return to innocence, its reversal in space' (Hesse 1974: 169).[5]

Harry Haller sets off on a journey among the mirrors of his own inner world. In the novel this is the 'Magic Theatre', shown to him by Pablo, who seems a shallow fellow but is actually a musician who has ascended to immortality. Pablo's speech to Harry is particularly interesting for our discussion:

> You long to leave this time, this world, this reality and enter another reality more suited to you, a world without time. Do that, dear friend, I invite you. But you know where this other world lies hidden, that it is the world of your own soul, that you are seeking. That other reality which you long for lives only in your own inner world. I

---

5.   Here again one sees the proximity of Hermann Hesse and Mircea Eliade, two intellectuals who regard the realm of spirit as the primordial place of freedom and, confronted with the total dehumanization of the world through two World Wars, as their personal refuge.

can give you nothing that does not already exist in you yourself, I can open no other hall of pictures than the one of your own soul. (Hesse 1974: 190f.)

The landscapes of the outer world of images are thus also a mirror of inner landscapes in *Steppenwolf*. Exactly as in modern esotericism, which has taken Hermann Hesse into its pantheon, we see the tendency to regard the outer world as a shallow illusion and beyond it the parallel inner worlds as the real realm of truth and knowledge.[6]

Neither Hesse nor Eliade took the path of transpersonal psychology. Harry Haller's soul worlds are not a suitable model for the collective unconscious, but are rather a realm of the spirit, accessible only to the person with 'one dimension too many'. For this reason, the adoption of Hesse's work by the New Age movement of the 1960s rests upon a misinterpretation. However, once again we see in *Steppenwolf* the Platonising tradition, which assumes parallel worlds and makes their mingling and reflection the focus of interest. Finally, it places the individual person at the centre of these worlds as the master narrator of his life and as a voyager beyond time and space, into the mirror world of his soul.

In his poem 'Es winkt zu Fühlung fast aus allen Dingen' ('Almost all things seek to touch'), Rainer Maria Rilke described how *inner space*, which extends through 'all beings', corresponds to the external world. In science fiction literature, especially in the second half of the twentieth century, the voyage to remote and unknown worlds in space can often be seen as a metaphor for the journey into the hidden worlds of one's own soul. The theme of *inner space* as a logical counterpart to *outer space* was introduced into science fiction by James Graham Ballard and applied to a whole series of novels in which he referred to Freud, Beckett, Jung and others. The 'New Wave' movement later caught on in the American scene, and Roger Zelazny's *Lord of Light* (1967) or Samuel R. Delany's *The Einstein Intersection* (1967) were soon regarded as influential examples of the new neo-Romantic trend.

The connection between outer history and inner processes of cognition was not only a theme of the 'New Wave' movement, but is plainly evident in George Lucas' *Star Wars* trilogy, surely one of the most successful science fiction productions of all time. In my view, this history is best interpreted as a 'gnostic' drama that revolves around the ideas of good and evil, the demiurge, archons, the fall and self-redemption. A key to its meaning occurs in the scene in Episode 5, in which Luke Skywalker (his name is a combination of 'Lucifer' [Light-bringer] and 'voyager in the heavens') is sent by his teacher Yoda (whose name also recalls a kabbalistic name of God) into a subterranean cave to encounter 'the dark side of power'. This

---

6.   'The premise is that the unconscious holds the answers to all questions', writes Wouter J. Hanegraaff (1996: 255), who concludes that the transpersonal movement identifies the angelic and demonic realms as realms of the human unconscious. '[T]his collective unconscious is in turn identified as an objective transpersonal realm accessed in the holotropic mode of consciousness. This is how the 'gods' that seemed to have been banned from heaven reappear—without losing any of their power—from the depths of the human psyche' (p. 252).

appears to him as the fearsome figure of a fallen Yedi knight (Darth Vader), who now serves the 'Imperator'. When Luke Skywalker succeeds in decapitating his opponent, the latter's head turns out to be his own. As in Harry Haller's case, he must learn to experience his own dark potential before he can expose himself to universal power. The external action involving a descent into the cave amid a swampy, fog-bound and dangerous landscape is a symbol for the journey into Luke's inner world.

AND THE 'NEW AGE'?

Everyone has somehow heard of the 'New Age' and connects it with 'esotericism', but no one really knows exactly what the term means. Worse still, this confusion not only applies to popular notions of the 'New Age' but also to the academic world. Although many books have been written on the subject, there is no settled consensus on its definition. Unfortunately, the collective term 'New Age' embraces so many varied currents, groups and identities, that any attempt at systematisation appears artificial. There are also different approaches. Although the history of ideas can demonstrate certain continuities among its constituent religious traditions, an empirical sociological analysis shows there is no united movement sharing common views. Moreover, those involved in the movement no longer refer to the 'New Age' and even regard it as a term of abuse.[7]

The idea of a succession of temporal eras is as old as the European history of religion. When one speaks of a 'new age', one cannot mean this general idea. The usage of the term actually goes back only as far as the nineteenth century. The English poet and artist William Blake (1757–1827) used the word as a catchword in the 1804 preface to his poem *Milton*, but this of course has little to do with the 'New Age' movement. Later the term was popularised through the books of the Theosophist Alice Bailey. The 'New Age' became generally known through American publications supporting the Californian protest movement of the 1960s and early 1970s. No one knew exactly how they envisaged the Age of Aquarius, proclaimed in the musical *Hair* (1968), but many people were fascinated by the idea that the Earth was passing through a process of transformation, which would imminently produce a new human consciousness. Even if the Age of Aquarius actually referred to the transition of the spring equinoctial point from Pisces into Aquarius, the term quickly cast off its narrow astrological connotation.

Individual authors played an important role in the development of the 'New Age'. David Spangler, an American who visited the alternative Findhorn com-

---

7. I am convinced that this academic dilemma can only be avoided if one undertakes an analysis of discourse as I have suggested for esotericism in general. This profiles the historical origins of this heterogeneous subject at the same time as showing the many transformations of the esoteric field of discourse in the second half of the twentieth century. By focusing on the esoteric field of discourse, one sees that the concept of the 'New Age' has no analytical function, but is itself the *object* of a discursive analysis.

munity in north Scotland at the beginning of the 1970s, broadcast the concept in his book *Revelation: The Birth of a New Age* (1976). Marilyn Ferguson spoke of the subversive 'New Age' in her book *The Aquarian Conspiracy* (1980) and the scientist Fritjof Capra combined Eastern ideas with Western physics in his work *The Turning Point* (1982).[8] Something approximating the 'New Age' movement emerged, once various advocates recognised that they were indicating a more or less common religious and political agenda. In the course of the 1980s and 1990s, these 'New Agers' came under fire from early members of the movement—regarded by many scholars as still belonging to it—so that the superficial unity of views soon proved fragile.

As an episode of Euro-American history of religion, the 'New Age' has been somewhat artificially prolonged by the labels of external critics and scholarly accounts. But it would be false to conclude from this negative view, that an examination of the underlying phenomenon is also redundant. Many sections of the wrongly termed 'New Age' scene can be aptly understood as modern esotericism.[9]

CHANNELLING

Channelling is a concept which became increasingly widespread in the 'New Age' scene from the 1970s onwards to denote a range of phenomena relating to communications between people and transcendental beings. Specially gifted or trained persons served as a channel for messages that came down into 'normal reality' from realms inaccessible to the ordinary senses. According to Michael Brown's definition: 'Channeling…can be defined as the use of altered states of conscious-

---

8.   On this topic, cf. Bochinger 1994; Kyle 1995; York 1995; Hanegraaff 1996; Heelas 1996; Corrywright 2003; Hammer 2005 provides a good overview.

9.   In his standard work *New Age Religion and Western Culture: Esotericism in the Mirror of Secular Thought*, Wouter J. Hanegraaff seeks to classify 'New Age religion' in the history of religion. Employing the characteristics of esotericism suggested by Antoine Faivre, he locates the origins of most themes prevailing in the New Age scene in the religious and philosophical context of the Romantic era. He regards the New Age movement itself as 'the cultic milieu having become conscious of itself as constituting a more or less unified "movement"' (1996: 97). The concept 'cultic milieu' was coined by Colin Campbell (1972), who sought to establish a sociological link between individualised cults and the growth of broad religious communities (see also Kaplan and Lööw 2002). In the course of his research Hanegraaff came to the conclusion that 'all manifestations of this movement [i.e. of this cultic milieu] are characterized by a popular western culture criticism expressed in terms of a secularized esotericism' (1996: 522). I believe that words like 'cult' and 'secularization' are not helpful in explaining this subject. 'Cult' derives from a distinction between *sect* and *cult,* while 'secularization' is a category in the academic study of religion used to explain the transformations of modernity, which now lie in the past. People, even in the West, are no less 'religious' today than they were two hundred years ago (cf. Fuller 2001). The separation of religion and state is by no means complete, as the concept of secularization suggests. However, if one speaks of a 'cultural milieu' rather than a cultic milieu, while using the category of discourse, then we may analyse the continuities and breaks of the New Age movement. We are then dealing with fields of discourse which refer to esoteric topics in the context of 'modernity'. What Wouter J. Hanegraaff describes as 'major trends in New Age religion' (see Hanegraaff 1996: 23-110), are from this point of view important cornerstones of an esoteric field of discourse.

ness to contact spirits—or, as many of its practitioners say, to experience spiritual energy captured from other times and dimensions' (Brown 1997: viii). This is a matter of religious or psychological practice to acquire information which, according to its practitioners, should benefit the development of the individual personality as well as humankind. One might speak of an 'articulated revelation', a process of revelation which is by no means new in the esoteric tradition, if one recalls John Dee's conversations with the angels.[10]

A brief survey of the most important representatives of channelling can make this clear. Besides Blavatsky, Bailey and other Theosophists, one might name Edgar Cayce (1877–1945), whose prophecies still attract considerable interest today. From 1963 onwards Jane Roberts (1929–1984) received 'announcements' from 'Seth', who described himself as the 'centre of energetic personality'. The Seth material is more sophisticated than many 'channelled' messages from the Virgin Mary, Jesus and others, whose trivial statements fill the shelves of esoteric bookshops today. Helen Schucman again received messages from 'Jesus Christ' and published them through the Foundation for Inner Peace in her voluminous work *A Course of Miracles* (1975), which has generated a whole network of seminars and magazines. David Spangler channelled an entity called 'Boundless Love and Truth', but later turned away from what he described as 'talkshow channels'. The most popular representatives of the movement are probably Shirley Maclaine and 'Ramtha', an entity which spoke through J.Z. Knight (b. 1946). In the beginning, Ramtha gave very positive messages (in accordance with 'New Age' expectations), but then made increasingly dark prophecies, which irritated many followers. In Germany one might name Varda Hasselmann, who organises seminars and public readings. Like Jane Roberts, she was not satisfied with trivial communications and speaks of a 'source' which should not be envisaged as a personality:

> The non-corporeal power, which communicates this information to us, is a transpersonal being upon the causal plane of consciousness. It is comparable to other causal teachers such as Seth and Lazaris… Our source is composed of 1164 individual souls whose energies have all coalesced.[11]

Finally, mention should be made of Neal Donald Walsch's extremely popular *Conversations with God* series (from 1995), which are based upon 'inner dictation' by a 'soft voice' inside his head, attributed to God himself.

The examples could be multiplied but their fundamental message would remain the same. Channelling is a cornerstone of twentieth-century fields of discourse, because here 'ultimate insights' can be gained from hidden dimensions of reality. Its premise is a cosmology that assumes a multiplicity of worlds, each influencing the others, and holds out the prospect that human beings can participate in the

---

10. One can therefore describe this field of discourse in Hanegraaff's words as a 'religion of revelation' (1996: 27). At the same time, Hanegraaff is correct in arguing that the term 'channelling' should be restricted to phenomena emerging in New Age discourse.

11. Hasselmann and Schmolke 1995: 476.

'true reality' of transcendental planes and draw knowledge from them. This field of discourse extends much further than the boundaries of channelling to include communication with creatures of power in so-called 'neo-shamanism', 'crystal travels' and drug mysticism, to the religion of nature expressed in the Wicca movement and neo-paganism (see von Stuckrad 2003c).

DEEP ECOLOGY AND NEW AGE SCIENCE

Holistic conceptions of nature and the translation of scientific approaches into spiritual practice form a major field of discourse in contemporary esotericism, which can be illustrated with reference to deep ecology and New Age science.

Deep ecology performs a similar function for the esoteric concept of nature, as does transpersonal psychology for the concept of the soul. Its spiritual practices are embedded in a supportive philosophical framework, which also provides ideological strategies. The concept was coined in 1973 by the Norwegian analytical philosopher Arne Naess as a radical polemic against the anthropocentric orientation of contemporary ethics and politics. From the outset, deep ecology conceived of itself as integrating ethics, politics, biology and spirituality for the first time in a common approach, an undertaking that was bound to attract harsh criticism from philosophical and scientific quarters. In fact, most writings on deep ecology are characterised less by coherent philosophical arguments than by moralising appeals and normative views. They all share a *biocentric* view, which rejects the incontrovertibility of the human perspective by granting each entity its own place and its own non-negotiable value. Deep ecology thus refers to recent ideas in biology, which regard the interdependence of ecosystems as the subject of investigation. According to Paul W. Taylor, a biocentric view means 'looking at the entire order of the biosphere of the earth as a complex but unified network of mutually linked organisms, objects and events' (Taylor quoted in Birnbacher 1997: 97).

It is interesting that the concept of 'ecology' came into use through Ernst Haeckel's work *Generelle Morphologie der Organismen* ('General Morphology of Organisms', 1866). If one recalls Haeckel's convictions with regard to the philosophy of nature and the religion of nature, links are obvious between the debates of deep ecology and such religious overlays in scientific research. They express in philosophical terms the result of a ritualised experience of nature in a spiritual respect. There is a recurrent overlap of deep ecological philosophy with spiritual concerns, which naturally accords with the self-understanding of leading deep ecologists. This is not just a matter of *knowing* about the interconnection of all levels of being, but also its *experience* and sensual communication.[12] Theory and

12. This has implications for the argument, as Dieter Birnbacher critically observes: 'In the philosophical writings of deep ecology, the discursive and argumentative element is largely sidelined by expressive and poetical formulations. Reverence for nature is no longer only described but invoked and visualized. Just as in the Romantic philosophy of nature, philosophy itself is assimilated into the intended process of a holistic, that is, no longer exclusively rational realisation of the individual self' ('Preface' in Birnbacher 1997: 9).

practice are thus both sides of the same coin; accordingly, most deep ecology publications contain not only theoretical discussions, but also invocations, meditations and spiritual exercises (see Seed *et al*. 1988).

It is a short step from here to the view of New Age science that the Earth is a living being. This idea became well-known through James Lovelock and his 'Gaia' hypothesis, while the concept was further explored by David Bohm, Ilya Prigogine, David Peat, Rupert Sheldrake and Fritjof Capra, to name but the most important (see Hanegraaff 1996: 62-76). Once again, we see the popularisation of academic knowledge, because most of these authors are scientists who, often in bitter opposition to 'established' interpretations of quantum physics and biology, present a holistic model of the cosmos against simple causal explanations to a wider public. The idea of *unus mundus* (the unity of the world), in which man and cosmos form a living whole, has always belonged to the interpretative repertoire of esoteric discourses. It is not therefore surprising that the Stoic conception of a 'sympathy' pervading all things should resurface in the context of New Age science (see Arzt *et al*. 1992).

THE SOUL, ONCE AGAIN

This book has repeatedly shown how closely esoteric thought is involved with Western conceptions of the soul. It is no wonder that the *sacralization of the Self*, already sketched in connection with Carl Gustav Jung, forms an important aspect of New Age thinking. Even if many transpersonal psychologists categorically reject being labelled as 'esoteric' or 'New Age', it is undeniable from the perspective of the academic study of religion that their development of Jungian ideas has had a major influence on contemporary esotericism. Transpersonal psychology relates to spiritual dimensions beyond the boundaries of the individual person. The development and dissemination of the transpersonal movement is directly linked with the genesis of the 'New Age' movement during the 1960s in the United States and had an important impact on notions of spiritual growth and the Human Potential Movement.[13]

The origins of the transpersonal paradigm can already be detected in Mesmerism, which Robert C. Fuller calls 'the first popular psychology in America' (Fuller 1982: 10), which then entered American transcendentalism and the New Thought Movement. Highly influential on this movement, Phineas Parkhurst Quimby (1802–1866) presented an interpretation of Mesmerism that characterised the health and disease of a person as the product of his or her imagination, a widespread idea among New Age thinkers.

The Psychology and Religion Movement of Ralph Waldo Emerson found its chief advocate in William James. James' works on the philosophy of religion combine Mesmerism and Swedenborgian mysticism with a specifically American form

---

13. The connection between transpersonal psychology and the human image of the New Age movement as well as its prehistory in the nineteenth century has been the subject of several studies; see Fuller 1982, 1986; Hanegraaff 1996: 482-513.

of functionalism. Catherine L. Albanese has called this collection of diverse currents a *physical religion*, which 'was, above all, *healing* religion—religion in which acts of caring and curing constituted the central ritual enterprise for believers' (Albanese 1991: 123). This American tradition of self-healing reinforced that psychologisation of religion and sacralisation of the psyche proposed by C.G. Jung. His concept of a 'collective unconscious' anticipated the view that the individual is not enclosed in his own limited inner world, but is linked to planes of reality shared by other human beings and which can ultimately be regarded as an all-embracing world of symbols.

Another, though lesser known, pioneer of transpersonal psychology is Roberto Assagioli (1888–1974). He was also one of the first to deplore the limitations of psychology and developed his 'psychosynthesis', which attempted to create an overall picture of the personality through the integration of personal, transpersonal and spiritual dimensions. Both Assagioli and the transpersonal movement seek to replace the predominant medical approach of psychology, even more so of psychiatry, with a model that emphasises the healthy rather than the pathological person. Such a model also sees the person's spiritual needs as an indispensable aspect of their total personality. The movement received further important momentum from representatives of humanistic psychology, especially Abraham Maslow and Anthony Sutich (see the survey in Grof 1985).

The American protest movement of the 1960s and early 1970s led to new explorations. On the one hand, there was enormous interest in Eastern meditation techniques, on the other extensive experiments with psychoactive substances. The LSD experiments of Stanislav Grof, research at the Esalen Institute in California and other initiatives close to the New Age movement attempted to investigate the phenomenon of altered states of consciousness on a systematic basis, which could reproduce the bandwidth of such states. Whole classes of potential transpersonal states of consciousness were constructed, and their authors claimed that these had been known and respected at all times and by all cultures. Only Western society had rejected and suppressed them.

The most important theoretician of the transpersonal movement alongside Grof is Ken Wilber. By distinguishing between the deeper and superficial aspects of mystical and religious experience, Wilber was able to profile the commonalities between shamanistic journeys, Christian mystics' encounters with angels, and the absorption of a Hindu with his *Ishta deva* by focusing on their contact with spiritual entities but without denying the differences between their individual experiences.[14]

Wilber thus presented a developmental model that related the various states of consciousness to transpersonal foundations. He thereby differentiated between perceiving progressively more subtle realms of the spirit ('subtle states'), extending over all objects and phenomena to pure consciousness ('causal states'), and

14. This explanation, even if Wilber would surely deny it, is unambiguously phenomenological, disregarding all the methodological issues arising from the contingency and determination of its comparative criteria to the neglect of historical contexts.

ultimately perceiving all objects and appearances as projections of consciousness ('absolute states') (Wilber 1995: Chapter 8). This evolutionary model leads to the evaluation of a phenomenon with respect to its transpersonal stage of development, for which Wilber has sometimes been criticised. He counters such charges by polemically distancing himself from culturally relativist positions and also resists the adoption of his theory by supporters of the New Age movement, whom he describes as naïve dreamers. According to Wilber, not every spiritual experience is a transpersonal one, for it is often confused with a prepersonal experience, that is a psychic regression to infantile fantasies of omnipotence, which are the very opposite of the transpersonal surmounting of the ego (Wilber 1995: Chapter 6). Ultimately Wilber is not interested in playing off various explanations of reality against each other, but in the integration of Western, Eastern and other methods in a comprehensive approach. The differences might only refer to individual perspectives falling in different places on the 'spectrum of consciousness', and confusion arises when one view is applied to other bands of that spectrum.

On first sight, the transpersonal movement might appear to have taken us a long way from the esoteric ideas of Marsilio Ficino, Emanuel Swedenborg or Helena Blavatsky. However, on closer examination, we see that transpersonal psychology, like channelling and deep ecology, basically continues the esoteric project by other means. These three fields of discourse are sections of the most recent chapter, so rich in ideas and rival theories, in the history of esotericism in Euro-American culture. One can be sure that the quest for perfect knowledge will continue into the future.

BIBLIOGRAPHY

Adler, Hans
1990   *Die Prägnanz des Dunklen. Gnoseologie—Ästhetik—Geschichtsphilosophie bei Johann Gottfried Herder* (Hamburg: Meiner).
Agethen, Manfred
1984   *Geheimbund und Utopie. Illuminaten, Freimaurer und deutsche Spätaufklärung* (Munich: Oldenbourg).
Ahern, Geoffrey
1984   *Sun at Midnight: The Rudolf Steiner Movement and the Western Esoteric Tradition* (Wellingborough: Aquarian).
Albanese, Catherine L.
1991   *Nature Religion in America: From the Algonkian Indians to the New Age* (Chicago/London: University of Chicago Press, 2nd edn).
Allen, Michael J.B.
1998   *Synoptic Art: Marsilio Ficino on the History of Platonic Interpretation* (Florence: L.S. Olschki).
Allen, Michael J.B., and Valery Rees (with Martin Davies) (eds.)
2002   *Marsilio Ficino: His Theology, His Philosophy, His Legacy* (Leiden: E.J. Brill).
Arzt, Thomas, M. Hippius-Gräfin Dürckheim and R. Dollinger (eds.)
1992   *Unus Mundus. Kosmos und Sympathie. Beiträge zum Gedanken der Einheit von Mensch und Kosmos* (Frankfurt: Peter Lang).
Assmann, Jan
1997   *Moses the Egyptian: The Memory of Egypt in Western Monotheism* (Cambridge, MA: Harvard University Press).
Assmann, Jan, and Theo Sundermeier (eds.)
1993   *Die Erfindung des inneren Menschen: Studien zur religiösen Anthropologie* (Gütersloh: Gerd Mohn).
Barnes, Robert B.
1988   *Prophecy and Gnosis: Apocalypticism in the Wake of the Lutheran Reformation* (Stanford: University of California Press).
Baßler, Moritz, and Hildegard Châtellier (eds.)
1998   *Mystique, mysticisme et modernité en Allemagne autour de 1900 / Mystik, Mystizismus und Moderne in Deutschland um 1900* (Strasbourg: Presses universitaire de Strasbourg).
BeDuhn, Jason David
2000   *The Manichaean Body in Discipline and Ritual* (Baltimore/London: The Johns Hopkins University Press).
Benavides, Gustavo
1998   'Modernity', in Mark C. Taylor (ed.), *Critical Terms for Religious Studies* (Chicago/London: University of Chicago Press): 186-204.
Benz, Ernst
2002   *Emanuel Swedenborg: Visionary Savant in the Age of Reason* (trans. and introduction by Nicholas Goodrick-Clarke; West Chester, PA: Swedenborg Foundation [1st edn 1948]).

Berchman, Robert M. (ed.)
  1998   *Mediators of the Divine: Horizons of Prophecy, Divination, Dreams and Theurgy in Mediterranean Antiquity* (Atlanta: Scholars Press).
Bibliotheca Philosophica Hermetica (ed.)
  2002   *Rosenkreuz als europäisches Phänomen im 17. Jahrhundert* (Amsterdam: In de Pelikaan).
Birnbacher, Dieter (ed.)
  1997   *Ökophilosophie* (Stuttgart: Reclam).
Blavatsky, Helena P.
  1888   *The Secret Doctrine: The Synthesis of Science, Religion and Philosophy* (2 vols.; London: Theosophical Publishing Company); vol. III edited by Annie Besant (London: Theosophical Publishing Company, 1897).
Blum, Wilhelm
  1988   *Georgios Gemistos Plethon. Politik, Philosophie und Rhetorik im spätbyzantinischen Reich (1355–1452)* (Stuttgart: Hiersemann).
Blumenberg, Hans
  1983   *Säkularisierung und Selbstbehauptung* (Frankfurt: Suhrkamp, 2nd edn).
Bobzin, Hartmut
  1995   *Der Koran im Zeitalter der Reformation. Studien zur Frühgeschichte der Arabistik und Islamkunde in Europa* (Beirut/Stuttgart: Orient-Institut der Deutschen Morgenländischen Gesellschaft).
Bochinger, Christoph
  1994   *New Age und moderne Religion. Religionswissenschaftliche Analysen* (Gütersloh: Chr. Kaiser Verlag).
  1996   'Auf der Rückseite der Aufklärung. Gegenwärtige religiöse Bewegungen als Thema religionswissenschaftlicher Forschung', *Berliner Theologische Zeitschrift* 13/2: 229-49.
Bonelli, M.L Righini, and William R. Shea (eds.)
  1975   *Reason, Experiment, and Mysticism in the Scientific Revolution* (New York: Science History Publications).
Bouwsma, William J.
  1957   *Concordia Mundi: The Career and Thought of Guillaume Postel (1510–1581)* (Cambridge, MA: Harvard University Press).
Brann, Noel L.
  1999   *Trithemius and Magical Theology: A Chapter in the Controversy over Occult Studies in Early Modern Europe* (Albany: State University of New York Press).
Brann, Ross
  2002   *Power in the Portrayal: Representations of Jews and Muslims in Eleventh- and Twelfth-Century Islamic Spain* (Princeton, NJ/Oxford: Princeton University Press).
Bremmer, Jan N.
  2002   *The Rise and Fall of the Afterlife: The 1995 Read–Tuckwell Lectures at the University of Bristol* (London/New York: Routledge).
Bremmer, Jan, and Jan R. Veenstra (eds.)
  2002   *The Metamorphosis of Magic from Late Antiquity to the Early Modern Period* (Leuven: Peeters).
Broek, Roelof van den, and Cis van Heertum (eds.)
  2000   *From Poimandres to Jacob Böhme: Gnosis, Hermetism and the Christian Tradition* (Amsterdam: In de Pelikaan).
Broek, Roelof van den, and Wouter J. Hanegraaff (eds.)
  1998   *Gnosis and Hermeticism from Antiquity to Modern Times* (Albany: State University of New York Press).

Brown, Michael F.
    1997   *The Channeling Zone: American Spirituality in an Anxious Age* (Cambridge, MA/
            London: Harvard University Press).

Burnett, Charles (ed.)
    1987   *Adelard of Bath: An English Scientist and Arabist of the Early Twelfth Century* (London:
            Warburg Institute, University of London).

Campbell, Colin
    1972   'The Cult, the Cultic Milieu and Secularization', *A Sociological Yearbook of Religion
            in Britain* 5: 119-36.

Campbell, Joseph
    1960–68   *The Masks of God* (4 vols.; London: Secker & Warburg).

Clark, Stuart
    1997   *Thinking With Demons: The Idea of Witchcraft in Early Modern Europe* (Oxford:
            Clarendon Press).

Clulee, Nicholas H.
    1988   *John Dee's Natural Philosophy: Between Science and Religion* (New York: Routledge).

Copenhaver, Brian P.
    1992   *Hermetica: The Greek* Corpus Hermeticum *and the Latin* Asclepius *in a new English
            Translation with Notes and Introduction* (Cambridge: Cambridge University Press).

Corrywright, Dominic
    2003   *Theoretical and Empirical Investigations into New Age Spiritualities* (Oxford: Peter
            Lang).

Coudert, Allison P.
    1980   *Alchemy: The Philosopher's Stone* (London: Wildwood).
    1995   *Leibniz and the Kabbalah* (Dordrecht: Kluwer).
    1999   *The Impact of Kabbalah in the Seventeenth Century: The Life and Thought of Francis
            Mercury van Helmont (1614–1698)* (Leiden: E.J. Brill).
    2001   'Seventeenth-Century Natural Philosophy and Esotericism at the Court of Sulz-
            bach', in Richard Caron *et al.* (eds.), *Ésotérisme, gnoses & imaginaire symbolique:
            Mélanges offerts à Antoine Faivre* (Leuven: Peeters): 27-46.

Coudert, Allison P. (ed.)
    1999   *The Language of Adam/Die Sprache Adams* (Wiesbaden: Harrassowitz).

Coudert, Allison P., Richard H. Popkin and Gordon M. Weiner (eds.)
    1998   *Leibniz, Mysticism and Religion* (Dordrecht: Kluwer).

Cranston, Sylvia
    1995   *H.P.B. The Extraordinary Life and Influence of Helena Blavatsky, Founder of the Modern
            Theosophical Movement* (New York: Putnam).

Craven, William G.
    1981   *Giovanni Pico della Mirandola, Symbol of His Age: Modern Interpretations of a
            Renaissance Philosopher* (Geneva: Librairie Droz).

Curry, Patrick (ed.)
    1987   *Astrology, Science and Society: Historical Essays* (Woodbridge/Wolfboro: Boydell).

Dan, Joseph
    1998   *Jewish Mysticism.* I. *Late Antiquity.* II. *The Middle Ages* (Northvale, NJ/Jerusalem:
            Jason Aronson).

Dan, Joseph (ed.)
    1997   *The Christian Kabbalah: Jewish Mystical Books and Their Christian Interpreters* (Cam-
            bridge, MA: Harvard College Library).

Davila, James R.
    2001   *Descenders to the Chariot: The People behind the Hekhalot Literature* (Leiden: E.J. Brill).

Debus, Allen G.
    1975   'The Chemical Debates of the Seventeenth Century: The Reaction to Robert Fludd and Jean Baptiste van Helmont', in Bonelli and Shea (eds.) 1975: 19-47.
    1978   *Man and Nature in the Renaissance* (Cambridge: Cambridge University Press).
Desmond, William
    2003   *Hegel's God: A Counterfeit Double?* (Aldershot: Ashgate).
Dillon, John
    1977   *The Middle Platonists: A Study of Platonism 80 B.C. to A.D. 220* (London: Gerald Duckworth).
Diner, Dan
    2003   *Gedächtniszeiten. Über jüdische und andere Geschichten* (Munich: Beck).
Dobbs, Betty J.T.
    1991   *The Janus Faces of Genius: The Role of Alchemy in Newton's Thought* (Cambridge: Cambridge University Press).
Dodge, Bayard (ed. and trans.)
    1970   *The Fihrist of al-Nadim: A Tenth-Century Survey of Muslim Culture* (New York: Columbia University Press).
Edighoffer, Roland
    1982   *Les Rose-Croix* (Paris : Presses universitaires de France).
Eliade, Mircea
    1959a   *The Sacred and the Profane: The Nature of Religion* (New York: Harcourt Brace Jovanovich).
    1959b   *Cosmos and History: The Myth of the Eternal Return* (New York: Harper [1st edn 1949]).
Faivre, Antoine
    1994   *Access to Western Esotericism* (Albany: State University of New York Press).
    1999   'The Theosophical Current: A Periodization', *Theosophical History* 7/5: 167-207.
Faivre, Antoine, and Wouter J. Hanegraaff (eds.)
    1998   *Western Esotericism and the Science of Religion* (Leuven: Peeters).
Faivre, Antoine, and Jacob Needleman (eds.)
    1992   *Modern Esoteric Spirituality* (New York: Crossroad).
Fanger, Claire (ed.)
    1998   *Conjuring Spirits: Texts and Traditions of Medieval Ritual Magic* (University Park: Pennsylvania State University Press).
Farmer, Steve A.
    1998   *Syncretism in the West: Pico's 900 Theses (1486). The Evolution of Traditional Religious and Philosophical Systems* (Tempe, AZ: Medieval & Renaissance Texts & Studies).
Farmer, Steve, John B. Henderson and Michael Witzel
  2000 (2002) 'Neurobiology, Layered Texts, and Correlative Cosmologies: A Cross-Cultural Framework for Premodern History', *Bulletin of the Museum of Far Eastern Antiquities* 72: 48-90.
Fauvel, John *et al.* (eds.)
    1993   *Newtons Werk. Die Begründung der modernen Naturwissenschaft* (Basle: Birkhäuser).
Ficino, Marsilio
    2000   *The 'Philebus' Commentary* (trans. M.J.B. Allen; Tempe, 7; Arizona Center for Medieval and Renaissance Studies).
Findlen, Paula
    2004   *Athanasius Kircher: The Last Man Who Knew Everything* (New York/London: Routledge).
Fine, Lawrence
    2003   *Physician of the Soul, Healer of the Cosmos: Isaac Luria and His Kabbalistic Fellowship* (Stanford, CA: Stanford University Press).

Flasch, Kurt, and Udo Reinhold Jeck (eds.)
    1997   *Das Licht der Vernunft. Die Anfänge der Aufklärung im Mittelalter* (Munich: Beck).
Force, James E., and Richard H. Popkin (eds.)
    1999   *Newton and Religion: Context, Nature, and Influence* (Dordrecht: Kluwer).
Fowden, Garth
    1993   *The Egyptian Hermes* (repr. Cambridge: Cambridge University Press [1983]).
Frick, Karl R.H.
    1973   *Die Erleuchteten. Gnostisch-theosophische und alchemistisch-rosenkreuzerische Geheim-gesellschaften bis zum Ende des 18. Jahrhunderts —ein Beitrag zur Geistesgeschichte der Neuzeit* (Graz: Akademische Druck- u. Verlagsanstalt).
    1975/78 *Licht und Finsternis. Gnostisch-theosophische und freimaurerisch-okkulte Geheimgesell-schaften bis an die Wende zum 20. Jahrhundert (Die Erleuchteten II)* (2 vols.; Graz: Akademische Druck- u. Verlagsanstalt).
Fuller, Robert C.
    1982   *Mesmerism and the American Cure of Souls* (Philadelphia: University of Pennsylvania Press).
    1986   *Americans and the Unconscious* (New York/Oxford: Oxford University Press).
    2001   *Spiritual, But Not Religious: Understanding Unchurched America* (Oxford: Oxford: University Press).
Gaiser, Konrad
    1988   'Platons esoterische Lehre', in Peter Koslowski (ed.), *Gnosis und Mystik in der Geschichte der Philosophie* (Munich/Zurich: Artemis): 13-40.
Garin, Eugenio
    1983   *Astrology in the Renaissance* (London: Routledge & Kegan Paul).
Geyer, Hermann
    2001   *Verborgene Weisheit. Johann Arndts 'Vier Bücher vom Wahren Christentum' als Programm einer spiritualistisch-hermetischen Theologie* (3 parts in 2 vols.; Berlin/New York).
Giller, Pinchas
    2001   *Reading the Zohar: The Sacred Text of the Kabbalah* (Oxford/New York: Oxford University Press).
Gilly, Carlos
    1994   *Adam Haslmayr. Der erste Verkünder der Rosenkreuzer* (Amsterdam: Bibliotheca Philosophica Hermetica).
    2000   'Das Bekenntnis zur Gnosis von Paracelsus bis auf die Schüler Jacob Böhmes', in Van den Broek and van Heertum (eds.) 2000: 385-425.
Gilly, Carlos (ed.)
    1995   *Cimelia Rhodostaurotica. Die Rosenkreuzer im Spiegel der zwischen 1610 und 1660 entstandenen Handschriften und Drucke* (Amsterdam: In de Pelikaan).
Gladigow, Burkhard
    1989   'Pantheismus als "Religion" von Naturwissenschaftlern', in Peter Antes and Donate Pahnke (eds.), *Die Religion von Oberschichten: Religion—Profession—Intellektualismus* (Marburg: Diagonal): 219-39.
    1993   '"Tiefe der Seele" und "inner space". Zur Geschichte eines Topos von Heraklit bis zur Science Fiction', in Assmann and Sundermeier (eds.) 1993: 114-32.
    1995   'Europäische Religionsgeschichte', in Hans G. Kippenberg and Brigitte Luchesi (eds.), *Lokale Religionsgeschichte* (Marburg: Diagonal): 21-42.
Godwin, Joscelyn
    1987   *Harmonies of Heaven and Earth: The Spiritual Dimension of Music from Antiquity to the Avant-Garde* (London: Thames & Hudson).
    1994   *The Theosophical Enlightenment* (Albany: State University of New York Press).
    2002   *The Pagan Dream of the Renaissance* (London: Thames & Hudson).

Goldammer, Kurt
    1991   *Der göttliche Magier und die Magierin Natur. Religion, Naturmagie und die Anfänge der Naturwissenschaft vom Spätmittelalter bis zur Renaissance. Mit Beiträgen zum Magie-Verständnis des Paracelsus* (Stuttgart: Steiner).

Goldish, Matt
    2004   *The Sabbatean Prophets* (Cambridge, MA/London: Harvard University Press).

Goodman-Thau, Eveline (ed.)
    1999   *Kabbala und die Literatur der Romantik. Zwischen Magie und Trope* (Tübingen: Niemeyer).

Goodman-Thau, Eveline, Gerd Mattenklott and Christoph Schulte (eds.)
    1994   *Kabbala und Romantik* (Tübingen: Niemeyer).

Goodrick-Clarke, Nicholas
    2002   *Black Sun: Aryan Cults, Esoteric Nazism and the Politics of Identity* (New York/London: New York University Press).
    2004a   *Helena Blavatsky* (Berkeley, CA: North Atlantic Books).
    2004b   *The Occult Roots of Nazism: Secret Aryan Cults and Their Influence on Nazi Ideology* (London/New York: Tauris, 3rd edn [1st edn 1985]).

Grafton, Anthony
    1991   *Defenders of the Text: The Traditions of Scholarship in an Age of Science, 1450–1800* (Cambridge, MA/London: Harvard University Press).
    1999   *Cardano's Cosmos: The Worlds and Works of a Renaissance Astrologer* (Cambridge, MA: Harvard University Press).

Grafton, Anthony, and Moshe Idel (eds.)
    2001   *Der Magus. Seine Ursprünge und seine Geschichte in verschiedenen Kulturen* (Berlin: Akademie Verlag).

Grafton, Anthony, and Nancy Siraisi (eds.)
    1999   *Natural Particulars: Nature and the Disciplines in Renaissance Europe* (Cambridge, MA: MIT Press).

Green, Arthur
    2004   *A Guide to the Zohar* (Stanford, CA: Stanford University Press).

Grell, Ole Peter (ed.)
    1998   *Paracelsus: The Man and His Reputation, His Ideas and Their Transformation* (Leiden: E.J. Brill).

Grof, Stanislav
    1985   *Beyond the Brain Birth, Death, and Transcendence in Psychotherapy* (Albany: State University of New York Press).

Groh, Ruth, and Dieter Groh
    1991   *Weltbild und Naturaneignung. Zur Kulturgeschichte der Natur* (Frankfurt: Suhrkamp).

Grözinger, Karl E.
    1993   'Reuchlin und die Kabbala', in Arno Herzig and Julius H. Schoeps, in collaboration with Saskia Rohde (eds.), *Reuchlin und die Juden* (Sigmaringen: Thorbecke): 175-87.

Gruber, Bettina (ed.)
    1997   *Erfahrung und System. Mystik und Esoterik in der Literatur der Moderne* (Opladen: Westdeutscher Verlag).

Gruenwald, Ithamar
    1971   'A Preliminary Critical Edition of Sefer Yeçirah', *Israel Oriental Studies* 1: 132-77.

Guthke, Karl S.
    1983   *Der Mythos der Neuzeit. Das Thema der Mehrheit der Welten in der Literatur- und Geistesgeschichte von der kopernikanischen Wende bis zur Science Fiction* (Bern/Munich: Francke).

Haeckel, Ernst

n.d. [1899]   *Die Weltiäthsel. Gemeinverständliche Studien über Monistische Philosophie*, Volks-ausgabe (151.-170. Tausend) (Stuttgart: Kröner); English edition, *The Riddle of the Universe* (London: Watts, 1929).

1917   *Kristallseelen. Studien über das anorganische Leben* (Leipzig: Kröner).

Hakl, Hans Thomas

2001   *Der verborgene Geist von Eranos: Unbekannte Begegnungen von Wissenschaft und Esoterik. Eine alternative Geistesgeschichte des 20. Jahrhunderts* (Bretten: Scientia Nova).

Hammer, Olav

2001   *Claiming Knowledge: Strategies of Epistemology from Theosophy to the New Age* (Leiden: E.J. Brill).

2005   'New Age Movement', in Hanegraaff (ed.) 2005: 855-61.

Hanegraaff, Wouter J.

1996   *New Age Religion and Western Culture: Esotericism in the Mirror of Secular Thought* (Leiden: E.J. Brill).

2001   'Beyond the Yates Paradigm: The Study of Western Esotericism between Counterculture and New Complexity', *Aries: Journal for the Study of Western Esotericism* 1: 5-37.

Hanegraaff, Wouter J. (ed.), in collaboration with Antoine Faivre, Roelof van den Broek and Jean-Pierre Brach

2005   *Dictionary of Gnosis and Western Esotericism* (Leiden: E.J. Brill).

Hanegraaff, Wouter J., and Ruud Bouthoorn

2005   *Lodovico Lazzarelli (1447–1500): The Hermetic Writings and Related Documents* (Tempe, AZ: Arizona Center for Medieval and Renaissance Studies).

Harkness, Deborah E.

1999a   *John Dee's Conversations with Angels: Cabala, Alchemy, and the End of Nature* (Cambridge: Cambridge University Press).

1999b   'Alchemy and Eschatology: Exploring the connections between John Dee and Isaac Newton', in Force and Popkin (eds.) 1999: 1-15.

Hankins, James

1990   *Plato in the Italian Renaissance* (2 vols.; Leiden: E.J. Brill).

1991   'The Myth of the Platonic Academy of Florence', *Renaissance Quarterly* 44: 429-75.

Hasselmann, Varda, and Frank Schmolke

1995   *Weisheit der Seele* (Munich: Goldmann).

Heelas, Paul

1996   *The New Age Movement: Celebrating the Self and the Sacralization of Modernity* (Oxford/Cambridge, MA: Basil Blackwell).

Herzog, Reinhart, and Reinhart Koselleck (eds.)

1987   *Epochenschwelle und Epochenbewußtsein* (Munich: Fink).

Hesse, Hermann

1943   *Das Glasperlenspiel* (Zürich).

1974   *Der Steppenwolf* (Frankfurt: Suhrkamp [English trans. New York, 1963]).

Hornung, Erik

2001   *The Secret Lore of Egypt: Its Impact on the West* (Ithaca, NY: Cornell University Press).

Howe, Ellic

1972   *The Magicians of the Golden Dawn: A Documentary History of a Magical Order 1887–1923* (London: Routledge & Kegan Paul).

Howell, Kenneth J.

2002   *God's Two Books: Copernican Cosmology and Biblical Interpretation in Early Modern Science* (Notre Dame, IN: University of Notre Dame Press).

Hughes, Aaron W.
  2004   *The Texture of the Divine: Imagination in Medieval Islamic and Jewish Thought*
              (Bloomington: Indiana University Press).
Hutton, Ronald
  1999   *The Triumph of the Moon: A History of Modern Pagan Witchcraft* (Oxford/London:
              Oxford University Press).
Idel, Moshe
  1988   *Kabbalah: New Perspectives* (New Haven: Yale University Press).
  1998   *Messianic Mystics* (New Haven: Yale University Press).
  2002   *Absorbing Perfections: Kabbalah and Interpretation* (New Haven/London: Yale
              University Press).
Jacob, Margaret C.
  1981   *The Radical Enlightenment: Pantheists, Freemasons and Republicans* (London: Allen &
              Unwin).
Jayakar, Pupul
  1988   *Krishnamurti—Leben und Lehre* (Freiburg); English edition, *J. Krishnamurti: A
              Biography* (New Delhi: Penguin, 1986).
Jenkins, Philip
  2000   *Mystics and Messiahs: Cults and New Religions in American History* (Oxford: Oxford
              University Press).
Johnson, K. Paul
  1994   *The Masters Revealed: Madame Blavatsky and the Myth of the Great White Lodge*
              (Albany: State University of New York Press).
Johnston, Sarah Iles
  1997   'Rising to the Occasion: Theurgic Ascent in Its Cultural Milieu', in Peter Schäfer
              and Hans G. Kippenberg (eds.), *Envisioning Magic: A Princeton Seminar and
              Symposium* (Leiden: E.J. Brill): 165-94.
Jüttemann, Gerd *et al.*
  1991   *Die Seele. Ihre Geschichte im Abendland* (Weinheim: Psychologie Verlags Union).
Kaczynski, Richard
  2002   *Perdurabo: The Life of Aleister Crowley* (Tempe, AZ: New Falcon Publications).
Kaplan, Jeffrey, and Heléne Lööw (eds.)
  2002   *The Cultic Milieu: Oppositional Subcultures in an Age of Globalization* (Walnut Creek,
              Oxford: AltaMira Press).
Kibre, Pearl
  1966   *The Library of Pico della Mirandola* (New York: AMS Press).
Kieckhefer, Richard
  1990   *Magic in the Middle Ages* (Cambridge: Cambridge University Press).
Kiesel, Wilhelm (ed.)
  2002   *Picatrix—Ghayat al-Hakim: The Goal of the Wise* (trans. Hashem Atallah; Seattle:
              Ouroboros Press).
Kingsley, Peter
  1995   *Ancient Philosophy, Mystery, and Magic: Empedocles and Pythagorean Tradition* (Oxford:
              Clarendon Press).
Kippenberg, Hans G.
  2002   *Discovering Religious History in the Modern Age* (Princeton, NJ/Oxford: Princeton
              University Press).
Kippenberg, Hans G., and Kocku von Stuckrad
  2003   *Einführung in die Religionswissenschaft. Gegenstände und Begriffe* (Munich: Beck).
Klaassen, Frank
  2003   'Medieval Ritual Magic in the Renaissance', *Aries: Journal for the Study of Western
              Esotericism* 3: 166-99.

Knysh, Alexander
  2000   *Islamic Mysticism: A Short History* (Leiden: E.J. Brill).
Koch, Klaus
  1993   *Geschichte der ägyptischen Religion. Von den Pyramiden bis zu den Mysterien der Isis* (Stuttgart: Kohlhammer).
Koselleck, Reinhart
  1973   *Kritik und Krise. Eine Studie zur Pathogenese der bürgerlichen Welt* (Frankfurt: Suhrkamp, 2nd edn); English edition, *Critique and Crisis: Enlightenment and the Pathogenesis of Modern Society* (Oxford: Berg, 1988).
Koyré, Alexandre
  1971   *Mystiques, spirituals, alchimistes du XVIe siècle allemand* (Paris: Gallimard).
Kuntz, Marion L.
  1981   *Guillaume Postel: Prophet of the Restitution of All Things. His Life and Thought* (The Hague: Nijhoff).
Kyle, Richard
  1995   *The New Age Movement in American Culture* (Lanham, MD: University Press of America).
Latour, Bruno
  1993   *We Have Never Been Modern* (New York: Harvester Wheatsheaf).
Lehmann, Hartmut, and Anne-Charlott Trepp (eds.)
  1999   *Im Zeichen der Krise. Religiosität im Europa des 17. Jahrhunderts* (Göttingen: Vandenhoeck & Ruprecht).
Lewy, Hans
  1978   *Chaldaean Oracles and Theurgy: Mysticism, Magic and Platonism in the Later Roman Empire* (Paris: Études Augustiniennes).
Ley, Michael, and Julius H. Schoeps (eds.)
  1997   *Der Nationalsozialismus als politische Religion* (Bodenheim: Philo Verlagsgesellschaft).
Linse, Ulrich
  1996   *Geisterseher und Wunderwirker. Heilssuche im Industriezeitalter* (Frankfurt: Fischer).
Magee, Glenn Alexander
  2001   *Hegel and the Hermetic Tradition* (Ithaca, NY/London: Cornell University Press).
Maier, Johann
  1995   *Die Kabbalah. Einführung—Klassische Texte—Erläuterungen* (Munich: Beck).
Markschies, Christoph
  2003   *Gnosis: An Introduction* (London: T. & T. Clark); German edition, *Die Gnosis* (Munich: Beck, 2001).
Marquard, Odo
  1987   *Transzendentaler Idealismus—Romantische Naturphilosophie—Psychoanalyse (ursprünglich Habilitationsschrift 1963)* (Cologne: Dinter).
Matt, Daniel C. (ed.)
  2003–   *The Zohar: The Pritzker Edition* (2 vols.; Stanford, CA: Stanford University Press).
  2004–   (trans./comm.) *The Zohar: Pritzker Edition* (Stanford, CA: Stanford University Press).
McCalla, Arthur
  2001   'Antoine Faivre and the Study of Esotericism', *Religion* 31: 435-50.
McIntosh, Christopher
  1987   *The Rosicrucians: The History, Mythology and Rituals of an Occult Order* (Wellingborough: Crucible).
McKnight, Stephen A.
  1991   *The Modern Age and the Recovery of Ancient Wisdom: A Reconsideration of Historical Consciousness 1540–1650* (Columbia: University of Missouri Press).

Meade, Marian
    1980   *Madame Blavatsky: The Woman behind the Myth* (New York: Putnam).
Meyer, Birgit, and Peter Pels (eds.)
    2003   *Magic and Modernity: Interfaces of Revelation and Concealment* (Stanford, CA: Stanford
            University Press).
Meyerson, Mark D., and Edward D. English (eds.)
    2000   *Christians, Muslims, and Jews in Medieval and Early Modern Spain Interaction and
            Cultural Change* (Notre Dame, IN: University of Notre Dame Press).
Miller, Clyde Lee
    2003   *Reading Cusanus: Metaphor and Dialectic in a Conjectural Universe* (Washington, DC:
            Catholic University of America Press).
Möller, Helmut, and Ellic Howe
    1986   *Merlin Peregrinus. Vom Untergrund des Abendlandes* (Würzburg: Königshausen &
            Neumann).
Monfasani, John
    1995   *Byzantine Scholars in Renaissance Italy: Cardinal Bessarion and Other Emigrés*
            (Aldershot: Variorum).
Moran, Bruce T.
    1991   *The Alchemical World of the German Court: Occult Philosophy and Chemical Medicine in
            the Circle of Moritz of Hessen (1572–1632)* (Stuttgart: Steiner).
Mörth, Ingo
    1978   *Die gesellschaftliche Wirklichkeit von Religion* (Stuttgart: Kohlhammer).
Müller-Jahncke, Wolf-Dieter
    1985   *Astrologisch-magische Theorie und Praxis in der Heilkunde der frühen Neuzeit* (Stuttgart:
            Steiner).
Mulsow, Martin (ed.)
    2002   *Das Ende des Hermetismus: Historische Kritik und neue Naturphilosophie in der Spätren-
            aissance. Dokumentation und Analyse der Debatte um die Datierung der hermetischen
            Schriften von Genebrard bis Casaubon (1567–1614)* (Tübingen: J.C.B. Mohr [Paul
            Siebeck]).
Nederman, Cary J.
    2000   *Worlds of Difference: European Discourses of Toleration, c. 1100–c. 1550* (University
            Park, PA: Pennsylvania State University Press).
Neugebauer-Wölk, Monika
    1995   *Esoterische Bünde und Bürgerliche Gesellschaft. Entwicklungslinien zur modernen Welt im
            Geheimbundwesen des 18. Jahrhunderts* (Wolfenbüttel: Lessing-Akademie).
    1999   ' "Höhere Vernunft" und "Höheres Wissen" als Leitbegriffe in der esoterischen
            Gesellschaftsbewegung. Vom Nachleben eines Renaissancekonzepts im
            Jahrhundert der Aufklärung', in Monika Neugebauer-Wölk (with Holger
            Zaunstöck) (eds.), *Aufklärung und Esoterik* (Hamburg: Meiner): 170-210.
    2000   'Esoterik in der Frühen Neuzeit. Zum Paradigma der Religionsgeschichte
            zwischen Mittelalter und Moderne', *Zeitschrift für Historische Forschung* 27: 321-64.
    2003   'Esoterik und Christentum vor 1800: Prolegomena zu einer Bestimmung ihrer
            Differenz', *Aries: Journal for the Study of Western Esotericism* 3: 127-65.
Newman, William R., and Anthony Grafton (eds.)
    2001   *Secrets of Nature: Astrology and Alchemy in Early Modern Europe* (Cambridge, MA:
            MIT Press).
Newman, William R., and Lawrence M. Principe
    2002   *Alchemy Tried in the Fire: Starkey, Boyle, and the Fate of Helmontian Chymistry*
            (Chicago/London: University of Chicago Press).
Noll, Richard
    1997   *The Jung Cult: Origins of a Charismatic Movement* (New York: Free Press, 2nd edn).

Novalis (Friedrich von Hardenberg)
  1999   *Gesammelte Werke* (3 vols.; Darmstadt: Wissenschaftliche Buchgesellschaft).
Oppenheim, Janet
  1985   *The Other World: Spiritualism and Psychical Research in England, 1850–1914* (Cambridge: Cambridge University Press).
Pagel, Walter
  1982   *Paracelsus: An Introduction to Philosophical Medicine in the Era of the Renaissance* (Basel/New York: Karger, 2nd edn).
Pagels, Elaine
  1979   *Versuchung durch Erkenntnis. Die gnostischen Evangelien* (Frankfurt: Suhrkamp); English edition, *The Gnostic Gospels* (New York: Random House, 1979).
Pauen, Michael
  1994   *Dithyrambiker des Untergangs. Gnostizismus in Ästhetik und Philosophie der Moderne* (Berlin: Akademie Verlag).
Pott, Martin
  1992   *Aufklärung und Aberglaube. Die deutsche Frühaufklärung im Spiegel ihrer Aberglaubenskritik* (Tübingen: Niemeyer).
Principe, Lawrence M.
  1998   *The Aspiring Adept: Robert Boyle and His Alchemical Quest* (Princeton, NJ: Princeton University Press).
Principe, Lawrence M., and William R. Newman
  2001   'Some Problems with the Historiography of Alchemy', in Newman and Grafton (eds.) 2001: 385-431.
Pumfrey, Stephen, Paolo L. Rossi and Maurice Slawinski (eds.)
  1991   *Science, Culture and Popular Belief in Renaissance Europe* (Manchester/New York: Manchester University Press).
Regardie, Israel
  2000   *The Golden Dawn: A Complete Course in Practical Ceremonial Magic. Four Volumes in One* (St Paul, MN: Llewellyn Publications, 6th edn [1st edn 1984]).
Reinalter, Helmut
  2002   *Die Freimaurer* (Munich: Beck, 3rd edn).
Reinalter, Helmut (ed.)
  1983   *Freimaurer und Geheimbünde im 18. Jahrhundert* (Frankfurt: Suhrkamp).
Ridley, Jasper
  1999   *The Freemasons* (London: Constable).
Riffard, Pierre
  1990   *L'ésotérisme* (Paris: Payot).
Robinson, James M. (ed.)
  1990   *The Nag Hammadi Library in English* (New York: Harper, 3rd edn).
Rossi, Paolo
  2000   *Logic and the Art of Memory* (Chicago: University of Chicago Press).
Ruderman, David B.
  1988   *Kabbalah, Magic, and Science: The Cultural Universe of a Sixteenth-Century Jewish Physician* (Cambridge, MA: Harvard University Press).
Rudolph, Kurt
  1990   *Die Gnosis. Wesen und Geschichte einer spätantiken Religion* (Göttingen: Vandenhoeck & Ruprecht, 3rd edn); English edition, *Gnosis: The Nature and History of Gnosticism* (San Francisco: Harper & Row, 1987).
Runggaldier, Edmund
  1996   *Philosophie der Esoterik* (Stuttgart: Kohlhammer).

Ruska, Julius
 1926 *Tabula Smaragdina. Ein Beitrag zur Geschichte der hermetischen Literatur* (Heidelberg: C. Winter's Universitätsbuchhandlung).

Rutkin, Darrel, Günther Oestmann and Kocku von Stuckrad (eds.)
 2005 *Horoscopes and Public Spheres: Essays on the History of Astrology* (Berlin/New York: W. de Gruyter).

Schäfer, Peter
 1991 *Der verborgene und offenbare Gott. Hauptthemen der frühen jüdischen Mystik* (Tübingen: J.C.B. Mohr); English edition, *The Hidden and Manifest God: Some Major Themes in Early Jewish Mysticism* (Albany: State University of New York Press, 1992).
 2002 *Mirror of His Beauty: Feminine Images of God from the Bible to the Early Kabbalah* (Princeton, NJ: Princeton University Press).

Schama, Simon
 1996 *Landscape and Memory* (London: Fontana).

Schlögl, Rudolf
 2001 'Hermetismus als Sprache der "unsichtbaren Kirche": Luther, Paracelsus und die Neutralisten in der Kirchen- und Ketzerhistorie Gottfried Arnolds', in Trepp and Lehmann (eds.) 2001: 165-88.

Schmidt-Biggemann, Wilhelm
 1999 'Christian Kabbala: Joseph Gikatilla (1247–1305), Johannes Reuchlin (1455–1522), Paulus Ricius (d. 1541), and Jacob Böhme (1575–1624)', in Coudert (ed.) 1999: 81-121.

Schmidt-Biggemann, Wilhelm (ed.)
 2003 *Christliche Kabbala* (Ostfildern: Thorbecke).

Schmied-Kowarzik, Wolfdietrich
 1996 *'Von der wirklichen, von der seyenden Natur': Schellings Ringen um eine Naturphilosophie in Auseinandersetzung mit Kant, Fichte und Hegel* (Stuttgart/Bad Cannstadt: Frommann-Holzboog).

Scholem, Gershom
 1962 *Ursprung und Anfänge der Kabbalah* (Berlin: W. de Gruyter).
 1991 *Die jüdische Mystik in ihren Hauptströmungen* (Frankfurt, 4th edn [1st edn 1957]); English edition, *Major Trends in Jewish Mysticism* (New York/Jerusalem: Schocken, 1941).

Schott, Heinz (ed.)
 1985 *Franz Anton Mesmer und die Geschichte des Mesmerismus* (Stuttgart: Steiner).

Schütt, Hans-Werner
 2000 *Auf der Suche nach dem Stein der Weisen. Die Geschichte der Alchemie* (Munich: Beck).

Seed, John, Joanna Macy, Pat Fleming and Arne Naess (eds.)
 1988 *Thinking Like a Mountain Towards a Council of All Beings* (Philadelphia: New Society).

Shapin, Steven
 1996 *The Scientific Revolution* (Chicago: University of Chicago Press).

Shapin, Steven, and Simon Schaffer
 1985 *Leviathan and the Air-Pump: Hobbes, Boyle, and the Experimental Life* (Princeton, NJ: Princeton University Press).

Sharot, Stephen
 1982 *Messianism, Mysticism, and Magic: A Sociological Analysis of Jewish Religious Movements* (Chapel Hill: North Carolina University Press).

Shumaker, Wayne
 1972 *The Occult Sciences in the Renaissance: A Study in Intellectual Patterns* (Berkeley: University of California Press).

Simonis, Linda
    2002   *Die Kunst des Geheimen. Esoterische Kommunikation und ästhetische Darstellung im 18. Jahrhundert* (Heidelberg: Winter).

Sladek, Mirko
    1984   *Fragmente der hermetischen Philosophie in der Naturphilosophie der Neuzeit. Historisch-kritische Beiträge zur hermetisch-alchemistischen Raum- und Naturphilosophie bei Giordano Bruno, Henry More und Goethe* (Frankfurt: Peter Lang).

Sonntag, Michael
    1999   *'Das Verborgene des Herzens'. Zur Geschichte der Individualität* (Reinbek: Rowohlt).

Stausberg, Michael
    1998   *Faszination Zarathushtra. Zoroaster und die Europäische Religionsgeschichte der Frühen Neuzeit* (2 vols.; Berlin/New York: W. de Gruyter).

Steiner, Rudolf
    1980   *An Autobiography* (New York: Rudolf Steiner Publications, 2nd edn).

Stuckrad, Kocku von
    2000   *Das Ringen um die Astrologie. Jüdische und christliche Beiträge zum antiken Zeitverständnis* (Berlin/New York: W. de Gruyter).
    2003a   'Discursive Study of Religion: From States of the Mind to Communication and Action', *Method & Theory in the Study of Religion* 15: 255-71.
    2003b   *Geschichte der Astrologie. Von den Anfängen bis zur Gegenwart* (Munich: Beck); English edn, *The History of Astrology: From Earliest Times to the Present* (London: Equinox, 2005).
    2003c   *Schamanismus und Esoterik. Kultur- und wissenschaftsgeschichtliche Betrachtungen* (Leuven: Peeters).
    2005   'Western Esotericism: Towards an Integrative Model of Interpretation', *Religion* 35: 78-97.

Swartz, Michael D.
    1996   *Scholastic Magic: Ritual and Revelation in Early Jewish Mysticism* (Princeton, NJ: Princeton University Press)

Stausberg, Michael
    1998   *Faszination Zarathushtra. Zoroaster und die Europäische Religionsgeschichte der Frühen Neuzeit* (2 vols.; Berlin/New York: W. de Gruyter).

Thomas, Keith
    1971   *Religion and the Decline of Magic: Studies in Popular Beliefs in Sixteenth and Seventeenth Century Europe* (London: Weidenfeld & Nicolson).

Torijano, Pablo A.
    2002   *Solomon the Esoteric King: From King to Magus, Development of a Tradition* (Leiden: E.J. Brill).

Travaglia, Pinella
    1999   *Magic, Causality and Intentionality: The Doctrine of Rays in al-Kindi* (Florence: Ed. del Galluzzo).

Trepp, Anne-Charlott
    1999   'Religion, Magie und Naturphilosophie: Alchemie im 16. und 17. Jahrhundert', in Lehmann and Trepp (eds.) 2001: 473-93.
    2001   'Im "Buch der Natur" lesen: Natur und Religion im Zeitalter der Konfessionalisierung und des Dreißigjährigen Krieges', in Trepp and Lehmann (eds.) 2001: 103-43.

Trepp, Anne-Charlott, and Hartmut Lehmann (eds.)
    2001   *Antike Weisheit und kulturelle Praxis. Hermetismus in der Frühen Neuzeit* (Göttingen: Vandenhoeck & Ruprecht).

Turner, John D.
    2001   *Sethian Gnosticism and the Platonic Tradition* (Leuven: Peeters).
Versluis, Arthur
    1999   *Wisdom's Children: A Christian Esoteric Tradition* (Albany: State University of New
                York Press).
Voegelin, Erik
    1953/54   'Philosophie der Politik in Oxford', *Philosophische Rundschau* 1: 23-48.
Walbridge, John
    2000   *The Leaven of the Ancients: Suhrawardî and the Heritage of the Greeks* (Albany: State
                University of New York Press).
    2001   *The Wisdom of the Mystic East: Suhrawardî and Platonic Orientalism* (Albany: State
                University of New York Press).
Walker, D.P.
    1958   *Spiritual and Demonic Magic from Ficino to Campanella* (London: Warburg Institute,
                University of London).
    1972   *The Ancient Theology* (London: Gerald Duckworth).
Wasserstrom, Steven M.
    1999   *Religion after Religion: Gershom Scholem, Mircea Eliade and Henry Corbin at Eranos*
                (Princeton, NJ: Princeton University Press).
    2000   'Jewish-Muslim Relations in the Context of Andalusian Emigration', in
                Meyerson and English (eds.) 2000: 69-87.
Weber, Max
    1982   *Gesammelte Aufsätze zur Wissenschaftslehre* (Tübingen: J.C.B. Mohr, 5th edn).
    1988   *Gesammelte Aufsätze zur Religionssoziologie* (Tübingen: J.C.B. Mohr, 9th edn).
    1992   *Wissenschaft als Beruf. Politik als Beruf* (Max-Weber-Gesamtausgabe I/17) (hrsg. von
                Wolfgang Schluchter; Tübingen: J.C.B. Mohr [Paul Siebeck]).
    2001   *Religiöse Gemeinschaften* (Max-Weber-Gesamtausgabe I/22-2; hrsg. von Hans G.
                Kippenberg in Zusammenarbeit mit Petra Schilm unter Mitwirkung von Jutta
                Niemeier; Tübingen: J.C.B. Mohr).
Wilber, Ken
    1995   *Sex, Ecology, Spirituality: The Spirit of Evolution* (Boston: Shambhala).
Williams, Gerhild Scholz, and Charles D. Gunnoe, Jr (eds.)
    2002   *Paracelsian Moments: Science, Medicine, & Astrology in Early Modern Europe*
                (Kirksville, MO: Truman State University Press).
Williams, Michael Allen
    1996   *Rethinking 'Gnosticism': An Argument for Dismantling a Dubious Category* (Princeton,
                NJ: Princeton University Press).
Wilson, David Sloan
    2002   *Darwin's Cathedral: Evolution, Religion, and the Nature of Society* (Chicago/London:
                University of Chicago Press).
Wind, Edgar
    1967   *Pagan Mysteries in the Renaissance* (Harmondsworth: Penguin [1st edn 1958]).
Wirszubski, Chaim
    1989   *Pico della Mirandola's Encounter with Jewish Mysticism* (Cambridge, MA/London:
                Harvard University Press).
Wolfson, Elliot R.
    1994   *Through a Speculum that Shines: Vision and Imagination in Medieval Jewish Mysticism*
                (Princeton, NJ: Princeton University Press).
    2005   *Language, Eros, Being: Kabbalistic Hermeneutics and Poetic Imagination* (New York:
                Fordham University Press).
Woodhouse, C.M.
    1986   *George Gemistos Plethon: The Last of the Hellenes* (Oxford: Clarendon Press).

Yates, Frances A.
  2002   *Giordano Bruno and the Hermetic Tradition* (London/New York: Routledge [1st edn
             1964]).
York, Michael
  1995   *The Emerging Network: A Sociology of the New Age and Neo-Pagan Movements*
             (London: Rowman & Littlefield).
Zika, Charles
  2003   *Exorcising Our Demons: Magic, Witchcraft and Visual Culture in Early Modern Europe*
             (Leiden: E.J. Brill).
Zimmermann, Rolf Christian
  1969   *Das Weltbild des jungen Goethe* (2 vols.; Munich: Fink).

INDEX

Printed in the United Kingdom
by Lightning Source UK Ltd.
133510UK00002B/238-267/P